of Paris in 1631

THE ILLUSTRATED HISTORY OF
PARIS AND THE PARISIANS

The Illustrated History of

This book was compiled under the general editorship of
ROBERT LAFFONT

Literary editor, director of pictorial research, captions
JACQUES BOUDET

Technical editor
PAUL RUDLOFF

Historical consultant
FRANÇOIS BOUCHER Honorary Curator of the Musée Carnavalet

Layout and montage
PHILIPPE GENTIL

Literary continuity
MAX-POL FOUCHET

Editorial board
JACQUES BROSSE, JOSÉ LACOUR, HUGUETTE RÉMONT,
JOSETTE BONDUELLE

PARIS and the Parisians

Illustrated with photographs, paintings, prints, drawings and maps

Translators
ISABEL QUIGLY, BARBARA BRAY

First published in the United States of America 1958.

Planned and printed in Paris, France, by Editions du Pont Royal.

DOUBLEDAY & COMPANY INC., GARDEN CITY, NEW YORK

Was love at the foundation of the City?

Who founded Paris? Paris, says tradition; one of the Trojan leaders who fled from the town besieged by the Greeks (1). In their flight, Aeneas founded Rome and the Roman people; Brutus founded Britain; Francion France. Paris founded Paris. This account of the birth of nations and their capitals is given in the 'Grandes Chroniques de France', the first book to be printed in French, though its pictures were still hand-painted (1). It is the primer of the annals of French history, compiled in 1493 by Vérard, a craftsman of Paris.

Ly cōmence le premier chapitre des grās croniques de
france et parle cōmēt les frācois descēdirent des troyes.

paris

eul d^{cc} ans xl et ix passez Du deluge: x
Outruytie hue : fonda en grand arroy D
Deuant qua rome euft des gens amassez

2

Did he who loved a queen console his exile where

It was to Venus that Paris awarded the apple. The most
handsome of men set beauty above power and intellect. It
was but natural, then, for this prince of love to found on
the banks of the Seine the capital city of charm. A pleasing
father for a town to own, one to whom a tapestry that
delighted the contemporaries of François I still pays
homage (2). Dressed as a nobleman of the Renaissance (3),
Paris quotes Ronsard against a background of the buildings
of Paris.

Later still, under the Revolution, at the Café Procope,
Citizen Jullian instituted the Phrygian cap, on the grounds
that the shepherd Paris wore it. And so the new ideas were
to go forward wearing the cap of the ancient fable.

6

But only a sinewy giant could really found Paris. On the way to the Garden of the Hesperides, Hercules gathered together the Parrhasians from the heights of Arcadia, settled them at the foot of Montmartre slope, and named them Parisians. Though she is sometimes the frivolous daughter of the Trojan shepherd, Paris can also be a city of harsh awakenings and laborious tasks; well may Hercules have presided at her birth. A good plump 'Gallic Hercules' was to welcome Henri II on his triumphal entry in 1549; and Louis XIV did not scorn to have himself portrayed as Hercules, club in hand, on the Porte Saint-Martin (4). For many years another Hercules received the homage of Christian congregations in Notre-Dame; but they baptised him St. Christopher.

But then at last Cuvier came upon the scene, and the myth was swept away. In the course of his reconstruction of the animal species the great palaeontologist threw devastating light on the family history of the capital. He discovered that Montmartre is a pie, crammed with the remains of all that ever lived there, animals and plants, swallowed up by time. The fleeting print of birds, the tracks of animals, skeletons: the earth preserved them all pell-mell. Cuvier put together the pieces of that enormous jigsaw puzzle, and to men's amazement restored to their mind's eye the lost world above which their city had arisen. Vague legend gave place to exact detail, and myth to knowledge; the founder of the city was not Prince Paris but a tiny shell-fish called a nummulite. Nearly three centuries before Cuvier, Jean Goujon, carving the Fontaine des Innocents, came close to scientific truth when he represented the tutelary spirit of Paris as a nymph of the Seine, whose body rested lightly on a couch of marine creatures (5). Like Venus, Paris was born from a sea-shell.

the river traced her remembered shape?

Eruptions and subsidences. Tides ebb and flow. Huge creatures are born,

Thirty to forty million years ago the monstrous ichthyosaurs and the huge triceratops had already vanished; the earth's crust had ceased its long trembling. The Eocene period of the Tertiary age had begun; the quiet morning of our planet. This was a crucial moment in the history of Paris: let us call it the Lutetian period, as the world's scientists have named it.

A sea bathed the site of the city, a warm shallow sea out of which arose islands covered with conifers. Fancy, rather than strict fact, recognizes in these islands Mont-Valérien, the heights of Chaillot and Belleville, Montmartre, and the 'mountain masses' of Bagneux and Meudon. A sparse fauna roamed here: tapirs, palaeotheriums, crocodiles, giant hares (dichobunuses), swine (cebocherus).

then disappear.   As man seeks a poem, so power seeks out its form.

But the sea, a vast aquarium of tepid water, teemed with life: traces have been found of 69 species of fish and 1858 species of mollusc, including the giant cerithus, twenty inches long; including also a shelled foraminifera, half animal, half vegetable, in great shoals: the nummulite. All this, after millions of years, became rock for the building of houses and monuments, stone for statues.

A lagoon fauna, through millions more years, at Montmartre, Ménilmontant, and Buttes-Chaumont, formed the deposits of gypsum that have made the famous plaster of Paris, which gave the ladies of Paris their face-powder, and perhaps the city its earliest name: Lucotetia or Lutetia, which means the 'white place'. And so a bounteous nature laid down all the materials for a great capital.

And now it rained. The tertiary age ended in a relentless stream of water that lasted a hundred thousand years, eroding, furrowing, undermining, disintegrating the earth. The great limestone plateau which covered north-west France was hollowed out, and in the valley a river flowed. It was sluggish, choked with sand and marshy far out from its banks; but on it converged all the slopes for a hundred and twenty miles around (7), towards it all that lived descended, and at its central and lowest point a little group of islands shone gently in the sun: the future cradle of Paris.

There, ninety feet above sea-level, man settled. Since then this chosen spot has been so constantly used – one might almost say worn – that no trace of the ancient days remains. The debris that man has left has banked it up nearly twenty feet above its original level ... (8).

A form is discernible

in the wastes of mud and the alluvial deposits :

an island.

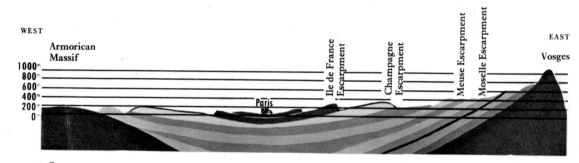

7

8

9

11

Only the little square at the prow of the Ile de la Cité, the Square du Vert Galant, now recalls, because it has remained at water level, what Paris was at the beginning.

And now the island,

still the water-logged expression of brute force, must be engraved and shaped...

10

This promontory (9), made up of several islets, is on the same level as the original Lutetia. Looking along the water-side to the Pont-Neuf, one can see the height that has been added by more than two thousand years of history.

This central island, convenient both for land journeys from north to south and for water transport from east to west, this platform from which to fish (10), to hunt water-fowl, and to gather rushes, was linked to the river banks by the first Parisians by means of the Grand Pont in the north and the Petit Pont (11) in the south. It was not long before the two powers, religious and civil, separated themselves out in a way that time has done nothing to change: the religious power in the east, upstream; the civil power to the west, downstream. Notre-Dame on the one hand, the Palais and the Préfecture on the other, were one day to arise on the very places where the first Parisians either called upon their gods or held their conferences.

11

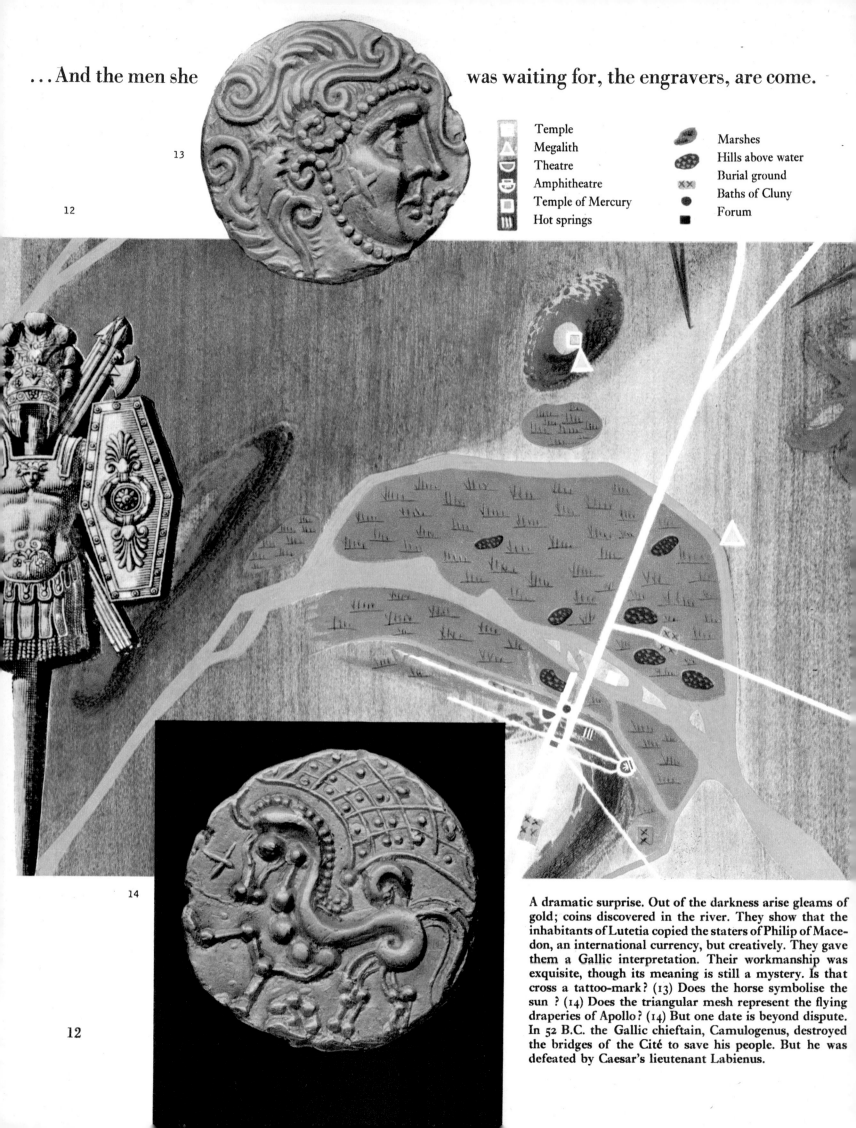

...And the men she was waiting for, the engravers, are come.

13

12

Temple
Megalith
Theatre
Amphitheatre
Temple of Mercury
Hot springs

Marshes
Hills above water
Burial ground
Baths of Cluny
Forum

14

12

A dramatic surprise. Out of the darkness arise gleams of gold; coins discovered in the river. They show that the inhabitants of Lutetia copied the staters of Philip of Macedon, an international currency, but creatively. They gave them a Gallic interpretation. Their workmanship was exquisite, though its meaning is still a mystery. Is that cross a tattoo-mark? (13) Does the horse symbolise the sun? (14) Does the triangular mesh represent the flying draperies of Apollo? (14) But one date is beyond dispute. In 52 B.C. the Gallic chieftain, Camulogenus, destroyed the bridges of the Cité to save his people. But he was defeated by Caesar's lieutenant Labienus.

They give expression, on stone or on metal, to power.

The bridges are lengthened into roads. The island is a hub surrounded by the spokes of a wheel.

The Roman occupation brought with it the age of the high-roads. A highway now bestrode the bridges of the Cité, and running through the 'pass' of La Chapelle joined Senlis or Rouen to Orléans (the present Rue Saint-Jacques and Rue Saint-Martin). On the left bank another, narrower road ran parallel to it – the 'via inferior', now the Boulevard Saint-Michel (12). One of its branches (now the Rue Saint-Antoine) crossed the marsh in the direction of Melun. But for Lutetia, built off the main thoroughfares of Gaul, the river remained supreme. Guards were set to watch over it. These are the first Parisians whose likeness has survived (15). They are armed, bearded, and staunch at their posts.

In 1711, under the apse of Notre-Dame, were discovered the fragments of a wonderful votive pillar, together with a whole collection of Gallo-Roman religious remains. One of them shows that under Tiberius, in about A.D. 37, the boatmen of Paris looked to Jupiter to bring them prosperous voyages. Failing Jupiter, or for other purposes, they worshipped Cernunnos, of the deer forests, an old prehistoric god, or Tarvos Trigaranos, the bull with three cranes (16), a horned being worshipped throughout Gaul. Tarvos Trigaranos, who gradually became a mere fatted ox, was honoured with colourful processions right up to the beginning of this century (17).

It is the wheel of the conqueror,

whose chariots cross the river.

Of all the gods Mercury was held in highest honour (18). This inventor of the arts and lord of travel and trade became the patron of the Celtic smiths and weavers. On Mount Mercury, the highest point in the town (now Montmartre), a temple was built to him from which the Christians were to find it by no means easy to dislodge him.

A small garrison town under an administration that concentrated its attention mainly on military matters, and, moreover, the victim of many vicissitudes, Lutetia did not preserve any important Roman buildings. Were there any? Many cities that are now much smaller seem to have had many more such buildings.

The men of the island hear new words, and mingle them with their own.

Lutetia is cleansed by the sword of Rome.

That is why, when a Roman amphitheatre was uncovered in the Rue Monge in 1869, Napoleon III thought it fitting that he should go in person to admire it (19). Paris at last had her arena. Alas, it was only a little one (20). It had been set against a slope, and was smaller than those of Poitiers, Autun, Arles and Nîmes. Nevertheless it could hold ten thousand people – quite a lot when you remember that Gallo-Roman Lutetia had only twenty thousand inhabitants.

On the site of the Panthéon, where the historians would have liked to imagine a majestic forum, all that has been found are some clay-pits and potters' kilns. Was there a great temple nearby? and a theatre on the site of the Lycée St-Louis? Fortunately there are the baths. It has not been possible to recover those of the Collège de France in their entirety, but the baths of Cluny, which are more than a hundred yards across, are thought to be among the largest Roman buildings of the first two centuries A.D. The frigidarium, a great refrigerated chamber with a pool (21) into which the Lutetians plunged after the hot bath, is still intact. The corbels, in the shape of ships' prows, that decorate the walls, reminded the customers that they were boatmen and ships' chandlers before they were bathers. This establishment saw a revival of popularity in the nineteenth century – in the Champs Elysées, in the form of a 'panoramic reconstruction' (22).

15

In A.D. 358 General Julian (25), nephew of the great Constantine, defeated the invaders on the Meuse. Going homewards via Lutetia, he was captivated by its vines, its fig-trees, and the limpid waters of the Seine. His pleasant dalliance was soon interrupted by an order to lead his Gallo-Roman troops into action in the Middle East. He refused. His grateful soldiers proclaimed him emperor of Rome in the Ile de la Cité. Another imperial coronation was not held there until 1804 (517).

Invasions

are the winters of history.

Lutetia was long acquainted

with the rule of force.

24

As late as the 17th century, on Midsummer Day in the Place de Grève, the people of Paris were to burn alive some cats and a fox shut up in wicker baskets. This cruel custom no doubt went back to the early days, when it was devised to propitiate some baleful native god. But it was the Roman deities who imposed themselves most firmly upon the Parisii.

This tutelary goddess of light (23), this proud effigy of Mars (24), born on the banks of the Tiber, soon won worshippers on the banks of the Seine. Three hundred years after the defeat of Camulogenus, their influence could still be traced in the gods of the Gauls, as well as in their art and in their thought. A dangerous partnership, an intellectual collaboration fraught with peril – for Rome was in decline.

26

Mercury occupied the highest point of the city. This was more than the missionary, Denis, could endure, and with the help of his friends Eleutherus and Rusticus, the holy man undertook to assail the heathen gods (26). It was a rash enterprise, and inimical to law and order. The governor Sisinnius had them beheaded (27). Denis picked up his severed head (28), and departed towards the country in the north-west, where he met Catulla, fortunately a convert, who buried him in secret. As recent excavations have shown, the three of them were buried in a pagan cemetery by the roadside, and there these pioneers of Christianity were to see arising over their tomb the most lofty and powerful abbey of Saint-Denis, which was to play such an important part in the history of the capital. The mount of Mercury was to become the 'mons martyrum': Montmartre. The saints were avenged.

27

28

But the Lutetia of Saint Denis

knew also the strength of the weak.

In 308, as a milestone showed, the name of Paris, the chief town of the Parisii, began to replace that of Lutetia. Between the Bièvre and the Seine, a little removed from the Cité and from the Roman quarter on the left bank, a Christian community was formed. The ancient quarries scattered thereabouts provided a convenient refuge in case of emergency. The greatest of these Christian settlers was Marcel (360–436), ninth Bishop of Paris. To him the city owed its deliverance from an enormous dragon that lurked along the marshy shores (29). Marcel reduced it to subjection by beating it with his crozier. Centuries later, at Rogationtide, the people of Paris were still to lead the dragon in procession, in remembrance of the days of the great marshes.

Already the inelegance of the pagan monsters offends her.

Fourteen centuries later a poet of Paris will say, 'Remember, Barbara...'

Marcel was not only a hunter of fabulous monsters. The sculptors of Notre-Dame delighted to show him baptising people (30). He was a great baptist. Thanks to him the bourg of Saint-Marcel became an important parish. Its inhabitants started a great Christian cemetery. They hollowed out the columns of temples and other Roman buildings, and buried one another in these improvised sarcophagi, head to the west, feet to the east, and for eternity a precious label – the monogram of Constantine entwined with the letters alpha and omega. It was in the bourg of Saint-Marcel in the 5th century that there died, at the age of twenty-three, the 'dulcissima Barbara', the most gracious Barbara, the first Parisienne whose sweet name has come down to us, through the medium of an epitaph discovered in 1656.

When the civil and military powers collapsed, it was a woman, Geneviève (423–512), who became the leading spirit of Paris's resistance to Attila and his Huns, lashing on the cowards, searching out the defeatists, sheltering refugees, organising supplies. When the danger was over, Paris vowed an ardent devotion to Geneviève, which Puvis de Chavannes portrayed as late as 1877 in his frescoes in the Panthéon (31). Soon the holy radiance shed by Geneviève became so great that Christian propagandists made use of it in the fight against pagan survivals.

In the church of Saint-Merry an anonymous painter of the 16th century immortalised one of the most striking features of the legend (32). The patron saint of Paris, disguised as a shepherdess for the occasion, watches her sheep in the middle of a circle of Druid stones which hold back a threatening flood. In the background two men are setting off on her instructions, which another miracle will enable them to fulfil, to find the necessary materials to build a chapel to Saint Denis. Thus the great patrons of Paris form a chain without a break.

31

Remember, Paris,

the first woman to save you, for you know how to find faith in gentleness.

32

Paris was no longer a child. She was to exchange the role øf a small garrison town, administratively subordinate to the old Roman province of the Lyonnais, for the new and more distinguished one of a capital. At this time Europe was riddled with the Aryan heresy. The Visigoths had spread it in Italy and as far north as Bordeaux. The Eastern Church was threatening to secede. In Rome the throne of Saint Peter trembled on its foundations. Then the man of destiny appeared, in the guise of a Frankish chieftain, Clovis, who vowed boldly to drive the Romans from the north of Gaul and the Alemanni from the east. Clovis was converted, baptised (33), and solemnly crowned at Reims in 496, a date of capital importance in the history of France, the history of the Church, and the history of Paris. In less than twelve years orthodox Christianity was restored in the south-west, and Clovis, nominated consul by the Roman ruler of the Eastern Empire, sought a capital. From what point could he best watch over both the Loire and the Rhine, the Elbe and the Pyrenees? Not from Tours, nor from Toulouse, nor from Orléans, but from Paris. Paris was to be the capital.

... As you know how to find greatness in faith. The dialogue

between gentleness and greatness begins on the banks of the Seine and in the hills.

Once it had become the capital, it was not fitting that Paris should show less of Christian splendour than Rome or Byzantium. One morning in the year 507 Clovis hurled his francisca (battle-axe) (34) and thus defined in regal fashion the bounds of an immense basilica. It was dedicated to Saint Peter and Saint Paul, and was the first church in Paris to have a cemetery, and the first royal burial-place in France. It was to receive into its crypts the body of Clovis himself, in 511; of Geneviève in 512, and of Queen Clotilde in 545. The Merovingian kings were also to remain faithful to this church, as were still more the people of Paris themselves, who gave it the name of Sainte-Geneviève.

35

36   All that now survives of the Abbey of Sainte-Geneviève (35) is a solitary belfry built in 1180, the Tower of Clovis (36); and, nearby, is the church built by Louis XV in 1744, which later became the Panthéon (36). Another feature of the cult was a procession bearing the splendid shrine of the patron saint of Paris; for centuries this was an annual event in the life of the capital, until the Revolution abolished it, after destroying shrine and relics and leaving the Abbey in ruins.
In 1220 a parish church dedicated to Saint-Etienne du Mont was built next to the abbey church. Later destroyed, but rebuilt again in 1626 (35), it still shelters a fragment of Geneviève's stone sarcophagus in a new shrine of gilded copper. The rood-screen, the only surviving one in Paris, dates from 1545 and is particularly beautiful.

21

The city reflects the soul. And the citizen is a warrior.

Although he murdered his nephews, Chilpéric the son of Clovis feared God. Besieging Saragossa in 542, he agreed to raise the siege if the defenders would hand over (37) the relics of Saint Vincent, which were venerated by the inhabitants. The relics were taken back to Paris and bestowed on an abbey founded in their honour on the left bank, outside the city, at the request of Bishop Germain (38). On December 23rd 558, when Childebert was dying, Bishop Germain dedicated the new sanctuary to Saint Vincent (39) in the presence of King Clothaire (40). It was to be the second burial-place of the Merovingians. Germain himself was buried there in 576.

This basilica, one of the finest of the period, could challenge comparison with those of Rome and Ravenna. The lower parts of its walls were faced with marble; its pavement was a series of mosaics; and the ceiling, the walls of the nave, and the roof of beaten tin were covered with gold. From a distance the whole building sparkled in the sun, and it was known as Saint-Germain the Golden. But alas, the Normans completely destroyed it. In the year 1,000 the basilica was rebuilt on much simpler lines, under the rural name of Saint - Germain - des - Prés (Saint Germain - in - the - Fields). The present belfry dates from this period (41).

Weary of violence, he encloses in the walls the treasures of lost gentleness. Paris, city of huntsmen; Paris, city of shrines.

Though they shared the Frankish kingdom between them, the heirs of Clovis – Chilpéric, Caribert, and Sigebert – left Paris undivided: a prudent compromise over a prize greedily coveted by each; but chaos was the result. It dragged on until 612, with a staggering train of crime, violence and treachery. Two women were outstanding in those days of savagery. The first was Frédégonde, wife of Chilpéric. She had no scruples about burning alive the witches supposed to be responsible for the death of her two children (42), and instigated many political murders.

It takes something of everything to make a soul.

It takes something of everything to make a city...

42

43

The second ferocious queen was Brunehaut, wife of Sigebert, King of Burgundy. Brunehaut happened to be in Paris, which she loved, when Chilpéric, disregarding his promise, came to set up his throne there. There was only just time to save the heir of Burgundy by lowering him over the ramparts in a basket (43). But Brunehaut too could be implacable. She came to a bad end: she was arrested, tortured for three days, and then, it is said, tied to the tail of a horse. She was eighty years old.

Naturally it was the people of Paris who footed the bill for this fratricidal warfare. But as if Providence considered that they had not suffered enough, in 583 a cyclone laid waste the valley of the Seine. This is the first great flood mentioned in the chronicles (44).

24

44

Peace returned to Paris under the reign, alas too brief, of good king Dagobert (629–639). He loved both Paris and its surroundings. He liked to reside sometimes at Clichy, sometimes at Reuilly or Epinay. He was devoted to the basilica of Saint-Denis, and had it sumptuously modernised (45). He also founded nearby the fair of Lendit, one of the most important international enterprises of the Middle Ages. At the age of 36, when he felt death approaching, he asked to be brought to Saint-Denis, and there he was buried.

Thus began Saint-Denis's history as a royal burial-place. At the same period, thanks to Eloi, the name of Paris appears for the first time on the coinage. Eloi was minister, bishop, and goldsmith. Not satisfied with striking coins, he enamelled chalices and reliquaries, made crowns and engraved them (46), and enclosed holy relics in shrines of marvellous beauty. He was as tolerant as he was gifted: he taught the people of Paris to treat their foreign slaves as friends. So well was the lesson learned that Clovis II, Dagobert's successor, married an Anglo-Saxon slave. Her name was Bathilda, and she died a godly death.

...The tyrant and the one who serves.

The murderer and the saint.

The ruffian and the goldsmith.

The man who destroys, and the man who builds.

But now a darkness fell which lasted three hundred years,
and from which emerges no monument, no scrap of drawing or painting.
In 751 the Merovingian dynasty died of its own excesses.
The east devoured the west: Austrasia annexed Neustria,
and the centre of the western world shifted between Rhine and Meuse.
Charles Martel just saved France from total collapse
by throwing back the Moslem incursions in 732.
His son Pepin was elected and crowned in Saint-Denis
with the Pope's blessing,
a brilliant new departure
by which the Carolingians' power received the backing of religious authority,
but one which did Paris no good.
It was in fact at Aix-la-Chapelle, from which he could command the whole of Europe,
that Charles Martel's grandson, Charlemagne, set up his capital.
By neglecting Paris
and concentrating too much on the south and east
the Carolingians left the Atlantic gateways unguarded.
In 840 the Normans entered by them,
and by March 29th, Easter Day, they were in Paris.
The first titular king of France, Charles the Bald,
paid a ransom to get rid of them,
and they left, but not before they had destroyed the left bank.
But they came back. They came back in 857,
they came back in 866,
they came back in 876,
then, growing more and more formidable,
they decided to sack wealthy Burgundy.
Paris, which had rebuilt its walls
and fortified its bridges, lay across the route of the invasion,
and suffered the first great siege in its history.
It lasted a year, from November 885 to November 886.
Meanwhile the throne had fallen vacant.
Charles the Fat, Emperor of Germany, was appealed to for help
and paid seven hundred livres for the safety of Paris.
From the battlements
the people of Paris watched the Normans set off towards the east,
dragging their galleys across the fields
because the Parisians would not allow them passage up the Seine.
In 888 they elected as king the valiant Eudes, count of Parisis.
A hero of the resistance,
Eudes belonged to the Robertian family,
who came from the banks of the Loire.
Even though the Carolingians briefly re-occupied the throne of France,
it was the Robertians, proclaimed 'Dukes of the Franks', who exercised real supremacy,
firmly based on the triangle Paris-Orléans-Tours.
There seemed to be no end to the calamities: political misfortune, famines, floods, plagues.
And a fateful day approached, which made the superstitious shudder: the year one thousand.

Man has two faces.

One of bright intellect, one of dim instinct.

One of peace, the other of murder.

One of quiet labour, the other of invasion.

47

And this is the mystery:

that these two faces are but one. And this face,

at once single and double, has for its mirror the city.

Every night must have an end. Just before the year 1000, Hugh Capet, a Robertian, installed his own dynasty on the throne of France. Paris, restored to its position as capital, was now to acknowledge for many centuries the family which in 1792 it rejected with violence. Provided at last with a king, the people of Paris no longer feared the emperor of Germany. In 978 Otto II encamped with his troops at Montmartre, but in spite of his warlike intentions he had to rest content with hurling his lance into one of the city gates. Thenceforward Paris remained unmolested for many years.

What a difference between the Paris of Hugh Capet and of François I! Here, in 1540, the Cité is covered with important buildings: Notre-Dame, the Hôtel-Dieu, the Palais, the Sainte-Chapelle. The Seine is spanned by two fine bridges, the Petit Pont and the Pont Saint-Michel. The left bank is studded with colleges, of Navarre, of the Lombards, of Beauvais, of Cambrai; with religious houses, the Carmelites, Sainte-Geneviève; with churches, Saint-Julien-le-Pauvre, Saint-Étienne-du-Mont; with picturesquely named streets where trades are plied, the Rue Pavée d'Andouilles, the Rue Perdue, the Rue des Rats, the Rue des Noyers, the Rue des Lavandières, the Rue des Poirées, the Rue Saint-Jacques.
Let us trace the progress of the village which after five centuries will deserve the name of capital.

49

It was intellectual supremacy that Paris attained first. As Pope Innocent III said, Paris became 'the oven where the bread of the whole world was baked'. From 1108 onwards G. de Champeaux, professor of rhetoric and theology, made the name of the Augustinian Abbey of Saint-Victor famous.

A philosopher is not necessarily any the less a man. The brilliant Abélard (1079–1142) quarrelled with Champeaux and put the finishing touch to the scandal by falling in love with Héloise, one of his pupils. Her jealous old uncle, a canon into the bargain, took her away, and punished him by the famous mutilation. Although in addition his teaching was condemned by a council and a pope, Abélard pursued his eventful life to the end, quarrelled and was reconciled with Saint Bernard, and taught the faith to three thousand pupils, of whom fifty became bishops, twenty cardinals, and one a pope. A capital in the Palais de Justice brings the faces of Abélard and Héloise together again (49).

Here is the Paris of Héloise and Abélard,

Of the love that acknowledged no law but itself.

Paris, the capital of passion.

The fame of Abélard does not eclipse that of the Abbey of Saint-Victor, nor that of G. de Champeaux. The great minds of the century, such as Saint Thomas à Becket, Adam, Richard, and Gilduin were among his pupils. But the monastery buildings vanished in 1790, to be incongruously replaced by the Halle aux Vins. Little remains to bear witness to the great abbey. A rare piece of evidence is a precious manuscript of the 15th century, a book of prayers of the infirmary. It shows the last dying moments of a monk (50), with Saint Augustine and Saint Victor at his bedside (51).

50   51

The Capetians' ambition was to organise and build. In about 1060 they created the post of provost to have charge of police and security. In about 1131 Louis VI founded the fair connected with the leper-hospital of Saint-Lazare, and in 1134 he founded the Abbey of Montmartre. Forty year later Louis VII decided to drain the marshes and put them under cultivation. But Philip Augustus (1180–1223) was the real builder of Paris (52); no mean achievement for one who spent most of his life fighting in foreign wars.

'Since evil

lies in wait for me,

says Paris,

'I will gird myself

with walls.'

Paris, left without kings or knights, had to protect herself. She became a fortress. Between 1190 and 1213 the city was encircled by an unbroken wall thirty feet high and between seven and ten feet thick, defended by thirty-three towers on the right bank and thirty-four on the left. Twelve gates were let into it. It was a solid piece of work, which time alone could break down, but of which many fragments remain – as in the Rue Clovis, the Rue Guénégaud, and this tower (54) in the Rue des Francs-Bourgeois, in the courtyard of the Crédit Municipal.

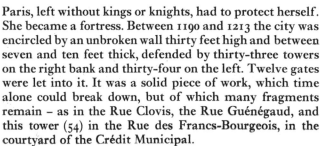

52

55

The streets were a slough. Some pigs wallowing in front of the church of Saint-Gervais caused the son of Louis VI to fall from his horse and break his neck. Philip Augustus, choked moreover with the pestilential stench, ordered the principal streets to be paved with stone. But even with the advent of paving-stones into the history of Paris, the pig was not quite banished. A stall in Saint-Gervais (55) preserves the memory of the creature beloved of Saint Anthony. In fact the religious of the Abbey of Saint-Antoine were the only citizens thenceforward permitted to let their pigs wander freely, and they sold great quantities of gingerbread pigs at their local fair, founded in 957, and now known as the Foire du Trône.

53

The rampart rendered superfluous the Grand Châtelet, built of wood in 870, then rebuilt in stone to defend the Grand Pont from the right bank. Philip repaired or restored its enormous towers (57), beneath which passed the new road leading to Saint-Denis, parallel to the old Rue Saint-Martin. The Grand Châtelet was to shelter beneath its roof prisons of sinister repute and halls of justice, for the provost of Paris made his headquarters here, with his advisers on civil and criminal law, and his police lieutenants, expert at applying the 'question' and its legal tortures. They did not deal lightly with the few malefactors, real

57

or alleged, who were caught at night in those perilous streets. Public exposure in the pillory or on the 'ladder', flogging, mutilation, the iron collar, these were the mildest examples of the provost's power. This power was shared, moreover, with the many special jurisdictions – seigneurial, academic, and ecclesiastical – which until the reign of Louis XIV had the right of punishment and could even give the death penalty.

56

The city wall increased the value of the land within. Where it was not covered with houses, numerous little enclosures sheltered and brought to perfection vines of repute. The vineyard of Montmartre (56), the Rue Vineuse, the Rue des Vignes, the Rue de la Goutte-d'Or, for long outside the city wall, are survivals of Paris's great wine-growing past.

'Come through the gate as a friend,
and I will give you wine from my vineyards.'

58

In 1202, in the west, where they still remembered the Norman terror, Philip had built a keep nearly seventy feet high, with walls fourteen feet thick at the base. It was called the 'Louvre', perhaps in memory of the Viking 'Leovar' or camp. It was a strong-room for the royal archives and a royal prison as much as a tower of defence. One of its deepest dungeons survives, its stunted pillars ornamented with carved heads (58). They looked down on the captivity of the Grand Ferrand, who was put in chains after his defeat at Bouvines; and later, on the punishment of the sinister Sire de Coucy.

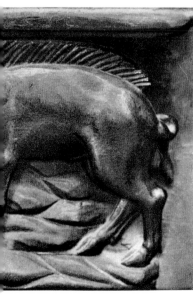

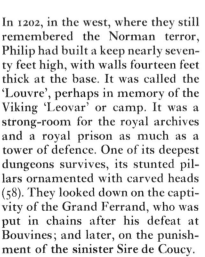

When he set off for the Crusades in 1190, Philip had no hesitation in entrusting power to some of the 'bourgeois'. This was a new class composed of craftsmen and merchants, whose prosperity derived from the building and provisioning of the capital, and on the trade and the taxes which the junction of land routes, rivers and bridges attracted. From 1135 onwards their activity was concentrated on the right bank, in the Marché des Champeaux (59). For this reason, in 1183, Philip decided to put up there two buildings especially designed for trade, enclosed within walls and shut up at night. These 'Halles' (60) or covered markets, which were first used only for the textile trade, were never to move from their original site.

Of all the bourgeois, the 'water-merchants'– i.e. those who provisioned or fitted out ships – were the first. They formed a syndicate or 'hanse', which exercised a monopoly over all river traffic from 1170 onwards. Their seal (61), a ship sailing on the Seine, already carried considerable weight when in 1220 Philip gave them authority over town-criers, the levying of taxes, and weights and measures.

'Enter my walls,' says Paris, 'and you will see — I am trade,

to do you service.'

Paris, now expanding, suffered from a shortage of water. For the new quarter, which was quite a long way from the Seine itself, Philip made a catchment of the springs from the heights of Belleville. The first public fountains appeared in the Halles and in the Charnier (Charnel-house) des Innocents, nearby. The Fontaine Maubuée (62), decorated with the arms of Paris and situated at the corner of the Rue Saint-Martin (No. 122), was to provide the citizens of Paris with water for seven centuries.

Here is another seal with a great future before it (63). It represents two scholars. Since the days of Abélard, Paris had been a city of learning. Students flocked from all over Europe England, Germany, Italy, Scandinavia.

The church schools of the Cité were now deserted in favour of the new quarter on the left bank. In 1180 Josse, an Englishman, opened the first residential hall for students.

A great community of scholars was formed, which took upon itself the title of University. From 1200 to 1220 laws and licences from King and Pope systematised its powers and confirmed its independence. The students, aged from fifteen to thirty, were not answerable to the civil power, i.e. the police – but they were obliged to speak Latin.

'I am knowledge. Books flourish beside the Seine. To make you wise.'

Paris learned to think on the left bank, but on the right bank she did not forget to pray. Like its counterparts Sainte-Geneviève and Saint-Germain-des-Prés, on the opposite bank the royal priory built in 1040 by Henri I on the extension of the Rue Saint-Martin gathered within its walls the religious activity of its own side of the river (64).

The Benedictines of Cluny made it an ardent centre of religious life, and it was within that orbit that the bourg or borough of Saint-Martin-des-Champs grew up. Its chapel was Paris's first Gothic building.

On the spot where faith had once quickened, the Revolution installed the Conservatoire des Arts et Métiers.

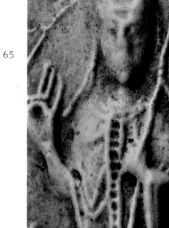

Notre-Dame, a determined leap towards the sky, is also a geometrical design covered with figures. It is 427 feet long and 157 feet wide. After the chancel (1163–1180), the transept and the nave (1180–1200), the west front was completed by 1250 and the south (67) and north fronts by 1270. Time has dealt fairly kindly with these wonders, but the great west front (68), with its three portals of Saint Anne, the Last Judgment, and the Virgin, its cornice showing the twenty-eight kings of Judah, its great rose-window and its arches, were attacked by the revolutionaries of 1792, and all its statues were destroyed.

'Enter,' says Paris. 'I am prayer. Here are my churches, to lighten your darkness.'

A great capital must have a lofty cathedral. In 1163 Pope Alexander III inaugurated a vast foundation on the site of the ancient Merovingian church dedicated to Our Lady. The first bishop, Maurice de Sully (65), the son of poor peasants, who baptised Philip Augustus there two years after the cathedral was founded, did not live to see it completed. Even when Philip Augustus himself died, only the chancel and the nave were finished. The foundations, reaching thirty feet below the ground, wait patiently for eternity. No one knows who built them. Architects of genius, and skilful craftsmen using tools as old as the world (66) bequeathed to posterity those imperishable masses of stone, but not their own names.

71

But the bishop's penitential ladder stood in the middle of the cathedral square. There was no more laughing or sleeping in the presence of this device. At its foot the guilty person confessed his fault, then he was perched up at the top, for hours if necessary, so that passers-by could enjoy his remorse (69). The ladder had plenty of customers: for example, the Grand Master of the Templars, Ravaillac, the Marquise de Brinvilliers, and Damiens the regicide, for whom it was the antechamber of death. Our humanitarian age has done away with such horrors: the place which was the foot of the ladder now marks the starting point for all the beckoning roads of France.

72   73   74

Notre-Dame is at once a vast mirror of moral, theological, and legendary lore, and a picture of the day-to-day life of Paris. The Jewish high priest finds his lost hands again on the Virgin's tomb that he tried to profane (70); Cruelty takes on the guise of a mistress spurning her servant; Discord brings a husband and wife to blows; Disobedience rebels against the bishop; Faithlessness is unfrocked. In peaceful mood, the Parisian gathers his harvest (71), threshes his corn (72), kills his pig (73), and feeds his birds (74).

'My cathedral is open,' says Paris. 'A public place, for your transfiguration.'

70

Though it is the stronghold of God, Notre-Dame was first of all the house of the people. It was the witness of royal marriages, the theatre for victorious Te Deums, the pyre for great obsequies, and also a place of gaiety. People gathered there for banquets, and to see mystery plays both sacred and profane. A Parisian could sleep there at night if he had no home, and find inviolable sanctuary when pursued either justly or unjustly.

75

'See,' says Paris,

'my cathedral has broad shoulders, like a porter in the Halles,

to sustain you.'

The towers of Notre-Dame rise 230 feet above the ground (75). On the left, in the south tower, Jacqueline still rings; she weighs thirteen tons and was recast in 1686, the gold and silver ornaments of pious Parisian ladies melted in with the bronze. On the right, in a tall oak belfry separated from the stonework that surrounds it, hangs the Great Bell, weighing fifteen tons. These giants are not easily moved. They speak only on the high festival days of the church, or to mark events of national importance.

As well as destroying the statues of Notre-Dame, the Revolution also plundered and scattered the great religious relics of Paris. But some were saved, among the most important of which were (76) the Sacred Nail, a fragment of the True Cross, and the Crown of Thorns, the acquisition of which was one of the major events of the reign of Louis IX (Saint Louis).

76

36

'If you find my cathedral too sturdy
look at her sister
Sainte-Chapelle. Champagne after
Beaujolais, to cheer you.'

REPRESENTATION DV PALAIS ROYALI! EN LA CITI

78

Saint Louis (77), grandson of Philip Augustus, dreamed,
like all the kings since Clovis, of making Paris the equal
of Rome and Byzantium. His faith gave him an idea which
would compel the attention of Christendom: he would
acquire the things that witnessed the Passion.

The Emperor of Constantinople sold him two pieces of the
Cross, a fragment of the spear which pierced Christ's side,
a piece of the sponge on which the vinegar was offered,
some shreds of clothing, the reed which was given to the
Son of God as a sceptre, and, most moving relic of all,
the Crown of Thorns.

The Sainte-Chapelle sheltered this sacred museum. It was
consecrated in April 1248. For a long time it stood alone in
the courtyard of the Palais (78). But after the fires of 1776
it was partly hidden behind new buildings, as if some evil
influence wished to conceal the mysterious glint of its
windows, fifty feet high. For these the master glass-makers
of the Ile de France fashioned 1,134 scenes, in which the
Old Testament, the Gospels, and the Apocalypse join
together in a sparkling mass of colour that remains
miraculously intact (79–83).

79

80

'In the contest

between light

and darkness in

architecture, the

creator of the

Sainte-Chapelle,

in the pride of

his victory,

built in light

itself.'

The only contemporary sequence in the fresco of coloured light is the solemn voyage of the Crown of Thorns, each stage of which is illustrated in minute detail.

In order to defend the Latin Empire of Constantinople, the young Emperor Baldwin had been obliged to pledge the Crown of Thorns to Venetian moneylenders. He offered it to Louis IX if he would redeem it. Two preaching friars were sent to Constantinople. The bargain was concluded, the price of purchase duly weighed out (79).

On 10th August 1239 the two emissaries arrived with their precious burden on the outskirts of Sens, and at Villeneuve-l'Archevêque the King himself took charge of it. On 18th August the Crown was exhibited for the people of Paris to do it reverence, in a Notre-Dame still noisy with the work of masons and hewers of stone (80).

The King and his brothers Robert, Alphonse, and Charles, took upon their shoulders once more the reliquary (81) which they had carried barefoot from Sens. Accompanied by the queen mother, Blanche of Castile, and by the Abbot of Saint-Denis and his monks, they brought the triple casket of wood, silver and gold, and set it down in the little palace church in the Cité until the Sainte-Chapelle should be built.

The Parisians who crowded the route of the procession saw a queen mother of stern aspect (82). But they loved her well, and she was a woman to be reckoned with. The daughter of an Englishwoman and a Spaniard, she found herself the widow of Louis VIII with a son of twelve. To escape from the lords and barons, who wanted to take her and the heir to the throne hostage, she sought refuge in the Château of Montlhéry, whence she appealed for help to the people of Paris. Then students, merchants and workmen were all to be seen hurrying through the Porte Saint-Jacques to bring back to their stout city the queen mother and the young King. Was she then so severe? Sometimes, as the sun goes down outside the Sainte-Chapelle, her face is visited by a secret gentleness.

81

82

The road through Paris, along which this ceaseless coming and going still continued as late as the 17th century, was dotted along all its length with pious foundations. In 1217 Dominique de Guzman sent seven of his followers to Paris, where they founded the convent of the Dominicans in the Rue Saint-Jacques, later called the convent of the Jacobins (85). Saint Dominic's successor as head of the preaching friars, a German, the blessed Jourdain of Saxony, was a pupil there, and in spite of his international responsibilities he used to return there in Lent to preach to the students. Another German, Saint Albert the Great, was a Dominican of the Rue Saint-Jacques, as was an Italian, the illustrious Saint Thomas Aquinas, who conceived the idea of the Summa Theologica there. One would have thought that so many great men would always attract young students; but their convent disappeared in 1800.

'Travel across me,' says Paris.
'I am port of call and
a thoroughfare.

You will go back
to your native lands,
but you will return to me:
to find yourselves again.'

So many objects of curiosity and beauty attracted crowds of people. While the Crusades were raging in the Holy Land, less warlike pilgrims flocked to Paris. They told of Charlemagne's expedition against the Saracens of Spain, and of his strange vision of Saint James the Apostle (84). From all the provinces of the north and the lands beyond the Rhine, thousands went down to Compostela to meditate at the supposed tomb of the Apostle. They arrived in Paris by La Villette, where the present church of Saint James and Saint Christopher was built in the 15th century; they were given rest and refreshment free of charge at the Confrérie Saint-Jacques; they passed the church of Saint-Jacques-la-Boucherie, built in 1060; they visited the Sainte-Chapelle and Notre-Dame, both newly completed; and then took again the Rue Saint-Jacques. The way ahead was still a long one: at the last halting-place, the Commanderie Saint-Jacques-du-Haut-Pas, they made enquiries, exchanged information, replenished their stores, and met old acquaintances. The way south, they were told, lay through the Porte d'Orléans.

40

Le chemin de monſieur

ſainct Iacques en Galice, dict Compoſtel, & combien il y a de lieuës de ville en ville, à partir de la ville de Paris.

DE Paris au Bourg la Royne. ij.l.
Du Bourg la Royne, à Long-ju-meau. iij l.
De Long-jumeau, à Mont-lehery. ij.l.
De Mont-lehery, à Chaſtres. ij.l.
De Chaſtres, à Eſtrecy le Larron. iij.l.
D'eſtrecy, à Eſtampes. ij.l.
D'Eſtampes, à Mont-neruille. iiij.l.
De Mont-neruille, à Angeuille la gaſte. ij.l.
D'Angeuille la gaſte, à Engeruille. ij.l.
D'Engeruille, à Toury. iij.l.
De Toury, à Artenay. iiij.l
D'Artenay, à l'Engenerie. ij l.
De l'Engenerie, à Sercottes. i.l.
De Sercottes, à Orleans. iij.l.
D'Orleans, à noſtre Dame de Clery. iiij.l.
De Clery, à S. Laurens des eaux. iiij.l.
De S. Laurens des eaux, à Blois. viij.l.
De Blois, à Chaumont. vij.l.
De Chaumont, à Amboiſe.
D'Amboiſe, à ...urs. vij. l.
... Chaſteau
De Tours, à ...ſon. iiij.l.
De Mu...ſ... ſaincte Catherine
De ſaincte ... ſaincte Maure.
De ſaincte M..., ...ort de Pille.
Du Port de P... ...ommes S. Martin
Des hommes ... Martin, à Ingrande.
D'Ingrande ... Chaſtelerault.
De Chaſtele... ... Tricherie.
De la Tricherie, à Poictiers. iij.l
De Poictiers, à Luſignen. iij.l.
De Luſignen, au Chenay. iij.l.
Du Chenay, à Melle. iij.l.
De Melle, à Ville-Dieu. iij.l.
De Ville-Dieu, à Eſconniau. v.l.
D'Eſconniau, à S. Eutrope de Saincte. iij.l.
De S. Eutrope, à Ponts. iiij.l.
De Ponts, à Plaſſa. ij.l.
De Plaſſa, à Mirrembeau. ij.l.
De Mirrembeau, à Torliers. iij.l.
De Torliers, à Blaye. iij.l.

De Blaye, paſſe ſur la Gironde pour aller à Bordeaux, qui dure huict lieuës. Somme de Paris à Bordeaux, il y a ſix vingts treize grandes lieuës.

De Bordeaux au petit Bordeaux. ij.l.
Du petit Bordeaux, à l'Hoſpital. iiij.l.
De l'Hoſpital, à la Tricherie. ij.l.
De la Tricherie, au Murel. ij.l.

Du Murel au Pontel. ij.l.
Du Pontel, à l'Herbe Famée. ij.l.
De l'Herbe Famée, à l'Hoſpital ſainct Anthoine.
De l'Hoſpital S. Anthoine, à la Ferme. ij l.
De la Ferme, à l'Eſperon. i.l.

Notez qu'à l'Eſperon, qui veut tirer à Nauarre, faut prendre à main ſeneſtre, & de là paſſer par la Biſquaye.

De l'Eſperon, à Chaſtel. ij.l.
De Chaſtel, à Mathicque. ij.l.
De Mathicque, à ſainct Vincent. iij.l.
De ſainct Vincent, à Hondres. iij.l.
De Hondres, à Bayonne. ij.l.
De Bayonne, à ſainct Iean de Lut. v.l.
De ſainct Iean de Lut, à ſaincte Marie de Hurin. ij.l.

Notez que c'eſt la fin du Royaume de France à vne riuiere qui eſt deçà ladite noſtre Dame de Hurin, pres Font-Arabie.

De ſaincte Marie de Hurin, à Arnany. ij.l.
D'Arnany, à Ville-Neufue. ij.l.
De Ville-Neufue, à Tholouſette. ij.l.
De Tholouſette, à Ville-Franque. iij.l.
De Ville-Franque, à Segure. iiij.l.
De Segure, au mont ſainct Adrien. ij.l.
... qui eſt aſſez haut, & p... ...ny le trou de ſainct Adrien ...
De ...oldodon, à Saluation. ij.l.
De Saluatiere, à Victoire. iij.l.
De Victoire, à Peuple. ij.l.
De Peuple, à Murande. iij.l.
De Murande, à Peucorbe. iij.l.
De Peucorbe, à Verbieſque. iij.l.
De Verbieſque, à Caſtille. i.l.
De Caſtille, à Monaſterio. i.l.
De Monaſterio, à Borges. v.l.
De Borges, à Tardaiges. ij l.
De Tardaiges, à Doruilles. ij.l.
De Doruilles, à Fontaines. ij.l.
De Fontaines, à quatre Souris. ij.l.
De quatre Souris, à Ponteroſe. iiij.l.
De Ponteroſe, à Boſeuille. ij.l.
De Boſeuille, à Formende. i.l.
De Formende, à la Rauanerie. i.l.
De la Rauanerie, à Population. ij.l.
De Population, à Carion. ij.l.
De Carion, à Caſedille. iij.l.
De Caſedille, à ſainct Sagon. iiij.l.

De ſainct Sagon, à Briſanne. ij.l.
De Briſanne, à Bourgue. i.l.
De Bourgue, à Religoux. ij.l.
De Religoux, à la Moyſelle. iij.l.
De la Moyſelle, à Lyon. iiij.l.
De Lyon, à ſainct Michel. ij.l.
De ſainct Michel, à Fontaines. ij.l.
De Fontaines, au pont de Laigue. ij.l.
Du Pont de Laigue, à Eſtorgues. ij.l.
D'Eſtorgues à l'Hoſpital ſaincte Catherine. iiij.l.
De l'Hoſpital, au Raneul. iiij.l.
Du Raneul, à Ville-Neufue. iiij.l.
De Ville-Neufue, à Moulins. ij.l.
De Moulins, à Quaux. i.l.
De Quaux, à Ponts Ferat. i.l.

Notez qu'icy eſt l'entrée du pays de Galice, & la fin du pays d'Eſpagne, & des bons vins.

De Ponts Ferat, à Pauie. iiij.l.
De Pauie, à Ville-Franq... ij.l.
De Ville-Franque, à Fum...re. ij.l.
De Fumeterre, à l'Hoſpit... la Côteſſe. ij.l.
De l'Hoſpital de la Côteſſe, ...ricaſtel. iij.l.
De Tricaſtel, à Ville-Miſer... iiij.l.
De Ville-Miſere, à Ponts-M...in. iiij.l.
De Ponts-Marin, à S. Iame l... il. ij.l.
De ſaincte Iame, à S. Iulian. ij.l.
De ſainct Iulian, à Chanle...r. iij.l.
De Chanleurier, à Arſe... ...t Ville-Neufue. ij.l.
De Ville-...eufue, à Vill...
De Vill...ſlée, à Vi...
De Vill...e, à ſainct...
De ſa... Mo...-jo...à Mo...
Iac... ...grande lieuë, ...
ris... ...Denys en France.

Somme ... Paris à ſainct Iacques en Galice ... trois cents cinquante & neuf lieuës.

A PARIS,
Chez IEAN LE CLERC, rue...
Latran, à la Salemandre Roy...
1621.

In a town of relics, of posting houses, and of saints, some shelter was needed for tired travellers. A touching legend gave rise to the building of such a shelter. Julien, a young nobleman, having been, through a mistake, the cause of his parents' death, renounced all wordly goods and with his wife became a hermit on the banks of a river. One day husband and wife, such was their humility, ferried a leper to the other side (88).

This poor man, abandoned by every one else, was really Christ come to bring Julien his pardon. It was no more than just that in the 6th century, on the banks of the Seine at the junction of the roads to Lyons and Orléans, a hospice and chapel should be dedicated to Julien l'Hospitalier. This charitable establishment was destroyed by the Normans, and replaced in 1170 by the little church of Saint - Julien - le - Pauvre, now the oldest church in Paris.

88

89

90

91

Opposite Saint - Julien - le - Pauvre stood the hospital of the Hôtel-Dieu. Saint Christopher, who carried the infant Christ on his shoulder through the flood, was its great patron. It was the only building in Paris which had a foot on either bank and spanned the river. It was huge. Its provisions were swallowed up by vaulted cellars ('cagnards') opening on to the Seine. Its own internal bridge, which was continually being rebuilt and improved, became a hospital ward in 1634. The public could pass through it by means of a double passageway, hence its name, Pont au Double.

For centuries kings and princes showered privileges upon this home of misfortune and suffering. But how overcrowded it was! The sick came there by land and by water (89). They waited four in a bed for death or for recovery, and death struck with equal hand the nuns who worked and the patients who hoped. The poet Gilbert died there in 1780, hapless guest at a banquet from which he was called away at the age of twenty-nine.

After being enlarged, altered and rebuilt several times, the Hôtel-Dieu was finally removed to the other side of the island. This was accomplished in 1865 by Haussmann, the great surgeon of Paris. Here is the building just before the operation (91).

'I care for both heart and soul.

The waters of my river are the elixir of life. The stones of my dwellings are

'The chief town of France, successor to Athens', as Bartholomew the Englishman termed her, Paris also strove to become a world centre of culture. Great minds abounded there. After the German Albert the Great and the Italian Thomas Aquinas came another Italian, Bonaventura, general of the Franciscan order at the age of thirty-six, and the Englishmen Duns Scotus and Roger Bacon.

Teaching was done in the open, in the Place Maubert or on the straw of the Rue du Fouarre; Saint-Julien-le-Pauvre, which rented out twenty-two houses to masters and students, was the heart of university Paris. Scholars had to wear caps and long gowns. Every college that belonged to a recognised 'nation' – France, Normandy, England, Germany, Picardy – rivalled the others to provide its scholars with teachers of reputation. The students had no written work, but had to attend long lectures (93). Their games and brawls took them as far as the Pré-aux-Clercs, near Saint-Germain-des Prés, and once a year, in a body, they paid a ceremonial visit to the fair of Lendit in the plain of Saint-Denis. Their rector was everywhere accorded princely honours.

The colleges began to climb the slopes: the Collège d'Harcourt, now the Lycée Saint-Louis, in 1280; the College of Cardinal Lemoine in 1302; the College of Navarre, now the Ecole Polytechnique, in 1304; the College of the Lombards, for Italian students, in 1333. There

92

93

were fifty-two of them by the end of the 15th century, and still to come were the College of Beauvais, where Ramus and Francis Xavier taught, and the College of Clermont, now the Lycée Louis-le-Grand.

In 1257, by a special act of Saint Louis, preserved in the Archives de France (94), secular priests were allowed to open a school near the Roman baths. Were they more able than the monks? Their success was soon manifest, to the delight of their director, the King's chaplain, whose name was Roger Sorbon. And so the Sorbonne was born.

94

philosopher's stones. When you are far away, you will still be near me; in dreams.'

95

Meanwhile Saint Louis increased the number of the monasteries. After introducing the Carmelites, mendicant friars, in 1230, he installed on the left bank the Franciscans, or grey friars. Their refectory, rebuilt on the right bank at the end of the 15th century, still survives as the Musée Dupuytren. In about 1254, near the Louvre, Louis also founded a hospice to receive three hundred blind persons, known as 'Les Quinze-Vingt'; and, at the instance of his sister Isabelle, an abbey at Longchamp. But for many years his most famous foundation was the Carthusian monastery of Vauvert, on the site of which the Luxembourg gardens now stand. It was then wooded country outside the city walls. There Druidic or Gallo-Roman remains harboured evil forces, in particular the devil Vauvert. It took the monks of the order of Saint Bruno no less than three days and nights to exorcise this tenacious fellow. On his late territory there then arose a great collection of buildings, dominated by the chapel built in 1326 (95). Nothing of this now remains.

Who can ever know the prayers

from which a Paris sky is woven?

May not the softness of certain evenings

come from lost orisons, lost as dusk gently falls?

So many monasteries must surely have left a haze of litanies in the air.

96

97

Of all the foundations of that time, the most famous was that of the Templars. These Knights of Heaven, whose order was founded for the Holy Wars and the protection of pilgrims, had been established for a hundred years in the east of Paris. In 1240 they built a fortified enclosure, where they settled in a body after the loss of the Holy Sepulchre (96). The Grand Master and the treasury were surrounded by four thousand persons, all enjoying immunity from the royal police and the claims of the exchequer. The keep of this fortress saw the passage of many events – the death of the Templars, the last agonies of the monarchy, the vagaries of the centuries; but in 1808 it too was to vanish in its turn.

The king had always lived in the west of the Cité. But the Palais was old. Philip the Fair ordered it to be modernised as was fitting for a great king. He built kitchens, a surrounding wall, and four defensive towers, later named the Clock-Tower, the Silver Tower, Caesar's Tower, and the Bonbec or blabbing Tower, so-called because it was there that torture loosened prisoners' tongues (99). The Palais was a triumph of Gothic art; even the vaults are of great beauty (100).

Paris continued to grow. The land was built on, parcelled out, sold to finance the Palestine adventure or to purchase the luxury which the East revealed. But hard times lay ahead. When the Crusades were ended and Philip the Bold was dead, after a reign too brief to be remembered, Philip the Fair (1285–1314) came to the throne, to grapple with the nobles, who thereafter lapsed into passivity, and with the needs of a now adult nation. They were cruel years, but judging only by his effigy in Saint-Denis, the king of iron turned a bland countenance upon all the tumults (98).

101

The Great Hall with its double nave (101) was the show-piece of the Palais. Stone statues of all the kings, from the legendary Pharamond onwards, stood there, gilt against a background of azure. In the centre was a huge marble table: banquets were held at it, plays were acted upon it. Leaving this hall to go to the Sainte-Chapelle, one crossed the 'Merchant's Gallery', a long public promenade where the citizens' handsome wives chatted in front of fashionable shop-windows.

Life and the city. A tour of the city.

Here is a waggon packed with travellers, there an apothecary crying his salves. A boat laden with casks wants to pass through, but a toll must be paid; meanwhile the revenue officer samples the wine (102).

102

103

A shepherd and his flock pass a countryman and his pig. Melons from Meudon, Chaillot or Nogent approach their mooring at a nearby wharf (103).

The age of the financier-king and 'voluntary confessions' was also an age of delightful artists. Master Honoré, the illuminator, was one of the first of the Paris School. He painted a life of Saint Denis for the King, in which sketches of Paris life also appear (102–8). The Grand-Pont (now the Pont-au-Change), bordered with houses and shops, which joined the Palais to the right bank, was a bustling commercial and business centre near to the Port de Grève where the provisioning of Paris was carried on. Let us examine this everchanging spectacle.

A day of life. Life changes. The city too.

Four men drag a barrel. A barefoot pilgrim walks with his shoes hung round his neck, while below is a commodity rarely seen on the Seine, coal (104).   104

The horsemen pay toll, but not the busker, whose marmoset makes the tollkeeper laugh. 'To pay in monkey-money', as the French say of bilking (105).   105

Where is that kennel-boy off to? To have a meal perhaps. At any rate the man with one leg has his eye on a fine pie. Below, a man holds his nose, ready to dive (106).   106

Life and the city. An old city. As old as life. Never old. Always alive.

109

Parisians also sang and played. An illustrated collection of popular songs, of about 1280, shows us their

110

diversions: hide and seek, blind man's buff, ninepins. They are still half rustic (109–110). The monk and the merchant pass by, the porter and the spinning-girl have stopped flirting, but the angler has thoughts only for his gudgeon (107).

107

108 Although a 'millers' bridge' was built in 1296, the paddle-wheels of the Grand-Pont continued to grind the grain of Beauce (108).

No. 3 Rue Volta was a well-to-do house, of unusual height, with a gable and two shops whose shutters folded back to form covered stalls. It is said that the mayor of the bourg of Saint-Martin-des-Champs lived here. The gable has gone, but the house is still standing; the oldest in Paris (111).

A horrible news item of 1290. A good woman who was very poor pawned her best clothes with Jonathan the Jew. 'I will give them back to you for Easter,' he told her, 'if you bring me the host from your communion.' She did so, and the scoundrel transfixed the host with his knife. Blood gushed from it. He cursed, and threw it in the fire. It remained whole. He plunged it in boiling water. The water grew red and boiled more furiously, and in the steam arose the image of a crucifix (112). This was enough to attract the neighbours, and make them burn Jonathan alive, which they lost no time in doing. To boil God – how horrible! A monastery called the Couvent des Billettes (Faggots) was built on the scene of the crime, and its cloister, rebuilt in 1408, is now the oldest in Paris (113). Napoleon allocated its church, rebuilt in 1756, to the Protestants.

113

Paris, city of gossip. Death is a scandal-monger.

It talks in order to kill. It kills in order to talk.

114

The houses on the banks of the Seine were bathed, so to say, in the water – some of them were actually built over the river – for there were no embankments. Two were built in 1313: the Quai de Nesle (now the Quai de Conti) and the Quai des Grands-Augustins. The monastic order which gave its name to the second had been installed on the left bank since 1293, but did not build its convent (114) until 1350, when it was provided with a hall so vast that it became a place of assembly and debate. Groups as diverse as the Chevaliers du Saint-Esprit (Knights of the Holy Spirit), the Parlements, the States-General, and the Chamber of Justice, met there till 1797, when the monastery was destroyed.

But it was around Saint-Séverin, rebuilt since 1230, that the activity of the left bank was most intense. The names of the streets speak for themselves: Rue de la Parcheminerie (parchment-makers), with its public scribes, copyists, and parchment-vendors; Rue des Enlumineurs (illuminators), now Rue Boutebrie; the Rues de la Hûchette-d'Or (Golden Bin), de la Bûcherie (woodmen), and des Sacs à Lie (lee sacks, i.e. winelees for treating skins), which has since become the Rue Zacharie.

The nearby Petit Pont made Saint-Séverin the travellers' church. They worshipped Saint Martin there, and dedicated their horses' shoes to him. Students went there too; the Macé bell sounded their curfew.

In the 15th century, galleries of charnel-houses were built there, as they had been near other churches; these were the only ones that survived thereafter in Paris (115). One day in 1474 a man condemned to death was operated upon there for the stone, and cured – an unprecedented surgical feat which earned the patient his pardon.

Saint-Séverin, many times restored and renovated, is the doyen of the parish churches of the left bank.

115   116

117

Where are your tongues, your skulls upon which Paris rests? You prattled in front of the pillory. Now you are as silent as your victims.

Every good social organisation included a pillory. Apart from that of the Abbey of Saint-Germain-des-Prés, which was kept up until 1636, Paris had only one: the pillory of the king's justice (117). A spendid device, its horizontal wheel could grip the heads and arms of six criminals at a time, and it turned a complete circle in two hours. After the reign of Saint Louis, someone had the bright idea of setting it up in the Halles, so that idlers who ran short of insults could shy rotten eggs and cabbage stumps at the people exposed there (petty rascals mostly). Sometimes there was a head that had just been lopped off, occasionally even a book. But Louis XVI abolished this strange object of amusement in 1786. Probably the only person really upset about this was the public hangman, who lived on the ground floor.

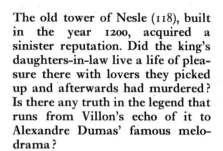

The old tower of Nesle (118), built in the year 1200, acquired a sinister reputation. Did the king's daughters-in-law live a life of pleasure there with lovers they picked up and afterwards had murdered? Is there any truth in the legend that runs from Villon's echo of it to Alexandre Dumas' famous melodrama?

118

Gossip. Legends of the boudoirs. Nothing escapes. What is not talked about?

Everything is talked about. Paris the scandal-monger. Paris the word.

119

There were three of them: Marguerite of Burgundy and her two cousins, Blanche and Jeanne, in their twenties, charming, perhaps a little harum-scarum. However, the scandal broke; they were thrown into prison. Then Philip, the strict father-in-law, died, and in record time, from 1314 to 1328, his sons, the kings of straw, succeeded: Louis X, the Headstrong, husband of Marguerite; Philip V, husband of Jeanne; and Charles IV, husband of Blanche. Marguerite died; Louis, who had doubtless connived at her murder, married Clémence of Hungary. He died, and Philip took his place. To repudiate Jeanne was a different matter: she had brought him Franche Comté as a dowry. What could he do? He died in 1322. Charles IV ascended the throne. Blanche was still imprisoned. An embarrassing situation. Why not divorce her? Monks and bishops made inquiry and counterinquiry (119), and at last the king was free to marry again. He did so, was left a widower, married yet again, and then died without a male heir; the end of the Capetians in the direct line. Only Jeanne remained. She came to beguile her widowhood in the Hôtel de Nesle, opposite the Louvre. It was said that the scholar Buridan visited her more often than was strictly necessary. That did not prevent him becoming a wise rector of the University.

121

Whenever the throne was unstable, Paris suffered. How many tragedies took place in those fourteen years! How many times was the sinister tumbril (120) seen taking the road north-east to the gibbet of Montfaucon (121, 131), which was from the time of Saint Louis the most terrible symbol of 'High Justice' in Paris!

In 1325 the wooden scaffold was replaced by sixteen stone pillars more than thirty feet high and joined together with heavy beams. Not only the living were brought there. The dead, already decapitated or boiled alive, broken on the wheel or quartered, were hung there also, the pieces of their bodies tied up in sacks. The corpses swung there (122) until their flesh, their bones, and the ropes they hung from had completely disintegrated, a process hastened by the birds. At their feet lay the ditch into which the last remaining fragments were tossed, and which provided a sinister framework for Victor Hugo's epilogue to 'Notre-Dame de Paris'.

122

What fury drove these kings of straw, incapable of setting their own house in order, to immolate their servants so cruelly, in particular the ministers of finance of the previous reign (121)? Philip the Fair's financial secretary, Enguerrand de Marigny, climbed the scaffold at Montfaucon in 1315. The corpse of Louis X's financial adviser was hung there in 1322, six years before Pierre Rémy, and nine before Macé de Maches, both from the same office. And sometimes a 'man' was cut down and rehabilitated, as happened to Enguerrand de Marigny – after he had swung for two years.

51

120

Let us talk. Let us talk. Of a new king. A new monastery. A minister of finance.

123

Let us acclaim the new king, John the Good, as he enters by the Porte Saint-Denis with his retinue in blue, pink and green (123). He was not to be a citizen of Paris for long. The English captured him on the field of Poitiers in 1356, and took him prisoner to London, where he eventually died in 1364. The young Charles, the first French prince to take the title of Dauphin, was to have a rough passage.

There was no king, no army, no money.

The barons were held responsible for the defeat. They had to give way, then, to the citizens of Paris. These had a political instrument in the States-General; a leader in Etienne Marcel, a prominent cloth-manufacturer and provost of the merchants; and an aim – to get rid of the boy Dauphin and put in his place the wily Charles of Navarre, who was John the Good's son-in-law, but hated him. These were the ingredients of the drama. Marcel gathered all the malcontents together and gave them a red and blue hood ('chaperon') for a uniform (124). The Dauphin, who was brave for all his eighteen years, faced the mob. But three thousand armed rioters invaded the Palais. Two marshals of the royal household were killed. Marcel himself saved the Dauphin by placing his own hood on his head (125).

124

125

Such sombre times did not ease the task of the Valois. But some new things were welcome: little Boccaccio, born of an Italian father and a Parisian mother in 1313; the monastery of the Cistercians (1338), where Pope Benedict XII made his profession (Rue de Poissy); the Faculty of Medicine, for its famous prescription against the Black Death, which claimed 80,000 victims in Paris, and even struck at the throne (1350).

But the Regent had meanwhile fled from Paris. Charles VII, Henri III, the young Louis XIV, and Thiers, would all do the same later, in similar circumstances. He fled only to return with advantage. The nobility were firm again. The provinces fell away from Charles of Navarre.

Etienne Marcel, the national hero, now seemed no more than the leader of a rebel town. The people, tired of making trouble for the sole benefit of the merchants, wavered in their loyalty. Marcel was suspected of conspiring with Navarre in the interests of the English who surrounded Paris. During the night of 31st July 1358, he gave the order to open the Porte Saint-Antoine to the troops of Navarre. The guard was loyal to the Dauphin. With the keys in his hand, Etienne Marcel was struck down with a hatchet (127); his corpse and that of his bodyguard were thrown on the rubbish heap (128–129).

The revolution ran its course. Its leader wanted to win for Paris the municipal autonomy enjoyed by the rich Flemish towns with which the Paris merchants traded. Premises were needed for this first 'commune'. Already, near the ancient Roman forum on the mount of Sainte-Geneviève, then, later, near the Grand Châtelet, there had been a 'citizens' parlour', where discussions and arbitrations took place. But new conditions called for new premises. Etienne Marcel bought a large porticoed house in the Place de Grève (126). This was the Hôtel de Ville of Paris, which was to remain there ever after. It was a fine place for the bourgeoisie: they aimed at making laws there, and bringing to heel both the city of Paris and the Dauphin, now Regent.

More taxes. Another reign.

Plague.

Poverty.

Processions.

Let us talk. Let us talk.

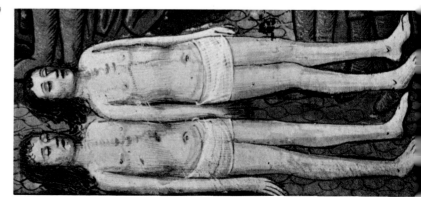

A full programme. It includes the stake. And the new Bastille.

130

When the English had been driven from France and order restored by Du Guesclin, it was necessary to make Paris safe from further assault. On the left bank, Charles V restored the ancient wall of Philip Augustus. On the right bank, which had been considerably developed, he built between 1367 and 1380 a new rampart (439), encircling the new quarters of Saint-Pol-des-Champs, the Temple, Saint-Martin-des-Champs, Saint-Honoré, and the Louvre. Two lines of moats completed this work of defence. The idea had been Etienne Marcel's. A wise prince does not scorn to use the ideas of a conquered rebel.

133

132

With Marcel defeated, Charles V re-entered Paris (130). In a city pacified and restored to prosperity he raised a new landmark. Beside the towers of the Palais, the scaffold of Montfaucon, and the lofty keep of the Temple, arose the great mass of the Bastille (131).

Since the massacre of 1358, the King had no great confidence in his palace. First a great gate was built, with four towers seventy feet high above foundations thirty feet deep, which closed the Rue Saint-Antoine.

By 1382 it had become a fortress with eight towers, and the street a cul-de-sac. A new Porte Saint-Antoine and a detour were made necessary. The King took up residence nearby in the Hôtel Saint-Pol, a huge up-to-date house with baths, sports-grounds, and aviaries. The nearby Celestine monastery became the major royal burial-place, after Saint-Denis. Now there is no trace of monastery, hôtel, or Bastille.

134

The King speaks. The people are silent.

136

135

Charles V sent to the stake the Turlupins, a group of heretics with somewhat wild beliefs. One, who died in prison, was even posthumously boiled in public in a vat (133).

The provost of the Châtelet, Aubriot, concentrated on the royal watch, or state police, rather than on the watch maintained by the Parisians themselves. In about 1380 he built the Pont Saint-Michel, and rebuilt and strengthened the Petit Châtelet, where students and travellers were screened on their way to the Cité via the Petit-Pont. He restricted the merchants' provost and the magistrates to the mere technical representation of communal interests, and imposed the King's authority on Paris and the nobles. He was to

smart for this later. But the citizens echoed Eustache Deschamps in singing: 'For pleasure and for beauty rare, Nothing with Paris can compare'.

Charles IV of Germany, the King's uncle, may have hummed these lines to himself during his state visit in 1378. The welcoming of a German Emperor was no ordinary occasion. The royal gold plate was brought out, and a great feast spread on the famous marble table in the Palais. The Archbishop of Reims and the King of the Romans were also bidden to the feast (136). Between the courses, strolling players acted scenes from the Crusades: the sermon of Peter the Hermit, the expedition of Godefroy de Bouillon, and the capture of Jerusalem.

55

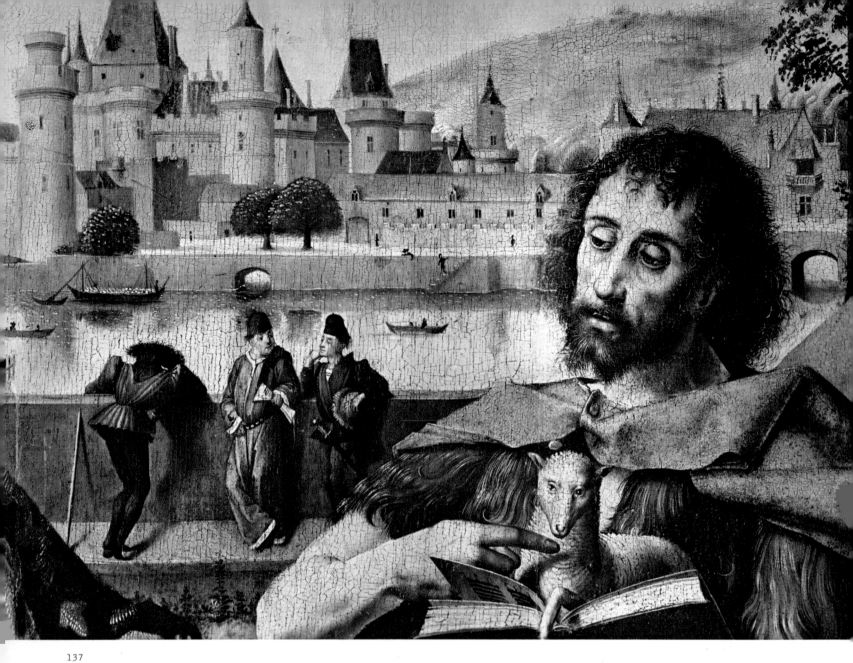

But the Seine flows on, more calmly than seems reasonable.

In truth, reason is lacking now.

Still troubled by the ghosts of his murdered marshals, Charles V handed over part of his palace to the Parlement of Paris. It was an unwise move: this supreme court of justice was to give future monarchs much trouble. The royal palace of the Romans and the Capetians thus became a palace of the lawyers, a palace of justice. But Charles held on to the Louvre. The keep was surrounded by the less forbidding living quarters, with turrets and weathercocks, of which the reredos of the Parlement of Paris gives us a charming picture (137). Inside was a library of 910 volumes, embellished with miniatures, the best of them from the hand of Jean Pucelle, the foremost in that art. At night thirty chandeliers lit up the cypress panelling and the cupboards of this quiet sanctuary, forerunner of the Bibliothèque Nationale.

LELOVVRE

138

56

139

1380. Charles V, who met a premature death, was succeeded by his son (139), whose brain hatched many disasters. Paris and the whole of France had cause to tremble.

140

Aubriot the Provost, the first victim of the new reign, was condemned to the ladder at Notre-Dame, to public penance and self-accusation (140), and to life imprisonment. The official reason? He sympathised with the Jews.

141

1382. Aubriot was released by the Maillotins, a group of Parisians who declared war on the Treasury, brandishing mallets. The Maillotins struck down the tax-collectors (141) and killed the Jews. Aubriot withdrew to Avignon. The Maillotins were crushed. That was the end of municipal rule.

A forest drives a king mad.

142

13th June 1392. The High Constable, Olivier de Clisson, another former adviser of the late Charles V, was attacked by Pierre de Craon (142), a nobleman of ill repute. The King, pursuing the criminal through the forest of Le Mans, got sunstroke. They had to take him home, bound, on a cart. He was mad.

Some maskers are consumed

143

Charles VI got better. He gave a masked ball which he and his friends attended attired in canvas covered with tow. Some merry fellow thought it would enliven the proceedings to set the tow on fire. Four of the masqueraders were burned to death (143). The King escaped, but without his reason.

by a fire of their own kindling.

57

144

This age of disorder, which heralded the decline of the Middle Ages, still retained the desire to live and to enjoy living. Is it possible to imagine, in those dark days, a pleasanter prospect than this of Paris (144), with two sumptuous royal trains greeting each other in the foreground? Fouquet painted it to illustrate the chronicle that told of the arrival in Paris in 1385 of the young Louis II, just crowned King of Naples. But Fouquet saw the scene in the light of the costumes and great lords of the 15th century. A later event gave him inspiration: the

meeting, in 1413, between Louis II, now grown-up, Yolande of Aragon, his wife, and Isabeau, the Queen of France. The little boy on horseback is Isabeau's third son, to whom the Anjous wanted to marry their daughter, Marie. He later reigned under the name of Charles VII. Isabeau is wearing a 'hennin'; it was she who introduced the fashion to Paris. It was a long-lived one, for in 1429, at the Abbey of Sainte-Geneviève, friar Richard preached against these tall head-dresses for six hours on end and for nine days running – without reducing their height.

The Paris that grew drunk with luxury could plead that at the same time she did harsh penance. It was at this time that the word 'macabre' first appeared and came into general use: the macabre which triumphed daily in the place of most resort, the charnel-house of the Holy Innocents (145). For over six hundred years, more than half the population found their last resting-place in the common graves of this great square near the Halles, and in its galleries where the bones were piled.

Paradoxically, this charnel-house was also the scene of lively activity: it was a place of promenade, of meeting, of business for small traders and public letter-writers. The great attraction was the dance of death, painted in 1416 (146–147): three gay and lively young men open a procession of gloomy pictures captioned with melancholy thoughts. It was believed that the English had caused these paintings to be executed, as a sort of psychological warfare, to undermine the Parisians' morale. But nothing like this happened. Engraved on wood and printed, the dance of death was a bestseller as late as 1484. An illuminated parchment from the library of Charles VIII restores its colours to us.

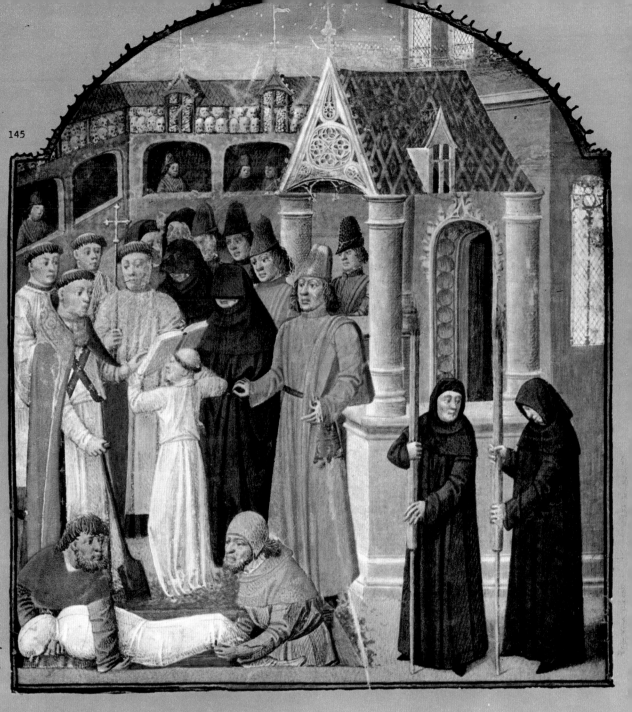

The peal of life. The peal of death. See them dance.

See them die. Paris dances in the charnel-house.

Le mort.   Le mort.

Here (148) is the Queen of France: Isabeau, daughter of the Duke of Bavaria and a Milanese princess. At eighteen, with her black eyes and fair hair, she was wildly acclaimed by the crowds on her state entry into Paris on 22nd August 1389. The young and beautiful Bavarian reigned first and foremost over Parisian fashion. She caused the 'hennins' to grow taller and taller, 'pointed as steeples'; ladies' coiffures grew so high that the ceilings of the Château of Vincennes had to be raised to allow them free passage. She set the fashion for a profusion of bracelets, necklaces, and trinkets. She already had five children when Charles V's madness became dangerous. She left the conjugal roof and went to the Hôtel Barbette in the Marais quarter. Louis of Orléans, her brother-in-law, was a frequent guest, and their love-affair was a public scandal. Isabeau of Bavaria went further and further along the sad path of dishonour. The slender sprite (148) was to coarsen into a fat old woman. The fresh young girl was to bear the burden of many sins and sorrows.

Death disguises himself as a young queen, whom the people acclaim.

Isabeau, if the King knew…

But the King knows nothing.

A terrible drama was about to be played out, in which all the actors wore crowns. Here (149) is Charles VI, the mad king, but still on the throne because a mad king may be ruled; his brother, Louis of Orléans, born in 1372, frivolous, spendthrift, sensual, but, it was said, a shrewd politician and the probable successor; Jean sans Peur (John the Fearless), his cousin, born in 1371, Duke of the rich land of Burgundy. And Jean de Berry, uncle of all three, in his mantle embroidered with swans (149), wanted to play the peacemaker. A grasping ruler of his province, but a prodigal patron, he attracted crowds of artists to both Paris and Bourges. Foremost amongst these were the brothers Limbourg, who painted for him the famous 'Très Riches Heures'.

150

Louis adopted as his rallying-sign a knotted club with the device 'Je l'envie' (I covet it). Thereupon Jean chose a carpenter's plane, and the device 'Je le tiens' (I have it). On 20th November 1407 the two cousins embraced. On the 23rd Jean had Louis cruelly assassinated in the street (150). After a short withdrawal from Paris, he became master of the city in 1409. But the Orléans party was re-forming. Charles, Louis' eldest son, and a poet, had married Bonne of Armagnac. His father-in-law, a powerful war-lord with his Gascon bands and his barons from the south, became the leader of the party in 1411. The Armagnacs adopted the white scarf and the nettle, the Burgundians the green hood and the cross of Saint Andrew. It was civil war.

He does not see the lover pay his homage. Death, love and madness: the ancient triangle.

151

152

Jean sans Peur, afraid of being murdered, built a veritable keep in the middle of his house, made to look like a bedroom. From the top of this square tower, which still survives (151), a strange sight among the crates of the Halles, he ruled over Paris, with his green hat, his Burgundian soldiers (152), and his butchers. The butchers of Paris. endowed with inalienable privileges and skilled in the use of mallet and chopper, had no fear of blood. This militia of slaughterers and skinners from the abattoirs ruled the streets of Paris. The chief skinner of the Hôtel-Dieu, Caboche, and his assistant Capeluche, a sinister executioner, led them to the carnage.

61

153

Blood on the stones of Paris.

Foreigners on her tattered soil.

During these two years first the Armagnacs, then the Burgundians, continually asked the English to intervene in their quarrel – a woefully misguided policy, which resulted in Henry V inflicting a heavy defeat on the Armagnacs on 25th October 1415 at the battle of Agincourt. The Armagnacs were out of the game. Isabeau ranged herself on the side of Jean sans Peur, while in June 1417 Charles the Dauphin became Lieutenant General of the realm. Poverty stalked the land. Plague came to add to the horrors, killing ten thousand Parisians a week.

By 29th May 1418 the Burgundians were again supreme. The Dauphin fled, and the butcher boys slew more than two thousand Armagnacs. But on 10th September 1419, it was the Armagnacs who murdered Jean sans Peur.

A mad king. A slut of a queen.

By the end of April 1413, Caboche and his butchers were undisputed kings of Paris. They marched against the Bastille, whose governor was hostile; a strange foreshadowing of a later revolution. They sought out the King and the Dauphin in their mansion and brought them back to the Louvre; they seized their advisers and lynched them (153). To calm public feeling Jean sans Peur and the University worked out a set of administrative reforms known by the high-sounding name of the Cabochian decree ('caboche' means a hobnail). This reorganised the public offices, taking away the royal prerogative of appointment, and simplified taxation. The Cabochians paid no heed, and indulged in such excesses that Jouvenel des Ursins rallied the moderates and treated with the Armagnacs. These latter soon made themselves masters of Paris, where they carried out a policy of merciless repression.

154

The civil war flared up more fiercely, to the great advantage of Henry V, and in spite of appeals for unity from the Bishop of Paris. On 21st May 1420, Isabeau and the Duke of Burgundy made Henry V heir to the throne of France. The King of England married Katherine, Isabeau's daughter, and on 1st December, with Charles VI taking part as a mere supernumerary, he entered Paris.

After the extortions of the Armagnacs and the Cabochians the people of Paris asked nothing better than order, from whatever quarter it might come; the merchants wished to retain contact with an English Rouen and a Burgundian Flanders; the University had fallen out with the Pope of the schism, a Frenchman suspected of sympathising with the Armagnacs. Paris, lamenting the madness of Charles VI, was content to become a French London.

It so happened that Charles VI and Henry V died almost at the same time in 1422. Henry VI of England was not yet one year old. Bedford, Regent of France, would have to look after London and Paris at the same time. It was too much.

155

England, the occupying power, was uneasy, and grew more and more so. She entered upon an intensive propaganda campaign, set up a strict security force, and sent agents even to wedding feasts. Montfaucon was not idle. Eight conspiracies broke out between 1422 and 1433, in which Parisians of every social class took part. A new party was formed around the Dauphin. The south declared for him, and gathered on the banks of the Loire. In 1429 the support of Joan of Arc played a decisive part in checking the English before Orléans, a focal point of this new force. On 17th July the Dauphin was crowned at Reims as Charles VII. Joan wanted to hasten matters. She presented herself at the gates of Paris and attacked the Porte Saint-Honoré (now the Place du Palais-Royal) on 8th September (156). Was this error a military or a political one? Paris did not surrender, and it was not long after that Joan, wounded and repulsed, met her death.

Paris rejected Joan. Paris wounded her. But Paris none the less was saved by her.

But the impetus once given did not die out. Little by little the provinces rallied behind Charles VI. The tardy coronation of young Henry VI in Notre-Dame brought no advantage to the English cause. In 1435 the army of the King of France hemmed Paris in on all sides. On 4th April it presented itself at the Porte Saint-Jacques. The garrison took refuge in the Bastille, and then were hooted out of the city. Charles VII made a ceremonial entry into Paris on 12th December 1437 (157). The sinister memory of Isabeau and Charles VI so haunted the Hôtel Saint-Pol that Charles VII took up residence at the Hôtel des Tournelles, where Bedford had lived. His example was followed by all the kings of France until 1559.

158 159 160

That sombre age produced not only traitors and cut-throats. Nicolas Flamel (1370–1417), who was at once an official public scribe, master of a large studio of copyists and illuminators, and a bookseller (158), grew so rich that his wealth was attributed to a knowledge of alchemy. With Dame Pernelle, his wife (159), he did his best to alleviate the many sufferings of the people of Paris. Their charities were innumerable. One of them remains: the free hostel for workmen, now No. 45 Rue de Montmorency, where the initials N.F. and the figures of angel musicians can still be seen carved on the façade.

Christine of Pisa (1363–1431), who came from Italy with her father, Charles V's doctor and astrologer, was Paris's first woman of letters (160). She lived by her pen, finding inexhaustible inspiration in the events of those terrible years. She wrote the first work devoted to Joan of Arc and her heroic deeds.

As before, as ever, Paris's suffering was bound up with that of a single heart.

164 165

Le rôdeau, que
fift ledit Vil-
lon quãt il fut
iugie.

161

163

Born at the end of the Terror, Villon (1431–1489), a Parisian, was to die without knowing the optimism and pride of the Renaissance (161). A student of the Latin quarter, he described the Paris of the taverns, vagabonds and women of the street; the criminals at Montfaucon (162); fine damsels, and the poor people who worshipped humbly in Notre-Dame.

For the illustrations to his edition of the comedies of Terence, the Parisian printer and engraver Antoine Vérard took his models from contemporary life (163). Who are these citizens, then? Without a doubt, leading members of the six guilds: drapers, furriers, grocers, mercers, hatters and goldsmiths, the pride of their trades.

The poet of the capital is called Villon. Paris, city of tragedy, finds her first town-crier in verse.

166

In spite of the difficulties of the occupation, Saint-Germain-l'Auxerrois was adorned in 1435 by an unusual porch, the only one of its kind in Paris, where all the characteristics of the flamboyant style are displayed (164). Under the roof of this church the canons preserved their treasure and their archives.

Both the century and medieval art came to a close with two buildings erected for civil purposes but which were nevertheless fortified against possible attack. In 1475 a fine town house (165) was built for the Archbishop of Sens, who remained head of the church in Paris until 1622. In 1605 it was temporarily allocated to the uses of Queen Margot, and in spite of many vicissitudes still survives today almost intact.

Between 1485 and 1498, on top of the ruins of the Roman baths, the abbots of Cluny built a fitting residence for their visits to the capital (166). Mary of England, widow of Louis XII, James V of Scotland, and Cardinal Charles of Lorraine were to be among its tenants. In 1844 a famous collector turned it into a museum.

168

At a time when Italian skill was combining with French taste to produce the Renaissance style, a laggard arose: the bell-tower of the church of Saint-Jacques-la-Boucherie (now the Tour Saint-Jacques) was built between 1508 and 1522 in the style of the previous century (168). Its height was put to good use by the people of Paris. Pascal conducted some barometrical experiments there. A maker of small shot demonstrated its usefulness, and thereby saved it from destruction, by dropping small pieces of molten metal from the top. Meteorologists still use it for making weather forecasts.

167

Paris consoles herself

with the flourishes of the flamboyant.

Neither of Charles VII's successors, Louis XI and Charles VIII, left Paris any great or lasting monuments to remember them by. The first, occupied with restoring France's territories, set himself to enrich the Loire valley; the second lived at Amboise, when he was not campaigning in Italy. Louis XII, who lived at Blois and was equally enamoured of Italian expeditions, was responsible for some improvements to the Palais de la Cité. But his stay in Paris is remembered because of some illustrated leaflets – printed ones, a new departure – which showed his state entry into the capital on 2nd July 1498 (167). Since 1470, when they set up their printing-presses in the Sorbonne, three Germans had been demonstrating this revolutionary process.

The printing - works of Paris produced not only religious and literary works. They also printed a 'provosts' regulation' which contained the rules governing all the river traffic of the Seine, with engravings showing the inspectors at work (169, 170, 174–8).

169

Here (169) is an inspector who never shirks: the wine-gauger. And here (170) one of Paris's most important officials, the controller of bridges, surrounded by his revenue officers. Nothing passed along the Seine without his having a hand in it.

170

Les rues de paris. Et finicremēt
se quartier des halles
La grant rue sainct denis
La rue sainct sausueur
La rue de beau repaire
La rue pauee
La rue de mont horgueil
La rue de quicquetonne
La rue au spon
La rue de mal conseil
La rue de merderel
La rue au signe
La rue de la grant truanderie
La rue de la petite truanderie
La rue de mandestour
La rue de petouet
La rue de la chāuoirerie
La rue de la coffonnerie
La rue au feurre
La rue de la charronnerie
Le cloistre saincte oppotune
La rue de la tabletterie
La rue de petrin gasselin
La rue de la barengerie
La rue de la saunerie
La rue de la megisserie
La rue sainct germain saucerrops
La rue des sauandieres
La rue de iehan soingtier
La rue guillaume poiree
La rue des recommandereffes

Les rues et les eglises de la ville.
de paris auec la despense qui se sait
par chascun iour

The first street directory appeared in 1489 (171). There are names in it which are still in use today: the Rue Saint-Denis, naturally, but also Montorgueil, Tiquetonne (spelt Quicquetonne), Mauconseil, Jean Lentier.

It was during the same period that craftsmen were working on a huge tapestry to deck the front of the Hôtel de Ville on days of public ceremony. It showed all the public buildings, private houses, and streets, before the changes of the Renaissance. But alas, nothing remains of this ingenious and detailed 'tapestry map' but a few fragments reproduced in gouache (48).

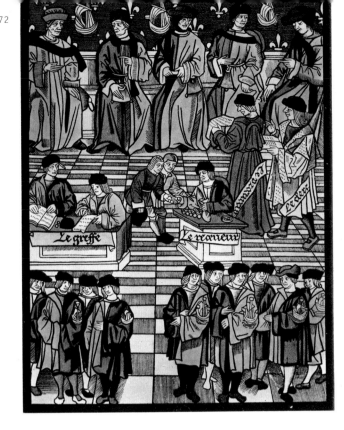

When prosperity returned and the kings of France deserted Paris for the châteaux of the Loire, the municipality (172) exercised a prudent surveillance over the organisation of public life and the guilds. The water-merchants, that is, those who specialised in the river trade, were not content merely to give the city their seal as a coat of arms, which was a ship with the device 'fluctuat nec mergitur' (61). Their provost also presided by right over the town council. Assisted by magistrates elected by the bourgeois, they had complete jurisdiction over the control of measures and prices, the policing of the ports, and the maintenance of public buildings.

Paris's last Gothic building (173) was the turret which Hérouet, secretary to Louis XII, built on to his house in the middle of the Temple quarter. Its function was no longer to defend or to keep watch against attack but to ornament, and to provide a good view on to the street. Feudalism had lost its ramparts, and a time was approaching when a commoner of Paris could emulate the nobility.

The merchant - provosts' regulations exhorted their inspectors to examine even onions with care (174), also trusses of hay (175), faggots (176) or poles, coal (177), plaster, and grain (178).

175

176

177

178

Paris broke through Charles V's wall, and spread out on all sides. Dyers from Flanders had set up their premises along the Bièvre. They brought with them a liking for beer. Pleasure gardens sprang up along the banks of the river, and even by the Seine itself. People went there to drink and make music, with a view of Notre-Dame and the Hôtel-Dieu in the distance (179). The more cultivated might repeat the words of Ronsard: 'I love the wave that babbles on the shore . . . . I love balls, dancing, masques; music and lutes, the enemies of care'.

179

180

The kings leave the banks of the Seine for the banks of the Loire.

Paris does not mind their unfaithfulness.

181

On 3rd February 1528, to a Paris where the pleasures of living had been rediscovered but where Protestant demands for reform were beginning to inflame men's minds, came Ignatius Loyola, a survivor of the Spanish wars, to devote himself to study and meditation. He indulged in demonstrations which alternately astonished and exasperated his mentors. One winter's day he plunged naked into the icy river to administer a shock to one of his friends, and thus prevent him from deserting his wife (182). His highly individualistic zeal resulted in his being condemned to be flogged by his comrades, but instead the head of the college knelt and asked his forgiveness (182).

Then, on 15th August 1534, Ignatius went up to Montmartre, and in the private chapel which marked the site of the famous martyrdom, he, together with several companions, vowed to dedicate himself to the salvation of souls (181). This was the beginning of the Jesuit order, which was to spread throughout the world.

68

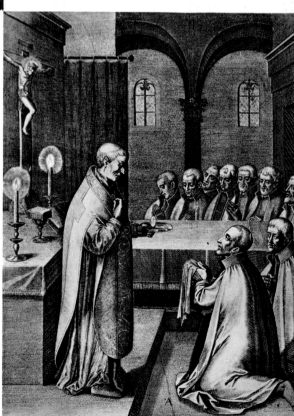

A. Parisijs in æde Virginis qui mons martyrum dicitur omnes socij Christi corpus suscipiunt et prima vota nuncupant. Lib. 2. c. 4.   B. Quod adolescer virgis cædere procumbens i

Paris sings in the taverns of the Bièvre.
Night is ending. It is a time of beauty,
a time of rebirth.

185

184

To the right of the Rue Saint-Martin, an old footbridge had been replaced by a stronger wooden structure known as the Pont Notre-Dame. On either side it supported a row of thirty-four houses numbered in red and gold – the first time street numbers were used in Paris. But in the autumn of 1499 the bridge was swept away by a flood. The city magistrates were held responsible for the catastrophe, and such heavy fines were imposed upon them that they had to go to prison until their debt was liquidated. A monk from Verona was employed to rebuild the bridge at their expense, and a new style appeared: the style of the Renaissance (180). The sixty-eight houses, built symmetrically of brick and stone, with gables and arcaded shops, had an air of great dignity.

182

Why should not the useful also contribute its share of beauty? The famous sculptor Jean Goujon was commissioned to brighten up the old charnel-house of the Innocents with a building in keeping with these more gracious times (184).
He built the fountain of the nymphs of the Seine, with its great female figures, upright or half reclining: nymphs (5), nereids, and tritons. It had no equal either in Greece or Rome. Unveiled amid rejoicing in 1549, it remained in the heart of popular Paris until Haussmann enclosed it in a gloomy and lifeless square, where it sank into disrepair.

186

François I (1515–1547) (183), who often went to Blois and Chambord, realised one day that he need not go so far afield for forests: Paris was surrounded by them. He came a little nearer, and the Palace of Fontainebleau sprang up on the site of an old hunting-box. The architects who built this marvel were Le Breton, Chambiges, and Castoret; the interior decorations were by Rosso and Primaticcio.
But Fontainebleau was still some distance from Paris. So a hunting-lodge was built in the Bois de Boulogne, the Château de Madrid, with interior decorations by the Florentine, Girolamo della Robbia. Then, for his mother, the king bought a large stretch of land near the Louvre, which had been used as a tile-works (tuileries). But it was on the Louvre itself that François lavished most of his attention.

183

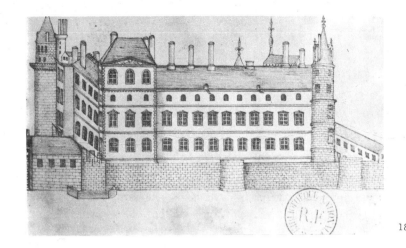

The people of Paris agreed to pay a large part of the ransom of François I, who had been beaten at Pavia in 1525 and was held captive in Madrid, on condition that he agreed to live in his capital. The King, who was 'marvellously given to building', chose to reside in the Louvre. In 1527 he pulled down Philip Augustus's great keep, and did away with the entrance on the Seine, retaining only the eastern entry. Pierre Lescot, a friend of Ronsard, rebuilt the south and west fronts in the Renaissance style. Androuet du Cerceau, a colleague of Lescot's, wrote: 'This stone frontage is so richly adorned with columns, friezes, and architectural devices of all kinds, of a beauty and symmetry so excellent, that one could hardly find anything to approach it in all Europe.' But the north and east fronts remained in the Gothic style (901).

187

And Ronsard sang of the celestial dance, which ever paused, and shifted,

and resumed.

188

189

Jean Goujon decorated the inner walls with poetic and musical divinities, and allegories of war and peace (188). On 1st January 1540 a distinguished visitor was welcomed to the new Louvre: the Emperor Charles V. 'Which is the greatest city in France?' he asked François I. 'Rouen, my honoured cousin,' came the reply. 'Not Paris?' 'No,' said the King. 'Paris is not a city. It is a country.'

A whole court sprang up around the King: nobles, fine ladies, scientists, scholars. For concerts and balls Jean Goujon built a musicians' gallery supported by caryatids in the Great Hall (189). Many ceremonies took place there: the marriage of François II and Mary Queen of Scots; the first performance of Molière in the presence of Louis XIV; the Institute's reception of Napoleon.

70

190

But after his marriage to Catherine de' Medici on 16th June 1549, Henri II started a tradition of sumptuous royal entries into the capital. Nothing was lacking: a live Hercules, a lovely maiden impersonating Lutetia, a rhinoceros with 'real scales'. Great rejoicing was followed by wild alarm. In August 1557 Paris trembled. The Spaniards, after a victory at Saint-Quentin, were marching on the capital. But the Duke of Guise drove them back, and in 1559 the peace of Cateau-Cambrésis was signed. To seal the pacification, Elizabeth of France was to marry Philip II of Spain. A great tournament was held to celebrate the occasion, near the royal Hôtel des Tournelles (now 62 Rue Saint-Antoine). In the jousting the King wore the colours of Diane de Poitiers, who was his real queen, although nineteen years his senior.

192

Henri II ruled in his turn (191). The flames already licked the faggots that were to consume the Lutherans, accused of having spread private and public disorder. On 3rd August 1546 Etienne Dolet, a printer, had been hung and burned in the Place Maubert. The reign began badly, with a duel. On 10th July 1547, on the terrace of Saint-Germain, the famous thrust of Jarnac laid low La Chataigneraie, the champion of the royal favourite, Diane de Poitiers.

Paris under the sign of Diana. A gay riding party returns, alas, in woe.

193

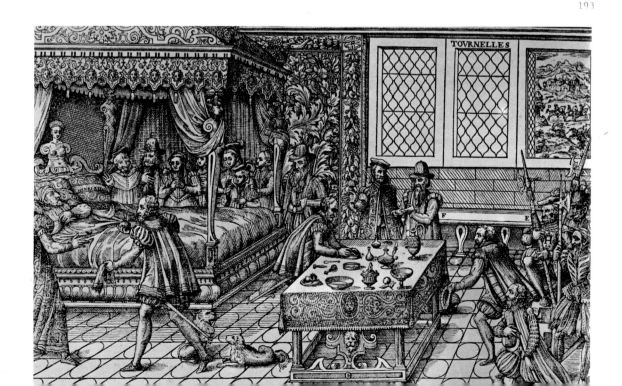

On 30th June, after being twice the victor, Henri broke his lance against that of Montgomery, captain of his Scottish guard (192). But his adversary's lance had shattered the King's vizor and pierced his eye. Ambroise Paré and Vésale, the famous surgeon of Brussels, were sent for, but in vain. After ten days of agony Henri died, and with him died the fragile peace of France (193).

The first sign of disaster was on the eve of the fatal tournament. The Parlement of Paris was divided over the case of some Protestants who had been found guilty of reciting psalms in the Pré-aux-Clercs. Henri had himself pronounced the sentence. Anne du Bourg, a city councillor and recent convert, had stood up and compared the King to the ungodly Ahab. The King's death, in which the Protestants saw the hand of God, did not prevent the execution of Anne du Bourg. On 21st December 1559, he was strangled and burned in the Place de Grève (194).

194

Three brothers succeeded each other swiftly in thirty years crammed with sensational events: François II, who reigned scarcely more than a year (1560) and married Mary Queen of Scots; Charles IX, king until 1574; and Henri III. The burden of government rested on the Queen Mother, inconsolable widow of an irresponsible husband who had given her nine children. Hers is a sombre face (195); in the eyes burns the fire of the Medici, those fabulous merchants of Florence who had climbed to the throne of France.

195

Several great noblemen, such as Coligny, went over to the Protestants. But twice, in 1567 and in 1568, the Protestant army tried in vain to capture Paris, which was passionately hostile to their cause. At last they came to terms. Coligny was admitted to the privy council. But conflict soon arose between the Catholic princes, Coligny, who thwarted Charles IX at every turn, and the Queen Mother, who saw power slipping from her grasp. Then, on 18th August 1572, when the King's sister was married to Henri of Béarn, the new King of Navarre (later Henri IV), and all the Protestant leaders were gathered in the capital, the people of Paris rose. All through 23rd August there were grave deliberations in the Louvre, and at two o'clock in the morning the bells of Saint-Germain-l'Auxerrois and the Palais rang out as a signal for the massacre of Saint Bartholomew.

On 22nd August Admiral Coligny had been shot and wounded by an assassin in the pay of the Guises (197).

Another hunt begins; the quarry is everywhere. The city no longer knows what she does.

During the night before the massacre of Saint Bartholomew, armed men broke through the gates of Coligny's house (198).

In the town they had murdered Coligny (198–200); in the Louvre they struck down the Protestant nobles. Presented with the alternatives of 'mass, death, or the Bastille', Henri of Navarre and Condé recanted for the time being, and escaped with their lives. The King's Huguenot nurse and Ambroise Paré were also spared, but the population of Paris had taken up arms in every quarter, and continued to massacre innocent and guilty alike. How many were struck down by pike and dagger and arquebus? Two thousand, it is said. Their corpses were swept away by the waters of the Seine (201).

The Admiral was savagely attacked and stabbed to death as he lay in bed. His naked corpse was thrown out of the window (199–200).

Paris, city of murder.

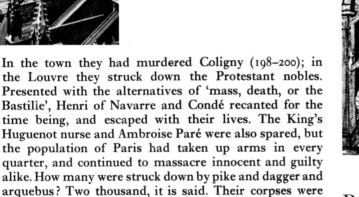

73

202

Cities suffer from the sins of their sons.

Les Tournelles, a sad place after the death of Henri II, was pulled down. The kings of France lived henceforward in the Louvre. For her own use the Queen Mother built a château designed by Philibert Delorme on the site of the old tile-works nearby. The stone came from the quarries of Vaugirard and were brought across the Seine by boat (hence the name Rue du Bac, or street of the ferry). The grounds, which were exquisitely laid out, included an Italian grotto with walls lined with ceramics by Bernard Palissy. Catherine wanted to join the Tuileries to the Louvre by means of a gallery, just as the Palazzo Pitti had been joined to the Uffizi in Florence in 1564. The foundations were laid in 1566. But the Queen Mother believed in astrologers and soothsayers, amulets and visions. An oracle pronounced by the Italian Ruggieri in 1572 told her that she would die near Saint-Germain. She immediately abandoned the Louvre and the Tuileries because they adjoined the parish of Saint - Germain - l'Auxerrois. From that time, it is said, misfortune hovered constantly over the Tuileries. It saw the fall of Louis XVI, Louis-Philippe, and the Second Empire, before the Communards set fire to it in 1871, reducing it to a magnificent ruin (202).

Catherine de' Medici employed Jean Bullant to build for her own use one of the most beautiful houses in Paris (its site is now occupied by the Bourse, or stock-exchange). The house itself disappeared in 1748, but its strange ornamental column, ninety feet high, still stands (203). It was Paris's first astrological observatory. The Queen Mother lived there for fourteen years, and died at Blois on 5th February 1589, attended by a priest called Julien de Saint-Germain. The oracle was right.

203

Henri III came from Cracow to reign in Paris. He has been called a comedy king, a petty oriental potentate of depraved habits. Is this true? Say rather he was demonstrative, sentimental, and given to excess. Henri III founded the Order of the Holy Spirit, the spectacular brotherhood of White Penitents; he made the pilgrimage to Chartres on foot and founded the academy of the Palais, forerunner of the Académie Française. He also laid the first stone of the Pont-Neuf, and set up the first public clock in the tower at the corner of the Palais (204).

204 Moreover—and this was considered an error by many—he condemned the massacre of Saint Bartholomew, and gave guarantees to the Protestants. The adherence to the Protestant party of the King's brother, the Duc d'Alençon, and of Henri of Navarre, led the Catholics to form a league of self-defence, which was supported by the Duc de Guise and his brother the Cardinal. Between the fanatic mobs and the intriguing nobles, the King stood alone.

The League, which was directed as much against the Crown as against the Protestants, recruited numerous members from all classes. On 3rd May 1588 Henri III was forced to flee from the capital, where barricades had appeared everywhere. In December he had both the Guises assassinated at Blois. Paris elected a Council of Sixteen, rose in rebellion, and chose a new King: a cardinal, and a prisoner! Henri III at once approached Henri of Navarre, heir to the throne since the death of the Duc d'Alençon. Their two armies joined together to surround Paris. The Parisians then provided Clément, a young Dominican monk, with weapons, and on 1st August 1589 he went to the camp at Saint-Cloud, asked for a private audience with the King, and stabbed him (205–206).

205

206

Paris suffers from fanaticism.

Though she will one day be freedom's capital, she now sins against liberty.

75

Henri of Navarre could not return to besiege Paris until May 1590. In the interval the League, financed by Spain, increased in strength. A quarter of the population was under arms: the priests of several large parishes spurred the people on; the more moderate ones were executed. A 'Catholic revolutionary commune'

was on the point of gaining control. On 14th May, on the order of the Bishop of Senlis and the Curé of Saint-Jacques, a great procession passed through the streets: 1300 monks in ranks of four, wearing accoutrements and cuirasses, with arquebuses on their shoulders – the officers of an army fifty thousand strong (208).

A tragic era finds

a tragic voice;

the voice of

Agrippa d'Aubigné

209

But Henri conducted a methodical siege. By August Paris was eating horses, asses, cats, grass, and even ground-up corpses. A Spanish relief force from the Netherlands created a dangerous but brief diversion.

The extremists executed Brisson, the president of the Parlement, on suspicion of being a moderate. Mayenne, the chief of the League, rallied the moderates and retired to the Bastille, and in December 1591, from this base, he wiped out the extremists.

Months passed by. A poem criticising the League, the Menippean satire; was circulated secretly, with huge success.

The people were weary and demanded a King. On 26th January 1593 the States-General met at the Louvre. Negotiations with Henri of Navarre were begun at Suresnes, and on 17th May he declared himself ready to be converted.

On 25th July 1593 Henri IV abjured the Protestant religion in Saint-Denis (209), amidst popular rejoicing. As Reims was still unsettled, he was crowned at Chartres.

212

'Man preys upon man; like a wolf he devours his fellow.

The father strangles the son; and a shroud

prepared by the son beckons the father.'

Paris was still dominated by the League and the Spaniards. But Mayenne, who saw which way the wind was blowing, had left the city, handing over his authority to Brissac, an extremist. Brissac however treated secretly with Henri, who promised a general amnesty, and that only the Catholic religion should be practised in the Paris region.

At last, on 22nd May 1594, in torrential rain, the royal troops entered the city. Some mercenaries were attacked and thrown into the Seine (210). The King appeared, put his scarf round Brissac's neck, and 'carried on the shoulders of the people', went to hear the Te Deum in Notre-Dame. The Spanish troops withdrew without disturbance. They marched past the new king, their arms at the salute. From a window in the Porte Saint-Denis Henri IV watched them go by. 'Give my greetings to your master,' he shouted to them, 'but don't come back!' (211).

From the first, the people of Paris saw prancing at the King's side his greatest friend, Maximilien of Béthune, later the Duc de Sully (212). In the space of five years this provincial was to become the most influential man in France: at once surveyor-general, master of the artillery, financial secretary, and controller of defence and buildings. Paris owed to him not only the reconstruction of the Arsenal, on the right bank to the east, with its public promenade which quickly became fashionable, but also large-scale modernisations.

211

Who can tell how many rebirths Paris has known?

213

214

On the evening of the day when he abjured at Saint-Denis, Henri IV had ridden to Montmartre to look from a distance at the city still forbidden to him (213). No king was ever more appreciative of the capital than this southern countryman. 'As soon as he was master of Paris, one saw nothing but stone-masons at work,' said the 'Mercure Français' in 1610. When the ambassadors who had known the troubled times of the League expressed astonishment and said, 'Sire, this city's appearance has indeed changed,' Henri replied, 'When the master is absent, all the house is in disorder. But when he returns, it is adorned by his presence, and everything is the better for it.' Between 1533 and 1603, the area of Paris grew from twelve to fourteen hundred acres, and the population from 260,000 to 300,000.

How beautiful Mary of England, Henry VIII's sister, had looked in 1514, a young royal bride, with Louis XII, a husband too old for her, at her side! So beautiful, indeed, that people crammed themselves into the Maison des Piliers, the porticoed house of the city magistrates, to do her honour. So it was decided that a new Hôtel de Ville must be built more in keeping with the present dignity of Paris and her people. Building was begun in 1533 according to the plans of Dominic of Cortona, called the Golden-voiced, and under the supervision of the contractor Chambiges it continued to grow. The guns were soon to fire a salute for the feast of Saint John in front of a beautiful brand-new building (214). The merchants' provost, François Miron, devoted a large part of his own fortune to its construction. Has Paris ever had a greater administrator? He was careful of the interests of both the king and the people; he wanted Paris to wear a humane and good-natured expression. 'It is not good to have the plump ones on one side and the skinny ones on the other; in the interests of our beloved King and of our fine city, it is better that they should be mixed.'

78

Who can tell of your journeyings, from life to death, from death to life again?

You lead yourself to the grave, then lift aside your own tombstone,

and live again more radiantly than before.

The aim of all the town-planning in the reign of Henri IV was to turn the banks of the river into the frame of a splendid prospect which both people and king could enjoy. Between 1598 and 1608, Jacques Androuet du Cerceau (the Second) completed the line of buildings five hundred yards long that Catherine de' Medici had planned (215). This riverside gallery cut boldly across the great wall of Charles V and joined the Louvre, in the city, to the Tuileries, a country estate in the suburbs (901).

On the ground floor the King set up a veritable school of fine and applied arts, to which the guild inspectors had no access. Restoration, amounting sometimes almost to reconstruction at the Tuileries end, changed the appearance of this gallery in later years.

215

The marriage of Henri IV and Marguerite (Queen Margot), daughter of Henri II, was so wretchedly unsuccessful that it was annulled in 1599. The following year, in Lyons, the King married Marie de' Medici. In 1622, to decorate the bare walls of the Luxembourg Palace, Rubens painted the story of the childhood and rise to the throne of this daughter of the Grand Duke of Tuscany. The pictures cover more than two thousand five hundred square feet of rich, grandiloquent canvasses (216), in which ancient myth is called upon to dignify the somewhat disorderly history of this latest Medici, who extended for a few more years the influence that Florence wielded under northern skies.

80

216

217

It was the
country-loving horseman
with the keen eye
who gave Paris
the perfect triangle of trees
between
the two gentle arms
of the Seine.

218

A rendez-vous at the point of the Cité: to the charming
square that he built in 1607 (217) on land reclaimed from
the royal gardens and from the Seine, president Harlay
gave the name of Place Dauphine, in honour of the heir
to the throne, later Louis XIII.

In the heart of the new Paris, the square opened on to the
Pont-Neuf (218), which Henri IV was the first to cross, on
horseback, in December 1605. The Pont-Neuf was the first
bridge to be built without houses on it. Another innovation
was the pavements. Such a huge crowd came to try them
that they stopped the traffic. Quacks, mountebanks, pickpockets, idlers from Paris and elsewhere, all stopped and
lingered by the shops set up in the semi-circular projections
over the piers (217 & 348). The pump of the Samaritaine,
the first to raise water from the Seine, was another great
attraction.

The islets of the Seine, now joined to the island of the Cité
(Square du Vert Galant) (218), supported, at the same level
as the bridge, Paris's first equestrian statue (219), a fine
likeness of Henri IV.

219

The Paris workman toiled for twelve or even sixteen hours a day, but there were eighty feast days a year, as well as Sundays. Paris was working hard to give France a centre of economic importance, but she also knew how to be entertained. The streets were stages where every Parisian was an actor. The May tree and the music called him out to dance, or play a game of skittles or quoits (223). But how was it that, amidst all this peaceful enjoyment, the King could murmur: 'God's mercy, I shall die in this city and never get away from it. They will kill me.'

A king who is moved by the human body. His hands have the secret of pleasure and of cure.

222

In 1598 the Edict of Nantes had restored religious peace for good and all, so men hoped. The throne was no longer in question. In spite of his rough and ready ways, Henri was accepted by all as the true repository of the sacred functions of the monarchy. On the first floor of the riverside gallery he received sufferers from scrofula in public audience. 'The King touches thee; may the Lord heal thee' (220).

221

220

In 1606 there was an outbreak of plague. The Hôtel-Dieu was not big enough. Outside the walls there soon arose a huge institution which was for years the most beautiful in Paris (221). With its four great single-storey buildings each over a hundred yards long, its double courtyards, double gardens and double walls, it kept those who carried infection completely isolated from the outside world. This true house of rest, which was named the Hôpital Saint-Louis, in memory of the illness and death of Saint Louis in Tunis, survives intact.

They killed King Henri.
But they could not kill the Vert-Galant.
Lovers are immortal in Paris.

Ever since the old days of Lutetia the Parisian had moved
about as best he could, on foot, on horse or mule. In 1550
coaches made their appearance: heavy contraptions
covered with leather, which could only pass through the
narrower streets with difficulty. This was well-known to
Ravaillac, the schoolmaster from Angoulême, a tall,
strapping young fellow with red hair, dressed in green,
who was inflamed by the same passion as the League had
inspired. On 14th May 1610, in the Rue de la Ferronnerie
(ironmongers), he took advantage of a block in the traffic
to assassinate the king (224). Was there some other arm
behind the bloodstained dagger (225)? The Spanish party,
perhaps, which was still influential at court and feared
another war. Ravaillac, though he was racked on 27th May
in the Place de Grève, never spoke (226). The funeral of the
King took place with great pomp at Saint-Denis (227).

In 1610 Louis XIII, aged nine, was installed in the Louvre, with Marie de' Medici as Regent. He was declared of age in 1614, and married a golden-haired Habsburg princess, Anne of Austria. But behind them (228) in the shadows, there loomed a number of great and little men, relations of the royal family and intriguing Italians belonging to the Queen Mother's retinue. The surf was beating even against the balconies of the Louvre.

Just as her duellists cross swords, so the roads of Paris, the old Roman roads, intersect.

But for the moment the late King still reigned in people's memories. In the middle of the Marais quarter, on the site of the old Hôtel des Tournelles, Henri IV had built an esplanade designed for equestrian sports and public promenade. Thirty-six houses of brick and white stone with arcades were built round this great square.

For three days during April 1612 Parisians watched with amazement the inauguration of this splendid group of buildings (229). Before ten thousand spectators, a hundred and fifty musicians played an accompaniment to the 'Tourney of the Glorious Cavaliers', a gigantic equestrian ballet punctuated by the sound of gunfire from the cannons of the Bastille.

Such was the beginning of the Place Royale, which attracted towards the eastern part of Paris all the activities of the city, great or small, which were military, financial, academic – or swashbuckling (230). Today it is the Place des Vosges (231), and is, alas, somewhat neglected.

The capital of the Grand Siècle, surrounded by windmills, is here spread out (234).

Paris has broken through Charles V's rampart. A bastioned wall has risen to defend the Tuileries (foreground), and the quarters of Saint-Honoré and Gaillon. The left bank, where the 'faux bourg' of the Abbey of Saint-Germain-des-Prés had begun to expand since the construction of the Pont Neuf, is still less developed than the right bank. The Paris of the Emperor Julian and of Philip Augustus can still be traced in the great intersection from north to south (Rue Saint-Martin and Rue Saint-Jacques) and from west to east (Rue Saint-Honoré to Rue Saint-Antoine). But looking down on this huge, harmoniously proportioned circle, who could believe that all below is noise and shouting and movement?

Who could imagine the stench of a mud which was legendary, the congestion in the narrow streets, the dreadful swamps? The Parisians of the Grand Siècle were anxious to transform this urban jumble. Descartes, the great philosopher, exhorted them to do so. 'These ancient cities,' he wrote in his Discourse on Method, 'have become so ill-proportioned over the years compared with those that an architect lays out regularly and according to plan on an open space, that although as much art is often found in the individual buildings of the one as in those of the other, or even more, yet seeing how they are arranged, here a large one, there a small, and how they cause the streets to twist and tumble, one would think it was chance rather than the will of reasonable men that had disposed them thus.'

233

The wheel of Paris; of chance; of fortune.

232

La Bruyère also criticised a city 'divided into separate societies, like so many small republics, each with its own laws, customs, languages and jests'. It was time that reason got out the rule and compasses and restored everything to fitting order.

234

One man wins.
Another loses.
For these the arquebus, the gallows, the axe, the fire.

The panic unrest of the city boiled over suddenly in a horrifying series of events that drenched the royal entourage in blood. The Queen Mother had given two of her compatriots, Leonora Galigai, her foster-sister, and her husband Concini, marshal of Ancre, preferment above their deserts. The councillors of Louis XIII, who did not rule but had a taste for power, decided to put an end to Concini's reign.

At ten o'clock on the morning of 24th April 1617, at the gate of the Louvre, Vitry, the commander of the bodyguards, arrested him, and he fell dead from three arquebus shots. It was said that the King appeared at the window to make sure that the operation had been successful (235).

That would have been enough.

Estime qui voudra la mort espouuantable,
Ce dernier iour des miens me semble le plus beau,
Et puis pour faire voir que ie l'ay agreable,
Et que ne la crains point, oste-moy ce bandeau.

But on the following day a gang of stone-haulers dug up the marshal's body, which they mutilated and hung up horribly at the end of the Pont Neuf (236). After parading the corpse through a Paris suddenly grown wild with xenophobia, they burned it. The stately background to all this, the steeple of Saint-Germain-des-Prés and the Tour de Nesle, had grown unaccustomed to such bloody disorders (237).

Leonora Galigai, the marshal of Ancre's wife, was beheaded in the Place de Grève. 'What a lot of people,' she said, 'to see a poor woman die.' The courage with which she met her death made the people of Paris pity her – when it was too late (238).

86

239

With only the solitary carpet factory of the Savonnerie at the foot of the slopes of Chaillot, founded in 1607, and the rural monastery of the Franciscans, known as the Little Ones or Manikins, it seemed improbable that Paris would spread westward. But the Queen Mother brought with

But others drive in their carriages along the Seine, whose every reflection is a wink of conspiracy.

240

her from Florence the fashion of going for a drive in the cool hours of the afternoon. She had four rows of trees planted in an avenue along the river, beyond the Tuileries (239). What crowds then thronged there! Masked ladies in silken gowns embroidered with gold; cavaliers in tall hats and high boots. The Comte de Bassompierre drove there in the first coach with glass windows. Sweetmeat-sellers and messengers with lovers' notes moved among the crowd. This 'oglers' Paradise' soon overflowed into the Tuileries gardens nearby.

Between 1615 and 1625 Marie de' Medici also built a house that recalled her native Florence. She bought the Hôtel du Luxembourg and its extensive grounds, and there Salomon de Brosse erected a palace with a large park (242). While they were still arranging the twenty-four panels by Rubens (now in the Louvre), the Queen Mother moved in. But not for long. It was there, on 10th November 1630 after a violent quarrel with Cardinal Richelieu, that for a moment she thought she had gained complete political control. But the next day Louis XIII recalled his minister and dismissed his mother. She was the victim of the 'day of dupes', and withdrew to Cologne, where she died in obscurity. The palace, which was used as a prison during the Terror, was assigned to the Senate in 1802. It is still called the Palais du Luxembourg. The park has been open to the public since 1650. A fountain-cum-grotto in the Italian style is the only thing that recalls the name of Medici – and even this has been moved from its original site and altered (243).

241

242

243

Richelieu, who left his mark on everything, left it on Paris. He amassed an estate stretching from the Louvre in the south to the city wall in the north, built a straight path through it (now the Rue de Richelieu), and divided the land on either side into building lots. There, between 1633 and 1639, Le Mercier built a huge house with eight courtyards, which the cardinal bequeathed to the King (244). Practically nothing remains of the Palais-Cardinal, as it was called. It was the residence of Louis XIV, and was then given to his brother, Philippe of Orléans.

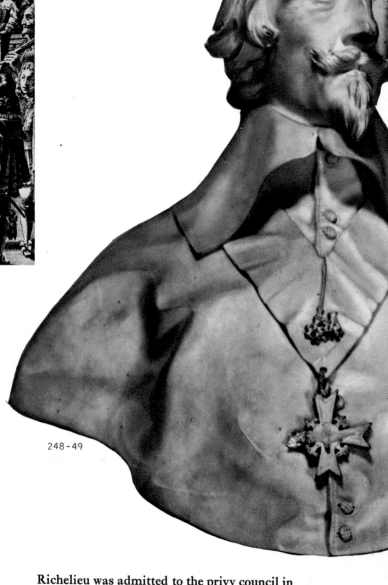

'An entire city, magnificently planned, seems to have arisen miraculously from an old ditch.' Corneille was the more lavish in his praise of the Palais-Cardinal in that he found there a patron and a stage. In 1636 a little room in the palace echoed to the verses of 'Le Cid'. In 1641 a larger stage was inaugurated with a performance of 'Mirame', a play by Richelieu himself. The whole royal family came to applaud (245). The theatre that was built on to the left wing of the palace in 1786, and later occupied by the Comédie Française, was justly called the Salle Richelieu.

Many architects were inspired by the Pantheon in Rome. In the Rue Saint-Antoine the Jesuits, copying the Gesù (Ecclesia del Gesù), introduced the cupola into Paris. But the Cardinal was attached most of all to the old medieval Sorbonne, of which he was chancellor and in which he wished to be buried. He rebuilt it at his own expense. But the modernisations of 1890 left only the church intact (246).

Richelieu was admitted to the privy council in 1624, and remained in power until 1642 (248). The Thirty Years War imposed austerity on the capital, but Paris was spared the real horrors of siege and civil war. The city, now the seat of a central power no longer in dispute, which set the fashion and named the virtues, had to pay the price: an arduous greatness, majesty, and severity.

246

250

On 13th March 1634 a small group of men of letters, who usually held their meetings at the house of the critic Conrart, accepted Richelieu's patronage and gave themselves the name of 'Académie Française' (250). There were nine of them at first, then twenty-seven, then thirty-four, and eventually forty. The Cardinal gave the Académie, the average age of whose members was thirty-six, authority over language and literature.

In 1631, Renaudot, the King's doctor, a man who was ingenious, inventive, and a Protestant, conceived the idea of a periodical miscellany containing home and foreign news and advertisements (251). Distributed by travelling pedlars (252) it proved a success, and came to the Cardinal's notice. He liked to support public spirit; so the King and he became contributors. The first modern newspaper was characteristically in line with official policy.

252

The century of the 'Discourse' begins.

251

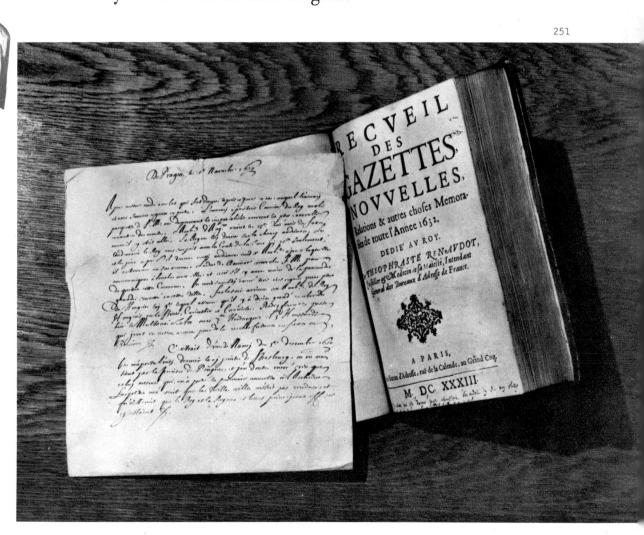

Paris dreams of a method. The city seeks a grammar for its streets. There is a new God, whose name is style.

253

Paris listens also to other

instructors:

the quacks of the bridges

and the squares.

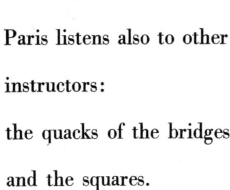

254

255

Throughout the ages the quacks – half doctors, half buffoons – had roamed through town and country-side selling their salves and herbs. But none made so fine an art of it as the tumblers of the Place Dauphine and the Pont Neuf. All Paris flocked to hear Signor Hieronymo, called the Orvietan after his native town, a pseudonym which became the name for a quack medicine. But the greatest was Tabarin (254). From 1620, he and Mondor, his compère, topped the bill for farce and improvisation. Pages, clerks,

gentlemen and pickpockets jostled each other to get into the front row (255). Soon a little boy called Jean-Baptiste Poquelin was among the spectators. He was to become famous as Molière. This elegant young couple (256) are only happy in the shopping arcades of the Palais de Justice, when they are not in those of the Place Royale. They are also to be met with in the nearby Hôtel du Louvre, where Madame de Rambouillet gives her literary parties and has founded a school of conversation and good taste.

The cheap-jacks of Paris

give Paris her savour.

90

256

257

Let us return to the Seine, the eternal theatre in which all the ceremonies of Paris have their setting, and which every government adorns with some new beauty. The bridges were magnificently rebuilt, stone replacing wood. The Pont Saint-Michel, after being swept away by floods no less than three times in less than a hundred years, entered on a new lease of life in 1624, with two rows of buildings each containing eight houses. The speed of the traffic was less important than its volume, and the money spent en route. The Pont-au-Change was rebuilt between 1639 and 1647, still with houses on it (257).

In 1618 the Ile Saint-Louis was joined to the right bank by means of the Pont Marie, with its fifty narrow houses; and in 1620 to the left bank by means of the Pont de la Tournelle.

The Ile Saint-Louis? How did this ship laden with houses come to rise suddenly out of the Seine in the wake of the Cité? In 1614 Christophe Marie and two financiers embarked on a vast scheme. They joined together the two islets –

the Ile aux Vaches and the Ile Notre-Dame – and divided them into building lots. The new Ile Saint-Louis, out of the way of the noisy crowds, became a peaceful subdivision of the Marais quarter (258).

Big town houses sprang up there, with underground passages opening on the river. Although the largest of these, the Hôtel Breton-villiers (1640), was foolishly demolished, the Hôtel Lambert (1640) still survives, where Voltaire lived, and Chopin; as does the Hôtel Lauzun, where Baudelaire had an apartment.

258

On 5th September 1638 a Dauphin was born, the future Louis XIV. He was baptised 'Dieudonné', God-given. In her gratitude Anne of Austria decided to transform into a great abbey the little monastery of Val-de-Grâce, in the Rue Saint-Jacques, where she often went into retreat. But François Mansart underestimated the extent of the quarries under the site (260), and the project had to be abandoned. It was the Gesù again and Saint Peter's in Rome which inspired his successors. The church was completed in 1665, and decorated by Mignard.

Molière praised that Val-de-Grâce, 'whose splendid dome ascending in the blue, Embellishes the city's splendid view'. The hearts of the dead princes and princesses of France were buried there up to the Revolution. In 1793 the monastery was converted into a military hospital (261).

Let M. de Vaugelas speak:

'There has never been a language in which one could write with

The Thirty Years War (1618–1648) gave the people of Paris one of their worst frights. In 1636 the Spaniards invaded Picardy, crossed the Somme, and sent advance-guards as far as Pontoise. The roads to the south were already crammed with coaches and fleeing horses when the army, hastily gathered together, came to the relief of the capital.

There was another cause of vexation, too. After twenty years of marriage the King and Queen, now to all intents and purposes separated, had no heir. In 1637 the King decided to place the crown and kingdom under the protection of Our Lady. He vowed to raise a monument in the cathedral, and to institute the solemn procession that takes place on 15th August. The painter Philippe de Champaigne depicted this dedication in his own mystical and grandiloquent style (259).

263

more purity and clarity than in our own, nor one which better

combined gravity and sweetness.'

In 1643 came another military threat. But at the battle of Rocroi a young prince of twenty-two with the profile of an eagle (262) – the Duke of Enghien, soon to be Prince of Condé – blocked the invaders' route to the capital. His victory caused a great sensation, and the captured Spanish colours were carried in state to Notre-Dame (263). But the people of Paris had had a fright, and if the new fortifications in the west were stout enough, the state of the wall built by Charles V, and of his Porte Saint-Denis (264), boded ill in case of serious attack.

265

264

On the other hand the spiritual defences were without flaw. In 1627 the Protestants were allowed to re-open their church at Charenton, and Catholicism too sprang into new life in Paris. The name of Pierre de Berulle, founder of the Oratory and the order of Mont-Carmel, was honoured everywhere. Jean-Jacques Olier, although of noble birth, became a simple curé in the Saint-Sulpice district, and opened a seminary which soon became famous. Vincent de Paul (265) had taken up his quarters at the old priory of Saint-Lazare. He founded the community of the Priests of the Mission (the Lazarists), and the Brotherhood of Charity (the Grey Sisters). The hardships brought about by the war, and the rigours of the political régime, gave them plenty of scope for their activities.

93

Here is the King (A), and the ship of Paris, sailing a dangerous sea with an ill-assorted crew (268): the Prince of Conti, the Duke of Elbeuf, and the Duke of Beaufort, soon to be known as the king of the Halles (B); the Duke of Bouillon (C), the Parlement and the municipality (D). Mazarin and his accomplices conjure up the storm, bringing the horrific figure of Concini (F) back to life for the occasion (268). Paris rose in revolt, forgetting that the good white loaves of Gonesse might suddenly grow scarce (269).

Paris continues to learn the alphabet of revolution.

269

New taxes goaded Paris past endurance (270). In June 1648 the Parlement and the high courts drew up a constitution limiting the power of the King. The Queen, as Regent, arrested Broussel, an elderly member of the municipal council, who was much respected by the people of his ward for his simple and austere life. On 26th August the city was full of barricades. The Queen and the young King, trapped in the Palais Royal, were obliged, with Mazarin, to yield. On 6th January 1649 they fled, while the Prince of Condé (262) and the royal, loyal army laid siege to the city.

Richelieu, Louis XIII, and Marie de' Medici, the Queen Mother, still in exile, all died between 1642 and 1643. The throne passed to Louis XIV, a little boy of five. Who was to rule the capital and France? The Queen, who was Regent? Mazarin, her minister? The princes? The Parlement of Paris? The malcontents, the bourgeois, or the mob? Parisians could not understand why the Italian Mazarin, the 'lay cardinal', stood so high in Anne of Austria's favour (267). He was the same age as the queen (41 when the king died) and this dark, handsome man, cheerful and agreeable, was the object of fierce popular hatred.

267

She has now got as far as revolt.

270

AVIS QUE DONNE UN FRONDEUR AUX PARISIEN QVIL EXORTE DE SE RÉVOLTER CONTRE LA TYRANNIE DV CARDINAL MAZARIN.

The Paris of the Fronde.

She little knew that this pebble would ricochet
for a century until finally it struck Goliath on the brow.

271

272

273

PLAN DE LA BATAILLE
DE S.ANTOINE,
Donnée le 5. Juillet 1652.
Entre l'Armée Royale
Commandée par les Maréchaux
De Turenne et de la Ferté;
Et l'Armée des Princes
Commandée par le Prince de Condé

274

275

The co-adjutor of the Archbishop of Paris, the Italian Paul de Gondi (271), later the Cardinal de Retz, organized the resistance against his compatriot Mazarin. But on 30th March 1649, the Parlement, fearful of the consequences of the blockade, opened negotiations with the Regent. At last they would be able to buy white loaves from Gonesse again!

But Condé was so proud of the victory he had gained that he in his turn now rebelled, aided by his brother the Prince of Conti, his sister the Duchess of Longueville, and Gaston of Orléans, the young King's uncle. Mazarin went into temporary exile.

A new citizens' uprising was incorporated willy-nilly into the uprising of the princes. On 1st July 1652, Turenne (272) and the King's forces surrounded Condé and the princes in the Faubourg Saint-Antoine (273). Condé would have been crushed back against the Bastille if the Grande Mademoiselle (274), Mlle de Montpensier, daughter of Gaston of Orléans, had not given orders from the top of the Bastille towers for the fortress's cannons to fire, and opened the gates of Paris for the rebel to escape.

The rebel princes could not agree among themselves. By the autumn the royal cause had triumphed. A stone statue showing the young King trampling rebellion underfoot was put up in the Hôtel de Ville (275). In 1687 Condé, of all people, bought it and set it up at Chantilly.

95

Louis XIV never forgot his childhood, harried by the Fronde. It was the memory of those days that made him move from the Palais Royal to the Tuileries, and soon afterwards to Saint-Germain and Versailles. To help to efface the memory of those difficult beginnings, the Parisian dawn of the age of the Roi Soleil was packed with public festivities. On 8th September 1656 the whole city was astir for Christina, Queen of Sweden. She was a person of note. Descartes had converted her to Catholicism and, after abdicating, she still half ruled her country. Mazarin and Paris gave her a great reception. Here she is entering the city (276), dressed in a scarlet jerkin. Fifteen thousand armed citizens welcomed her, together with the royal guard, all the public authorities of Paris, and three hundred archers. The pro-gramme included a Te Deum in Notre-Dame, a stay in the Louvre, and a visit to the Académie. The impetuous daughter of France's great ally. Gustavus Adolphus, was worthily received.

Paris on parade. When the cavalry prances through the streets,

278

On 2nd August 1660 Louis XIV and the young Maria Theresa made a magnificent entry into Paris after their marriage at Saint-Jean-de-Luz. A huge throne was set up on a special site constructed at the end of the Faubourg Saint-Antoine, and all the official bodies filed past to pay homage with such pomp that the spot was known long after as the Place du Trône. Then an enormous procession escorted the young couple to the Louvre (277). From the balconies of a house in the Rue Saint-Antoine Anne of Austria, Henrietta Maria, widow of Charles I, Turenne, and Mazarin, together with many great noblemen and ladies, watched the triumphant procession (278).

After this, the crown of all his diplomatic endeavours, Mazarin did not need to stay longer. He died, leaving a magnificent town house with two galleries full of works of art. In 1720 the Regent housed the Royal Library there.

she cannot but see herself as an equestrian city, a city of finery and bunting.

282

281

280

On 5th and 6th June 1662 a great equestrian show was given on a parade ground constructed between the Louvre and the Tuileries. The amphitheatre held fifteen thousand people, who thronged there to watch the evolutions of the king (279) and the princes of the blood (280), leading five brigades of Romans, Persians, Americans, Turks and Indians. Each brigade, decked with gold, silver, precious stones, plumes and ribbons, had its own colour (281–282). The splendid cavalcade crossed Paris twice, to the sound of trumpets and drums, and the plaudits of spectators packed to the very roof-tops. One vestige remains of these festivities: the name of the Place du Carrousel (tournament).

LE DVC DE GVYSE, ROY AMERIQVAIN.

Pauure côe Iob

Salade à Caute

A l'Hospital

re chetif et malbeureü
nt subict aux enuieux

veut, ni ne vaut

grand Hospital

Il va tousiours son grand chemin

Le grand chemin de l'hospital

And the flags that are tatters:

The honest citizen of Paris feared the darkness. In order to make the streets safe from the murderers, robbers and vagabonds that lurked there, whose numbers were estimated at fifty thousand, Louis XIV created the post of lieutenant of police, to which he appointed Nicolas La Reynie in 1667 (283). There still survived from the middle ages many culs-de-sac and blind alleys, known as 'cours des miracles', where so many outlaws and down-and-outs had entrenched themselves that the eight hundred archers of the watch did not even try to enter them. These nests were systematically surrounded and destroyed. In the winter the city was lit by 6,500 lanterns.

283

Paris raises those too.

285

In 1656 the Parlement had voted the setting up of the Hôpital Général, a kind of public assistance comprising several endowed institutions. Applications for help were soon overwhelming (284). The ancient château of Bicêtre sheltered the men.

It was soon necessary to enlarge the Salpêtrière, the annexe of the Arsenal, which took in the women and young children (285). In 1669 Libéral Bruant began building a great church with eight separate naves to accommodate the different kinds of patients (285).

288

But when one looks at them closely, in the pictures drawn from life, the ordinary people of Paris look a more cheerful lot than their officials, or the courtiers of Versailles. On the Quai de la Mégisserie (tawery wharf), where two boats have moored to enjoy a little celebration, work is not allowed to get in the way of entertainment (286). The fisherman sells his wares, or protects his servant-girls from the advances of a too enterprising customer. A group of young men are drinking and dancing with the laundresses.

286

If the Salpêtrière was over-crowded, it was because Paris often felt the pangs of hunger. Natural disasters added to the difficulties caused by the war. In the very place where the sumptuous tournament had taken place in 1662, and in the same year, a public centre had to be set up for the distribution of corn. A setier (about 8 pints) of flour, which cost 18 livres in 1692, cost 51 in 1694, and in 1709, during the severe winter when the Seine froze in the middle of Paris, the price of a setier of flour rose to 69 livres.

But she depends on her own resources more than on charity.

Nor are they any gloomier in the Vallée market, which was moved in 1679 to the Quai des Grands-Augustins, at the end of the Pont Neuf. Poultry, butter and eggs are the speciality there (287). Cocks and hens run about between the carts and the coops. A stall-keeper respectfully salutes the steward of some great house, or a food-inspector. Two tradeswomen are having a fight, and a water-carrier has just filled his buckets at the river.

289

287

288b

291

Paris, city of soldiers, of the low, the obscure, those without rank.

City of foot-sloggers. She gives to the survivors of her battles

The Sun King's plan to transfer his court and seat of government to Versailles encouraged the development of the western suburbs.
Louis XIV bought a part of the great undeveloped 'plain' of Grenelle, and on 12th March 1670 ordered the construction of a hospital to give board and lodging to disabled soldiers and veterans who had nowhere to go in their old age. The first stone was laid on 30th November 1671, but the key was not handed over to the King, who came with all his court for the ceremony, until 1706 (291–293). The completion of the capital's most beautiful monumental group of buildings took over thirty years.

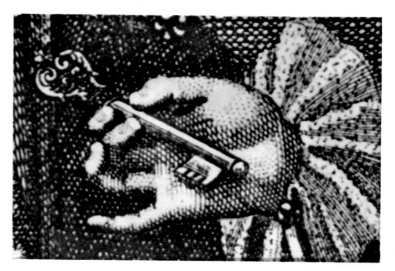

292

a panorama of stone, topped by a helmet of gold with plumes of cloud.

Who was really the father of the Invalides? Bruant, who built the main ranges, the courtyards, and the church of Saint-Louis? Louvois, simultaneously controller of buildings and minister of war? Jules Hardouin-Mansart, who built the royal chapel? Mansart, who was architect to the King from 1676 onwards and succeeded Louvois as controller of buildings, was technically responsible for all the great architectural achievements of the age of Louis XIV. It was he who raised the 350 foot dome dedicated to the sufferings and honours of war; at its restoration in 1934 two hundred and fifty tons of lead were used, and 360,000 sheets of gold leaf, weighing . . . thirteen pounds.

295

293

The Hôtel des Invalides, built without resort to special taxation because the money was included in the ordinary military accounts, has a frontage 230 yards long, and is a masterpiece of classical grandeur (294). Decorative masks, braziers, helmets, and prancing horses are its only ornaments; against the roof the dormer windows stand out in the shape of trophies, each one different (295). It is not every military budget that allows for such successful and creative projects.

294

Although affairs of state were managed at Versailles, Paris remained the undisputed setting for the grandeur of those years. Frivolous, brilliant or hardworking, useful to the state or harmful, all the queens and kings contributed to this splendour in their own fashion. Ninon de Lenclos (296), who died in 1705 at the age of 85, made herself, first by her conquests, then by her literary salon, one of the most important personalities of the Marais quarter. Boileau read his satires aloud at her house, and Molière his 'Tartuffe'.

296

Mlle de Fontange, who was said to have more beauty than intelligence, and who died at the age of twenty for love of the Sun King, would not be remembered here if she had not had the idea, one windy day when out with the hunt, of restoring her hair to order with the aid of ribbons. This coiffure (297), which grew taller and taller and more and more intricate, was all the rage from 1682 to 1713, in spite of the disapproval of the King himself.

297

A Grand Siècle confers royalty upon its women.

299

Another fashion, rather more obnoxious, was that for poisons founded by the Marquise de Brinvilliers, who killed her father and brothers by this means. She was beheaded (293) and burned in July 1676.

298

In 1668 Mme de Montespan, aged twenty-seven (298), supplanted Louise de La Vallière, aged twenty-six, in the affections of Louis XIV. She was to bear him eight children. Paris, a large city in which secrets can be hidden, welcomed this semi-royal brood in a beautiful house at Vaugirard. Mme de Montespan had a sharp wit, but that did not prevent her from driving the Italian players out of Paris because of the sharpness of theirs.

301

302

300

If the king is the Sun, they are the Danaë.

Mme de Maintenon (300), widow of Scarron, a true poet of Paris, and governess to the children of Mme de Montespan, superseded her mistress. She even married the King, secretly, in 1684. Her religious zeal brought austerity to Versailles, and was a contributing factor to the persecution of Parisian Protestants.

302b

303

Colbert (303), chief minister from 1664 to 1683, would have liked to make Paris a new Rome in respect to architecture, a new Venice or Amsterdam for commercial and industrial wealth. But foreign affairs left him no time to carry out his plan completely. He always regretted that Paris was not a sea-port.

309

304

Barrême (304), a mathematician and citizen of Paris, invented simple tables for the conversion of currency and the calculation of interest, and modernised the methods of accountancy.

305

Showers of gold? That was the business of great ministers.

306

307

308

Louvois (306), the docile executor of the King's wishes, though he was more of a soldier than a builder, was nevertheless the King's controller of buildings from 1685 to 1691. Jules Hardouin-Mansart, the architect, found him a useful ally. However great kings may be, they are not necessarily good financiers: Samuel Bernard (308) remedied this deficiency.

At a time when private individuals did not entrust their money to the state, this Protestant banker paved the Roi Soleil's footsteps with gold. He also made Passy and the Place des Victoires fashionable. In the first he built himself a château; he attracted banking and commercial interests to the second.

311

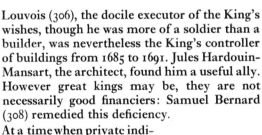

310

On the banks of the Bièvre, the Gobelins turn Paris into Smyrna or Ispahan.

Among the Flemish crafts-men (dyers and fullers) who had frequented the banks of the Bièvre since the 15th century, a certain family

312

313

Veüe d'vne partie de l'Hostel Royal des Gobelins, ou sont establies les Manufactures des meubles de la Couronne.

The shuttles of the Gobelins still weave their brilliant tapestries. But what has become of the wooded Bièvre, beloved of the Parisian laun-dresses, on the banks of which Rousseau was soon to botanise? Its waters, though they grew more and more polluted, continued to give a living to dyers and tanners until quite recent years (314), but now all that remains is the memory of frozen ponds in the name of the Glacière quarter. The Bièvre, now little more than a sewer, is siphoned off under the Seine.

314

called Gobelins had risen so quickly to wealth and pre-eminence that they had given their name to the whole quarter, where other dyers and Flemings had also established the art of tapestry-making. They brought it to such a degree of perfection that Colbert bought the whole place in 1666 and turned it into a royal factory, 'Les Gobe-lins', which he visited ac-companied by the King himself (312).

Provided with designs by the great artists of the day under the direction of Le Brun (312) and his successor Mignard, the Gobelins was a hive of ceaseless activity; its two hundred and fifty workmen, each with his own house and garden, made up a whole commu-nity, in which there were opportunities for amuse-ment (313) as well as orders for work.

In gambling-houses and at fairs, the gold coins roll, bright with the image of Louis XIV.

Paris, city of gamblers.

The making of playing-cards was a flourishing industry. This manufacturer (315) of the Place Dauphine enjoyed not only the finest view of Paris – the Seine from the Louvre to Chaillot – but also, no doubt, an equally splendid clientèle. At Versailles they were reckless gamblers, and even in Paris the meanest gambling-den called itself an 'Academy' to attract the bourgeois.

The ordinary people preferred less costly pleasures. There was a ceaseless coming and going at the great fair which since 1486 had flourished under the protection of the Abbey of Saint-Germain-des-Prés (316). It was a place of brawling and fighting no less than of amusement and trade; there were to be found such rare and fashionable novelties as tea, chocolate, and tobacco. All the tradesmen of Paris were represented at the fair of Saint-Germain, but especially French pastry-cooks, Italian sellers of soft drinks, and managers of dance-halls.

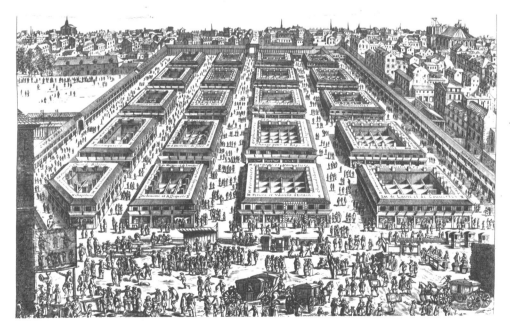

Let us hear the King,

Marie de' Medici and then Anne of Austria liked to have their private chambers in the little gallery of the Louvre which joins the wing that Lescot built to the riverside gallery. In 1661 it was ravaged by fire. The architect Le Vau rebuilt it, and Le Brun the painter decorated the first floor with frescoes showing the triumph of the chariot of the Sun. This gallery of Apollo (317) is an obvious compliment to the King.

in the royal palaces:

319

For the cyma of the central pediment, Perrault selected from the quarries at Meudon an immense monolithic block which he had hewn in two. The two halves, each nearly sixty feet long and over eight feet wide, were so heavy that to bring them on to the site and hoist them to the top a special machine on rollers had to be used (319), similar to those the ancient Egyptians employed. An innovation was the use of invisible iron girders to reinforce the wide span between the peristyle and the wall behind.

'Reason commands that we obey before reason itself those impulses and blind instincts, apparently sent from heaven, which are common to all men,

When he commissioned Le Mercier to build the Pavillon de l'Horloge (clock), Louis XIII had intended to make the Louvre four times as extensive as the old square château of Philip Augustus (901). His successor gave Le Vau orders to complete the new quadrangle. This was done by 1664, and it was decided that there must be a new and magnificent entrance front. The plan drawn up by Bernini, who came to Paris in 1665, was not approved. Le Brun, Le Vau, and above all Claude Perrault (a doctor not an architect) had the idea of imposing on a storied building the façade of a great Roman temple. The colonnade attributed to Perrault was begun in 1667, and introduced the 'colossal' style into the Parisian landscape (318).

318

But in 1678 the king and his court forsook the Louvre and the Tuileries. Perrault's colonnade remained roofless and unconnected with the façade on the Seine. Tenants of all kinds moved into the palace: the various academies, and, in the wake of the artists, a crowd of intriguers and undesirable hangers-on who lingered there until Napoleon sent them packing.

But the entrance from the great colonnade into the Cour Carrée, and that of the Pavillon de l'Horloge, already showed the direction in which modern Paris was to develop. Slightly out of line with the axis of the Tuileries, it established the east-west alignment according to which the planners were to construct Paris, from the Place de la Nation to the Rond-Point (circus) de la Défence, passing through the Arc de Triomphe du Carrousel, the Champs-Elysées, and the Arc de Triomphe de l'Etoile (321).

321

and especially worthy of consideration in those whom heaven itself has set above the rest.'

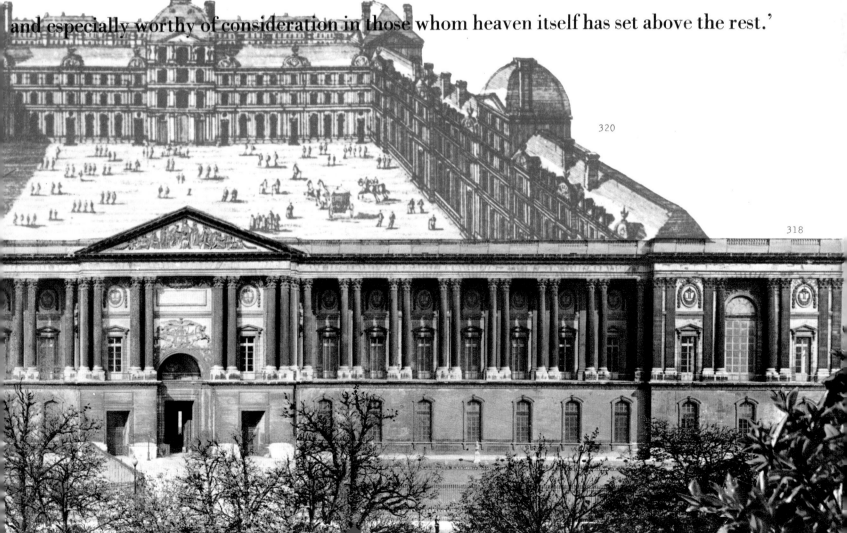

320

318

323

In 1667, Colbert, not to be outdone, and anxious to see the French fleet sail the seven seas, ordered the construction of an Observatory. In the high and barren district of the quarries, Perrault erected a building that corresponded to strict astronomical requirements (324). The Paris meridian cut it in two equal halves. It contained no wood or iron, and its terraced roof was specially designed for the taking of observations. Less useful since the sky over Paris has become obscured by smoke, it now shelters a speaking clock (325).

322

Mazarin had left two million livres to provide a French education and Parisian surroundings for sixty boys from the new royal provinces of Piémont, Alsace, Artois, and Roussillon. In 1663 the Hôtel and the ancient Tour de Nesle were demolished, and in 1684 in their place, according to plans drawn up by Le Vau, was built the Collège des Quatre Nations. This new institution was to pass through many vicissitudes during the Revolution; finally Napoleon transferred it to the academies which together formed the Institute.

The cupola of the old church (322) has become famous because of the receptions of the Academy which attract large crowds of spectators. A large portico leads to the Mazarin library (323), open to the public in accordance with the wish of the cardinal minister.

325

324

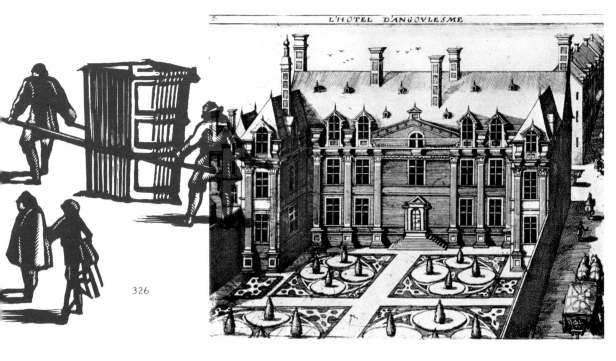

And Malherbe: 'Paris has had my heart since I was a child;

how many excellent things have come to me through her.'

Who is the guest on his way by chair (326) or coach to this house (327) in the Marais, built by Diane de France, Duchess of Angoulême, in 1584 and rented since 1658 by Guillaume de Lamoignon, first president of the Parlement? Is it Bourdaloue, Regnard, Racine or Boileau? This peaceful garden, this Corinthian façade so daring for that time, are eternally vowed to literature. A fervent bibliophile housed a collection there of 20,000 books about the capital, the first historical library of Paris. The poet Delille and Alphonse Daudet lived there.

The sharpest of wits was exercised not far from here, at the Hôtel Carnavalet, a large Renaissance house rebuilt in the classical style by

328

François Mansart. Mme de Sévigné (328), who rented it in 1677, was enchanted with it. 'A healthy air, a fine courtyard, a lovely garden,' she wrote. The great men of literature, the arts, politics, and the army all passed through its salons. In them the famous Marquise's letters, grave, gay or fearful, were written. In 1880 it became a historical museum of the city of Paris. In its main courtyard (329) stands a statue of Louis XIV by Coysevox, the only one to survive the Revolution. It was spared because it had been commissioned and paid for by the municipality.

But the Marais quarter was going out of fashion. A footbridge had replaced the ferry that used to connect the Tuileries to the left bank. Then, between 1685 and 1689, at the personal expense of the King, a new bridge was built, the Pont Royal of today, the ninth bridge of Paris but the first to cross the whole river from bank to bank without the aid of any island. The combined efforts of the architect Gabriel and the Dominican friar François Romain were needed to produce the Pont Royal, a bridge with no houses on it, a work of simple and beautiful proportions, and of easy access (330). Soon the Pré-aux-Clercs (the clerks' meadow), the huge public parks of Queen Marguerite, were to be no more than a memory. They gave place to the noble Faubourg Saint-Germain, which was adorned by two hundred great houses between 1690 and 1789.

330

332

About fifty of these hôtels have survived assault and the ravages of time, with their gateways on to the street, their great courtyards, and their main buildings each with its loveliest façade facing on to inner gardens. Many of them have escaped decay by being taken over as embassies or ministries, as in the Rue de Varennes, the Rue du Bac, the Rue de Lille, and the Rue de l'Université.

What a wealth of magnificent salons, splendid staircases, and beautiful entrances, such as that of the house (331) built for letting out by the seminary of Foreign Missions (120 Rue du Bac). The Clermont-Tonnerre family gave it its name. Chateaubriand died there. What beauty even in the details of these famous houses; for example, the doorknocker of the Hôtel de Cavoye (332), one of the finest houses in the district, built in 1643 and occupied in 1687 by a childhood companion of Louis XIV, a friend of Racine and Turenne.

Just nearby, for Anne's son, soon to be Cardinal-Archbishop of Strasbourg, the same architect built the Hôtel de Rohan. To decorate the passage leading to the stables, Le Lorrain carved the horses of the sun (334), which brings a scene of horses being watered to the heart of Paris. After the peace of Nijmegen in 1685 the Maréchal de La Feuillade, that whimsical muddlehead and heroic scatterbrain,

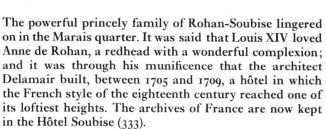

The powerful princely family of Rohan-Soubise lingered on in the Marais quarter. It was said that Louis XIV loved Anne de Rohan, a redhead with a wonderful complexion; and it was through his munificence that the architect Delamair built, between 1705 and 1709, a hôtel in which the French style of the eighteenth century reached one of its loftiest heights. The archives of France are now kept in the Hôtel Soubise (333).

Height does not matter so much as perspective. The sun needs space.

offered the Roi Soleil a statue and a square for it to stand in. Hardouin-Mansard designed it, and put up a statue of the King, on foot, crowned with laurels (335). Four lamps which were lit up at night were placed round it. But the fine symmetrical lay-out of the Place de la Victoire has not survived, and after adventures yet to be described, Louis XIV found himself back in the saddle (335b).

335b

336

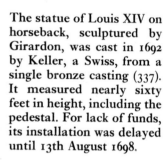

337

The statue of Louis XIV on horseback, sculptured by Girardon, was cast in 1692 by Keller, a Swiss, from a single bronze casting (337). It measured nearly sixty feet in height, including the pedestal. For lack of funds, its installation was delayed until 13th August 1698.

Louvois, jealous of La Feuillade, planned to create a complete administrative area built round a vast octagonal space, also with a statue of the Roi Soleil in the middle. To make the Place Louis-le-Grand (now the Place Vendôme) he had to buy up a huge hôtel, displace the Capuchin monastery, and carry out large and lengthy building operations under the direction of the architects Hardouin-Mansard and Boffrand. In the end the expenses were so enormous that the buildings round the square had to be sold to private individuals. Once a year the fair of Saint-Ovide drew large crowds there with its pastry-shops and theatres (336).

Several prosperous financiers, including Law and Bourvallais, were the first residents of the Place Louis-le-Grand (338). Today the Ritz Hotel, the Ministry of Justice, fashionable dressmakers, jewellers, perfumiers, and big business establishments occupy the setting in which Chopin died and Napoleon III fell in love with Eugénie de Montijo.

338

This is the age of lyrical order.

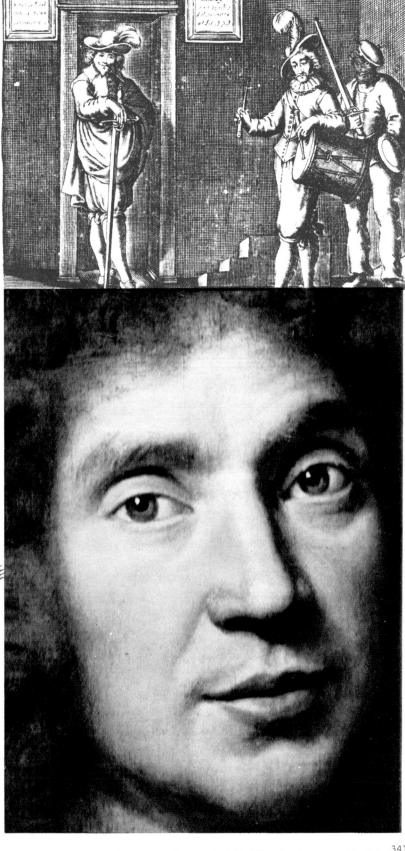

On the Pont Neuf, and at the fairs, three baker's boys, Turlupin, Grosguillaume (339), and Gaultier - Garguille (340), delighted Parisians with their flour-throwing farces. Richelieu himself took great pleasure in their antics.

The Salle (or theatre) de l'Hôtel de Bourgogne had become the first theatre in Paris (342). Richelieu arranged for the popular flour-throwing comedians to perform there. The Italian players came too. There the masterpieces of Corneille were performed, and all the plays of Racine.

In 1643 Jean-Baptiste Poquelin, called Molière (341), a true Parisian, founded a company of amateurs, the Illustre Théâtre, which was not successful. For twelve years he remained in the provinces perfecting his art. Back in Paris in 1658, he put on 'Le Dépit Amoureux' (The Amorous Spite) and 'Les Précieuses Ridicules' (The Bluestockings) at the Hôtel du Petit Bourbon, near the Louvre, his performances alternating with those of the Italians. He won fame at the Palais Royal, in the theatre built by Richelieu, and died on its stage in 1673.

The Italian players, established in Paris since 1570, went on from success to success. With their masks and gestures, Scaramouche (343), Harlequin, Pantaloon, Trivelin and Aurelia gave the Commedia dell'Arte a dazzling style. But Mme de Montespan claimed they had caricatured her; in 1697 they were expelled, returning twenty years later to even greater adulation.

At the King's command Molière's company amalgamated with the players of the Marais, and established themselves in Saint - Germain-des-Prés. Seven years later Louis XIV added to their numbers the actors from the Hôtel de Bourgogne. The three companies which had created the masterpieces of Corneille, Molière, and Racine, now formed a single troupe, the Comédie Française, which gave its first performance on 25th August 1680.

And as the city submits to it, so does the theatre, whose noblest century this is.   113

People rushed to buy Chardin's account of his travels in Persia and elsewhere. Soon Montesquieu was to present Paris as a new and amusing Ispahan.

346

The power of the theatre, the major art form. Nature is the setting

Louis XIV, a born actor (346), turned every public event into a great spectacle. As, for example, when on 18th November 1663, before the altar of Notre-Dame, he and Lefèvre, the ambassador, renewed on oath the Franco-Swiss alliance, in the presence of representatives of the thirteen cantons (344). But the people of Paris witnessed much stranger ceremonies. Louis dreamed of Eastern and Far Eastern alliances. In 1669 the envoy of the Grand Turk arrived in Paris, and in 1684 the Parisians watched with astonishment a procession of Siamese mandarins. In February 1715 they jostled each other in the Place Royale to get a closer look at the Persian ambassador (345). For the whole duration of his visit, which lasted eight months, he was the centre of attraction in the capital: his pipes, his coffee, and the weird goings-on of his suite were the subjects of conversation for the whole of Paris.

for real life actors. Paris is the theatre of life.

345

St Denis en France

Mont-Martre

Carosse de Madame la Regente

Officiers de la Maison du Roy

Le Clergé de St Denis

Carosse de Madame la Douairiere

Les Gentils homme de la maison du Roy

Pages de la grande et petite Ecurie du Roy

Carosse de Mons.r le Regent Duc d'Orleans

Carosse du Roy

Les Escuyers du Roy

Corps du Roy

Gardes du Corps du Roy

Ausmoniers du Roy avec les Herauts d'Armes aux 4 coings du Corps

Les Cents Suisses

Chez J. Chiquet a Paris.

Marche et Convoy funebre de Louis le Grand Roy de France et de Navarre; de Versailles a St Denis en France lieu de sa sepulture avec les autres Roys de France le 9.e septembre 1715. le quel estoit mort le 1.re du mesme mois; son Coeur ayant esté porté aux Jessuites a Paris, et ses Entrailles a n. Dame Cathedrale de Paris.

On 1st September 1715, a reign which had lasted almost three-quarters of a century came to an end. Louis XIV breathed his last at Versailles. Paris was weary. The repeal of the Edict of Nantes, the persecution of the Jansenists, the terrible winter of 1709, the shocking deaths of the heirs to the throne, all had combined to darken the atmosphere of his later years. But the people of Paris, on foot or in their coaches, crowded the route to Saint-Denis to watch the midnight funeral procession of France's greatest monarch (347). During the reign of Louis, the Roi-Soleil, Paris had sometimes gone hungry, but she had come to be respected, admired and wondered at throughout the world.

Death is a scene from a play. The curtain falls on a sunset where the gold is swallowed up in a dark and bloody sky. The great show is over.

L'Hôtel de Conty....... 5 Le Mône de Calvaires 9 Quay des quatre Nations Ce grand Ouvrage fut entrepris Sous le Regne de Henry
L'Abbaye de Saint Germain des prez 6 Les Theatins 10 Les Pont Neuf...... la Ville de Paris y fit mettre la dernière main en l'An
Le Collège des quatre Nations 7 le Quay d'Orcai 11 le Pont Royal Cheval, a esté fait a Florence par Jean de Boulogne, C
Les Invalides 8 Quay Malaquais 12 le Cours de la Reine qu Pré et les ornements par Pierre Francheville Na

348

The new age is young, and so is the King. Give thanks with Racine:

The world smiles at the waking sun,

1726: the great gallery of Paris. A crowd of onlookers – a haberdasher, a wounded soldier, a Capuchin monk, a vendor of honeycombs – all greet the new King and Queen as they cross the Pont Neuf. Let us look in detail at the beauties added to this landscape by three reigns and a hundred years. The kings and queens, leaving to the working people the congested island of the Cité, and to the nobility the Marais quarter, have built up in the open spaces of the west the regal and symmetrical order that Descartes

it Jetter les fondations en 1578. Et le Roy Henry IV. qui aimoit
La Statue Equestre du Roy Henry IV. le 23 Aoust 1614. Le
meux Michel Ange, La Figure du Roy par un Sculteur nomé
bray   Paris chez P. Gallays, rue St. Jacques a St. François de Sales.

13	La Porte de la Conférence.	17	Port St. Thomas du Louvre.	21	Le Quay de l'Ecolle.
14	Le Quay de la Conférence.	18	Le Louvre.	22	La Samaritaine.
15	Les Tuileries.	19	Le Garde meuble.	23	Le Carillon.
16	Les Galleries du Louvre.	20	Porte des Tuileries.		La largeur du Pont neuf est de 1. en y comprenant l'espaisseur du P.

'The bright and rosy-fingered one prepares the way for him who follows.

And shades sink back into night's hollows.'

desired (see p.85). But beware: this new king has a taste for irregular charms, for opulent curves, and for caprices in stone, rather than for academic and geometrical majesty. To underline the changes that the coming metamorphosis was to bring, go back to 1st September 1715, when the great reign ended and Louis XV became king, the only surviving representative of the royal line, at the age of five and a half. 'The world has nothing so sweet as the air we breathe in Paris,' Racine had written. How long would this be true?

117

Frivolous Paris, lover of gaiety, feasting and pleasure. How many times, having won back liberty, have you forgotten that it exacts more sacrifice?

The Parlement of Paris was given the responsibility of opening and executing the dead King's will. All the capital was at the windows or in the streets on 12th September to honour the young King on his way to hold a 'lit de justice' at the Palais. Before he entered the Great Chamber the new sovereign was welcomed at the Sainte-Chapelle with a great display of many-coloured uniforms and ladies in their finest array (349). But contrary to the last wishes of Louis XIV, there was to be no Regency Council. The Duke of Orléans was appointed sole Regent, and the Parlement seized this opportunity to exercise again the famous right of remonstrance, of which they had been deprived for forty years. They would willingly have gone further in this direction. The new reign began badly. The Regent, who at first was generally esteemed, began to indulge in senseless debauchery at the Palais Royal. But no one seriously considered the possibility of another Fronde. During the whole of the Regency, until 1723, the court resided in Paris.

The Opéra balls were inaugurated. Everyone danced, philosophised, tried to make money, and criticised the government; but without resorting to arms. The Paris of Louis XV was to be a city which, after the vigours and rigours of preceding reigns, wished to enjoy the pleasures of society and the joys of living, real or illusory. By chance, there were some eminent and responsible men, such as Michel-Etienne Turgot, provost of the merchants from 1730 to 1740, who watched over the interests of the city with scrupulous care. And there was always the Seine, the eternal bearer of bread and work, the great purveyor of amusement. Why worry about tomorrow? The painter Raguenet bids you to a water-tournament, which brings crowds of cheerful Parisians to the Pompe and the Pont Notre-Dame (350). Can you see a Parisian who sells pictures in a shop on the bridge leaning out of his window to applaud? That is Gersaint, and Watteau, the painter, has just made him a shop-sign. Watteau! A new Paris. A new age.

A Tsar embraces Paris

351

The treasury nevertheless remained empty. In 1716 the Regent listened to the proposals of Law, a Scot, who suggested that the State should give paper money in exchange for gold and silver, and vice-versa. At the same time people were buying shares in great foreign enterprises. The Mississippi was a name to conjure with. Everyone shared the craze for paper money. Crowds thronged the Rue Quincampoix (352) to buy or sell shares (353). Masters and servants made fortunes overnight.

But more were ruined. There was a panic in 1720, and it was found that notes worth three thousand million francs had been issued against five hundred million francs' worth of gold. There was one slender consolation: the pillory was working overtime. A financier and a bailiff were hauled there one after the other (354).

352

Peter the Great came to Paris in 1717. His visit was a triumphant success. He went all over the city, attended the Opera, and drank with wounded veterans at the Invalides. He was delighted by the medal that was specially struck for him, showing him, quite simply, about to embrace the young King (351). The only thing he found too fine and too extravagant was the luxury surrounding the royal family.

353

354

120

DECLARATION
DU ROY,
QUI REGLE LES LIMITES DE PARIS.

Donnée à Chantilly le 18. Juillet 1724.

OUIS par la grace de Dieu Roy de France & de Navarre : A tous ceux qui ces prefentes Lettres verront, SALUT.
Pour renfermer noftre bonne Ville de Paris dans de juftes
limites , & prévenir les inconveniens qui feroient à craindre
de fon trop grand accroiffement , les Rois nos Prédeceffeurs
ont fait en differens temps des défenfes de bâtir aucunes Mai-
fons dans les Fauxbourgs , lieux prochains , & hors les Portes,

The government's brief stay in Paris gave rise to some new
building. But there had to be a limit. Great stone columns
were to be set up at the ends of the streets, and no one was
allowed to build beyond them. A city which grows too fast
condemns itself to death. A wise principle, which Louis XV,
now of age, laid down by edict five times in forty years!
And every time in vain (355).

Louis XV returned to Versailles, and
the money merchants became the
new kings of Paris. In 1718, in a quiet
corner of the Faubourg Saint-
Honoré, the Comte d'Evreux built
himself a splendid residence which
later became the Elysée Palace
(356).
In place of the fortifications, which
Louis XIV had had pulled down,
there extended an almost deserted
avenue (now the Grands Boulevards). The Marquis d'Antin, controller of buildings, had a big house
built there with a road leading to it
(the Chaussée d'Antin), which was
soon much frequented. In 1721, in
the stately Faubourg Saint - Germain, the Hôtel Matignon arose,
and in 1722 the Palais-Bourbon (358),
with its great terrace overlooking
the Seine.

357

358

359

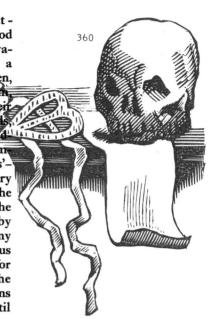

360

The little graveyard of Saint-Médard where the tombstone stood was the setting for endless extravagant scenes (361). To induce a trance, men, and especially women, got others to trample on them, wound them with axes, pierce their tongues. Some swallowed live coals, others bibles, complete with binding. Sects quickly formed: the 'jumpers', the 'mewers', the 'barkers'—until the King closed the cemetery in 1732 and sent the leaders to the Bastille (362). A wag scribbled on the gate: 'The Lord is forbidden by Louis his Grace To perform any miracles in this place.' The religious ladies who mewed in chorus for hours on end were silenced by the threat of the whip. But convulsions continued to be held in private, until the Jesuits, the enemies of the Jansenists, were themselves accused!

In the classical age reason triumphant had reigned without opposition.   But this left

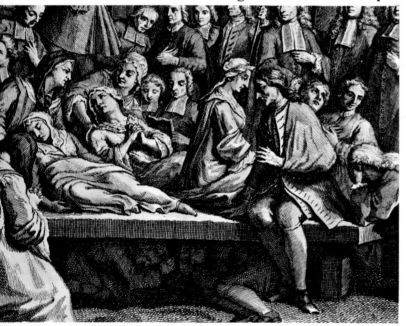

361

The people of Paris, always so willing to call themselves sceptics, nevertheless witnessed and to a certain extent took part in a strange and unearthly series of events. The Jansenists, persecuted by Louis XIV, resumed their activities. Cardinal Fleury, now chief minister, once more embarked on the struggle against them, invoking the bull Unigenitus. In 1727 there died at the age of thirty-six François de Pâris, son of one of the councillors in the Parlement (359). After he had been ordained deacon at Saint-Médard, a Parisian parish where Jansenism was rife, he had lived a life of privation, asceticism and mortification of the flesh (360). His tomb soon acquired a reputation among the devout for inducing fits which ended in marvellous ecstasies.

362

Not far from Saint-Médard, in the Jardin des Plantes, strict reason and vegetable calm prevailed. It had been founded in 1626, and already in 1641 contained 2,500 different kinds of plants. But it was during the reign of Louis XV that it became one of the Parisians' favourite haunts. The silt of the Seine, the mud of the Bièvre, and the refuse left by generations of Parisians made an invaluable leaven in the soil. One hillock in particular, a veritable mountain of detritus, became a favourite spot where there grew a maze of most beautiful shrubs, and the flowers most propitious to amorous or scholarly converse (363). The brothers Jussieu, all three ardent botanists, joined in bringing honour to the Jardin des Plantes. It was said that in 1734 Bernard de Jussieu brought back a cedar from Syria in a hat, and watered it with his ration of drinking water. The tree in question, which as a matter of fact had only crossed the Channel, has triumphantly borne the weight of the years (364).

364

ut of account the imagination of Paris.

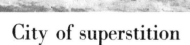

City of superstition

363

Buffon (365), promoted curator of the Jardin des Plantes in 1739, added new land to the plantations, and surrounded himself with eminent colleagues. He had enormous success. One of his lesser inventions attracted the curious: above the maze he erected an observation tower surmounted by an iron sphere which formed a kind of sundial; and this, by a cunning arrangement of pendulums, was made to sound twelve strokes at noon (363).

as well as of logic.

365

What must the voice of Paris have been, when a thousand voices echoed in her streets,

366

A strange custom produced a tragic result (366). If you have dropped anything in the Seine, call upon good Saint Nicholas and put in the water a piece of wood carrying a lighted candle and a piece of consecrated bread. In the place where the candle goes out you will find what you have lost. Alas, in 1718 a widow whose son had been drowned decided to try this remedy. The piece of wood was swept away in the current, the candle set fire to a boat carrying hay, and the blazing vessel hit against the wooden scaffolding of the Petit-Pont. The bridge burned for three days, together with the twenty-two houses that stood on it. It was rebuilt for the eleventh time, but without any houses. The Hôtel-Dieu nearby escaped this time, but it was not so fortunate either in 1737 or 1772, when 1,500 patients are supposed to have been burned to death.

crying their wares of fish and fruit and fowls?

Was the Paris of Louis XV so different after all from the Paris of Philip the Fair? Street criers still boasted their wares at the tops of their voices, their shouts rising above the din of the crossroads. Bellows-menders, water-carriers, secondhand-hat merchants, sellers of fresh fish and vegetables, all contended to attract customers as piercingly as possible (370 & 375-9).

124

370

367

This century of 'joie de vivre' was also a century of great fires: the Chamber of Accounts in 1737, the Pont au Change in 1746, the Opéra in 1763, and in 1776 the Palais, in a conflagration which destroyed the old medieval castle. During the night of the 16th to the 17th March 1762, the vast caravanserai of the Fair of Saint-Germain was burnt out. There was a north wind blowing, and so the finest wooden structure in the whole of Europe was reduced to ashes (368). When the

368

69

alarm sounded, monks specially assigned to the task, Capuchins chiefly, rushed to the spot and at the risk of their lives fought the blaze with huge casks of water (367), buckets, crosses, axes and hose-pipes. Thanks to M. de Sartine, lieutenant of police, a corps of firemen was organised which was at last equipped with pumps (369).

But this was by no means the end. In 1763 the Opéra, now in the Salle de Richelieu in the Palais Royal, burned to the ground (371). It was rebuilt nearby. But in June 1781 a rope on the forestage was set alight by a Chinese lantern, and curtains, scenery, gilded boxes, all were burned. What use were pumps when the reservoirs were dry! Fourteen people were 'reduced to ashes'. A new Opéra was hastily built in the Boulevard Saint-Martin.

370 b

371

125

The appeal of these boulevards was so strong that the revolutionaries of 1792 were to welcome the advent of the Chinese baths at 29 Boulevard des Italiens, which was also a café and restaurant (374).

376

The age of Paris can be counted by the boulevards she outgrows,

375

In the boulevards that took the place of the fortifications pulled down by Louis XIV, only the two gates in the form of triumphal arches to the glory of the Roi Soleil, the Porte Saint-Denis (1672) and the Porte Saint-Martin (1674), recall the fact that the growth of Paris halted there for many years. The Grands Boulevards remained for a long time virtually deserted, but at last they became fashionable. Theatres sprang up, such as the 'Variétés' (372), which, although it moved later to various other sites, eventually returned there. In the Boulevard du Temple was to be found the Café Turc, the biggest and finest of them all (373). Excellent ices, chess and dominoes inside. Tops, quoits and swings under the cool branches. Green arbours. Music. Specially recommended for matrons. Absolutely no admission to servants.

373

as that of a tree can be seen from the circles in the trunk.

374

380

Like the fair of Saint-Germain (380), now rebuilt, the boulevards had a great star-attraction: Nicolet, manager of a troupe of tightrope walkers, tumblers, singers, actors, acrobats, clowns, and dancers, not to mention a performing monkey. 'Always one better, as at Nicolet's,' was the slogan of this wonderful establishment. It was in the neighbourhood of the Boulevard du Temple, which remained in vogue for a whole century, that the crowd was thickest (381). All classes of society rubbed shoulders there: officers, lawyers, gentlemen, priests, financiers, foreigners, fine ladies anxious to see and be seen. The Boulevard de la Madeleine, on the other hand, was the site chosen for many quiet and comfortable town houses (382). In 1780 Deshayes, the farmer-general of taxes, commissioned Aubert to build him a charming house with a roof-garden at the corner of the Rue Caumartin. The first storey was ornamented with fine statues in bas-relief, but these were hacked down in 1908 to make room for advertisements (383); goodbye to another quiet shady spot.

381

Strollers, idlers, passers-by – here is a city that will fit its pace to yours.

383

382

AU TAMBOURG

Ce qui vient de la flûte
retourne au tambourg.

384

The signs of Paris.

In 1761 it was made compulsory to fix shop-signs flat against the buildings from which they hung, instead of allowing them to dangle out dangerously over the street. In this way Paris preserved a few signs that dated back to the middle ages. The origin of one of the oldest can be traced back to the 13th century. Renaud de Bréhon, son-in-law of the Prince of Wales, had come to Paris in 1228 to make an alliance against England. He was attacked by five Englishmen, and defended himself valiantly with the aid of his faithful servant. This servant later inherited his master's house, and opened a tavern there called 'At the Sign of the Armed Man', in memory of the fracas (386). Other signs a hundred or a hundred and fifty years old are: 'La Coquille d'Or' (the golden shell) (385); 'Le Bon Puits' (the pure well) (387); 'La Biche d'Or' (the golden hind) (387); and 'La Petite Chaise' (the little chair); they conjure up memories less distant but more peaceful.

Other signs read: 'Au Petit Maure' (the little Moor), 'Au Pied de Mouton' (sheep's foot), 'Au Puits Sans Vin' (a pun on 'puissant vin', strong wine), 'Aux Envieux de la Vertu' (haters of virtue), 'Aux Trois Forbans' (three stout benches), 'Au Pauvre Diable' (poor wretch); picturesque names which still stand at street corners.

385

The night shines like a jeweller's display.

388

386

A picture album, the blazon of our desires.

389

In the reign of Louis XV it was a man called Ramponneau (389) who was responsible for the most famous sign. In the suburb of Belleville, notable for its pleasure gardens, he opened a tavern called 'Au Tambour Royal' (royal drum) (388), where he served a little local wine, sparkling and gay. Teller of stories, master of ceremonies, the ancestor of all the song-writers and impresarios of the Paris cabarets, he established himself in 1760, near to the Chaussée d'Antin, at 'La Grande Pinte' (full measure) or 'Aux Porcherons' (swineherds). Great ladies did not scorn to rub shoulders there with waggoners, soldiers, and the stone-masons who were building this new district. The place could hold six hundred people. Ramponneau's wine was cheaper by half than anywhere else.

387

The popularity of tennis (390), the favourite sport of all, showed no sign of waning. In the reign of Louis XIV there were 114 covered courts in Paris. It was in one of these that the actor-playwright Molière made his début. The Florentine Lulli had likewise won dazzling success with his operas performed in an indoor tennis-court. It was in another of these in 1734 that Favart launched the first great series of comic operas. By 1850 only one tennis-court remained.

Lotteries were so much the rage that in 1710 the state took a hand and tempted the Parisian with 490 cash prizes. Several great religious buildings such as Saint-Roch, Sainte-Geneviève (Panthéon) and Saint-Sulpice owe their existence or completion to special lotteries (391).

In 1740 Peyrenc de Moras, a barber, was able to build himself a fine house in the fashionable Faubourg Saint-Germain, thanks to a lottery. In 1776, to avoid the possibility of fraud, Louis XVI made lotteries a state monopoly.

In August 1739 the five Ruggieri brothers, newly arrived

391

from Italy, gave a firework display over the Seine in honour of the Treaty of Vienna and the marriage of the King's eldest daughter to Philip of Spain. There was an orchestra of 190, a procession of 60 boats lit by 11,000 coloured lights, 6,000 rockets, 32 cascades, a sun 72 feet in diameter, and, it was said, 500,000 spectators (392).

392

Dancing invaded the salons and the parks. Ladies' gowns, worn with 'panniers' as they were called, grew wider then ever (393). The upper classes were also greatly addicted to horse-racing, a form of both sport and gambling imported from England.

One of the secrets of Paris : let nothing be done without elegance.

394

395

Riding contests brought the Bois de Boulogne area into favour (394), especially as the Abbey of Longchamp, though closed to the public, was the object of a sumptuous annual 'pilgrimage,' which gave the experts their chance. The prevailing taste for uniforms and finery (395) also inspired something more lasting. The new royal favourite, Mme de

Pompadour, and the financier, Pâris-Duverney, had the idea of founding an establishment where poor gentlemen could train as officers. Between 1751 and 1768, J.-A. Gabriel put up an immense group of buildings in the hitherto empty plain of Grenelle (396). In front was a vast open space where 25,000 armed men (397) could manoeuvre: the Champ de Mars.

396

397

The dazzling beauty of the Marquise de Pompadour, a Parisienne from the lower middle classes whose real name was Jeanne-Antoinette Poisson, was transitory (398). But to preserve the unique 'happiness of being with the king', the Marquise created about her an atmosphere of luxury and effortless distinction. She acted as patron to authors, painters and decorators, and had the Marquis de Marigny, her brother, made controller of buildings.

398

399

Nothing could be done except through the women. With what rapt attention J.-J. Rousseau, Rameau, Bouchardon, Soufflot, Van Loo, and d'Alembert listen to the actor Le Kain reading from some learned page (399). The hostess, the wealthy Mme Geoffrin, corresponded with the whole of Europe: the King of Poland addressed her as 'mama'. And friendly or rival salons were plentiful: at the houses of Mmes de Lambert, d'Epinay, du Deffand, de Tencin, de Houdetot.

Voltaire had left Paris in 1750. He returned in 1778 at the age of eighty-four. On 30th March the Comédie Française staged an apotheosis during a performance of his 'Irène'. A bust of Voltaire was crowned with laurels in his presence (400). Franklin, American Ambassador since 1776, asked him to bless his son. This excess of glory exhausted his strength and he died on 30th May.

400

It is as necessary to a gown or a game as to a speech or a book.

131

401

Was the King resentful against Paris? In May 1750 popular anger was aroused by police raids among beggars and young people to recruit colonists for the Americas. Twenty people were killed, many wounded. Louis retaliated by avoiding Paris when he crossed that part of France. The 'route de la Révolte' was hastily built between Versailles and Saint-Denis. But when he fell dangerously ill at Metz it was to the patron saint of Paris that he turned. The abbey church of Sainte-Geneviève was falling into ruins, and the King made a vow to replace it. Marigny commissioned his friend Soufflot to build a new church with a cupola nearly two hundred and seventy-five feet high (402). Louis XV himself laid the first stone in 1764. Soufflot aimed at combining the Greek beauty of the temple of Paestum, the majesty of the Pantheon at Rome, and the lightness of Gothic art. The difficulty of the problem killed him. The noble building he achieved was to be known under various names: the Temple of Fame in 1791, the church of Sainte-Geneviève in 1806, the Panthéon in 1830, the National Basilica in 1851, and in 1885, the Panthéon again.

When they wished to do something on the grand scale, it was to Rome or Athens that the architects of Paris turned. In 1733, to complete the church of Saint-Sulpice, begun by Le Vau in 1646 and one of the largest in Paris, the Italian Servandoni conceived the idea of an enormous façade with a two-storied colonnade surmounted by a great pediment (401). But his plans for the towers were not carried out, and the rococo style beloved of the age of Louis XV triumphed inside. The people of Paris came to marvel at the huge Tridacna clam-shells which were used as holy-water stoups, and at 'Our Lady of the Second-Hand Plate', a massive silver statue which the impetuous and zealous Abbé Languet de Gergy had made from the silver he had stolen (for the furtherance of religion) at weddings and banquets.

402

Paris has always looked with a loving eye on the cities of antiquity.
It is a kind of elegance to hold up a mirror which reflects their glory.

403

Another monument borrowed from Rome was built between 1771 and 1777 on the Quai de Conti by Antoine, an architect aged thirty-five, to house the Mint (403). Here, in a regal setting, furnaces, rolling-mills, presses and scales struck many beautiful medals and coins of gold and silver.

The people of Paris lacked faith. More churches were crumbling into decay and being demolished than were being built. But between 1774 and 1784, in the still sparsely inhabited quarter of du Roule, Chalgrin built the church of Saint-Philippe-du-Roule in the Graeco-Roman style (404).

But imitating the ancients did not rule out delicacy. In 1782 Rousseau, the decorator and architect, designed this charming little palace for the Prince of Salm-Kirbourg (405), with gardens stretching right down to the Seine. The Hôtel de Salm, which was won in a lottery in 1795 by a wig-maker who had made his fortune but was later thrown into prison, afterwards became the Swedish Embassy before it was given over to the Chancellory of the Legion of Honour in 1804.

404

05

Crowds of foreigners were attracted as much by the shops of Paris (407–408) as by her theatres and salons. The most Parisian of Parisians were Englishmen: Bolingbroke, Hume, Walpole, Arthur Young, and Watt, a Scotsman; or Germans: Glück, Prince Henry of Prussia, Holbach, Grimm; or Swedes: Creutz, Lafrensen, who called himself Lawrence, and the future Gustavus III; or Italians: Galiani and Piccini; or Swiss: like Necker. The Parisian Houdon went to America to sculpture a bust of Washington from the life. In every capital of Europe 'models from the Rue Saint-Honoré', the harbingers of fashion, were eagerly awaited.

A LA TESTE NOIRE. FRANÇOIS ANDRY MARCHAN EPICIER DROGUISTE, RUE DE L HARPE PRÉS CELLE DE S. SEVERI A PARIS. 1758.

France lost the Seven Years War (1757–1763), she lost Canada and her Indian colonies. Anglomania raged, but Paris still reigned over Europe. The fame of the cabinet-makers Boulle and Crescent, of the great goldsmiths, of the porcelain - manufactures of Sèvres, spread as far as Moscow and Washington. In the Faubourg Saint - Antoine Réveillon made beautiful painted wall - papers, and in his factory not far away Saint - Gobin turned out sheets of plate glass, using a remarkable new process which made his fortune (406).

406

It is a kind of elegance to hold up a mirror where the worl may see itself...

Paris was infatuated with the experimental sciences. Many private individuals had their own more or less elementary physics laboratories and mineral collections. Fine ladies crowded the house of the Abbé Nollet (409) to be given an electric shock, and went into raptures about his levers and pendulums and furnaces. He was more successful than M. de Silhouette. This minister of finance came and went so quickly and left the treasury so empty that his name became synonymous with a shadow.

In 1749, as the result of the imposition of new taxes, the Parlement of Paris, supported by the parlements of the provinces, entered upon a struggle with the Crown that did not end until 1789. On 5th January 1757, at Versailles, Damiens, a madman, stabbed the King. It was the general climate of feeling rather than any particular conspiracy that had instigated the attempt.

He was quickly dragged to Paris, where he was subjected to tortures (410) all the more cruel because everyone concerned secretly knew himself to be guilty.

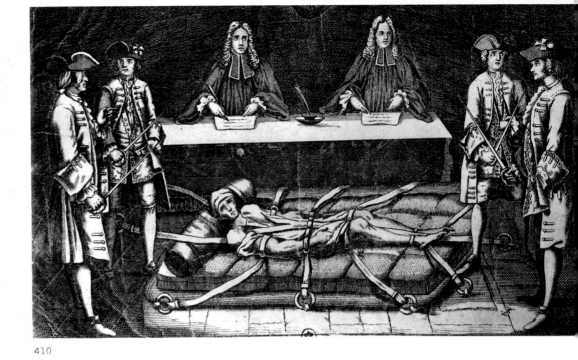

410

where the glory and the suffering of men are reflected.

The Parlement of Paris, to its shame, condemned young La Barre to death in 1765 on suspicion of irreligion. But it revealed itself incapable of any constructive policy in the field of finance, where it nevertheless had the monopoly. In January 1771 the members of the Parlement were sent into exile. Terray, the chief minister, imposed a tax on rents in Paris. Maupeou undertook the reform of the state. The wealthy middle classes, nobles and chief magistrates (411) were put in their place; but the people of Paris, who could not make head or tail of what was going on, allied themselves with these against the government.

411

The Jansenists of Paris, still numerous and some of them influential, continued to be active. They carried on a vigorous campaign against the Jesuits. The people of Paris, who were resistant to Rome's claim to authority over the clergy and saw the Jesuits as instruments of the power of Rome, ranged themselves on the side of the Jansenists. On 6th August 1761 the Parlement of Paris ordered the closing of all Jesuit establishments, and in 1762 the suppression of the Jesuit order (412). But this coalition of natural opposites was an ill-assorted one, with no definite political programme.

412

DESTRUCTIONS DES JESUITES DE FRANCE PAR LES ARRETS DES PARLEMENTS en 176

The political situation was becoming
more and more embittered: but one of
the most beautiful urban areas in the
world (the Place Louis XV, now the Place
de la Concorde) was brought peacefully
to completion.

To give thanks to the King for the peace of
Aix-la-Chapelle (1743), the municipality
had decided to erect a statue to him in the
middle of a specially constructed site.
Following a suggestion of J.-A. Gabriel,
they chose the undefined area beyond the
Tuileries, hitherto used as a store-ground.
With the Cours-la-Reine and its circus
opposite the Invalides (413), where a
hundred carriages could drive at the
same time (now the Place du Canada),

413

414

415

and the Champs-Elysées (414), already
a favourite place of promenade, the area
presented a very attractive appearance.
Along the Seine the Tuileries were now
joined to the Champs-Elysées by another
fine square, which differed from all its
predecessors by not being entirely enclosed. On the north side, between 1760
and 1772, Gabriel built two great identical
houses, each over three hundred feet long,
divided by the Rue Royale. Though they
owed their inspiration to the colonnade of
the Louvre and the houses of the Place
Vendôme, they were built in a style that
was finer and more delicate than these.
The octagonal Place Louis XV (415) – here
curiously engraved in reverse – was bordered by wide, deep ditches, in which
were plots of lawn and flowers reached
by means of stairways concealed in eight
little corner pavilions.

416

The equestrian statue of the King in the centre of the square (416) was a remarkable and curious piece of work by Bouchardon which was cast all in one piece. This figure of the King as a Roman Emperor (417) was erected in 1763; Pigalle's statues of the virtues of Strength, Prudence, Justice and Peace decorated its pedestal. But the Parisians felt cool towards their King; they had disliked the Marquise de Pompadour, and jeered, with good reason, at the new favourite, the Comtesse Du Barry. A malicious couplet went about: 'Beautiful statue, beautiful base! With the virtues on foot, and vice on a horse.'

People might be cool towards the King, but they flocked to the square called after him. In 1716 an Augustinian monk had thought up the idea of a swing bridge at the Tuileries, and it had never been so successful as it was after the Place Louis XV was laid out. Since 1719 it had been flanked by two winged horses (418) sculptured by Coysevox for the Château of Marly, with Mercury riding one and Fame the other. 'Each of these groups is made out of a single block of marble twelve feet high, with nothing added, not even Fame's trumpet, which has been preserved intact with infinite care.' In 1795, the two horses by Coustou which were to have replaced them at Marly were taken to Paris as well and set up at the entrance to the Champs-Elysées.

418

Here is a new theatre, large enough for Paris and its citizens since it covers 100,000 square yards (419). It had a bad start. In 1770, during the celebrations for the marriage of the Dauphin and the Archduchess Marie-Antoinette of Austria, the authorities failed to keep order and there were incidents with the fireworks; the result was a terrible panic, with 103 dead and hundreds injured. It seemed a gloomy omen. A great deal of Paris's history, joyful or dramatic, was to unfold here: revolutions, celebrations, military parades.

421

In 1784 Franklin and Lavoisier opened an official inquiry into these collective and sometimes hysterical healing sessions organised by Mesmer, which was the end of his famous tub. But just at this time the Parisians, who extolled reason, critical philosophy, and scientific knowledge, were taken in by an adventurer calling himself Count Cagliostro (421), a prophet, curer and manufacturer of the elixir of life, who was under the protection of the powerful Cardinal de Rohan. The great politicians of the day unhesitatingly consulted this dangerous quack, who was finally exiled in 1786.

In 1774 Louis XVI succeeded Louis XV, and the blessings and hopes of Paris went with him. But it was a period of deceptive calm; some sinister characters, as well as men of good will, were busy behind the scenes. In 1778 the German wonderworker and magnetiser, Mesmer, had so many customers, male and female, that he invented a collective remedy consisting of an oak tub with a number of metal rods sticking out of it (420) which the patients laid on whatever part of them needed curing. The King seriously offered Mesmer 20,000 louis to put mesmerism at the disposal of all.

420

With her nose in the air, Paris follows the balloons like a bored schoolboy watching flies.

422

Credulity was rife. The sale of miracle-drugs was forbidden, but there were still plenty of charlatans to preach the powers of astronomy and alchemy to the crowds (422). The German Curtius made astonishingly lifelike wax figures of kings, great writers, pretty women and notorious thieves. Neither his niece, Madame Taussaud, who set up in London, nor the Musée Grévin in 1882, were to do any better.

424

Paris kept looking skywards all through the memorable year of 1783, and learnt with great excitement that on 5th June the Montgolfier brothers had sent up a paper balloon filled with hot air into the sky at Annonay. Supervised by Charles, a physicist, the Robert brothers began to construct another balloon, this time of oiled silk and filled with hydrogen. It took off from the Champ de Mars on 27th August, watched by a huge crowd. Franklin (423) greeted the dawn of the future from the terrace of his house at Passy.

On 19th October the daring Pilâtre de Rozier and the Marquis d'Arlandes went up in a balloon moored in the garden belonging to Réveillon, the wall-paper manufacturer and friend of the Montgolfier brothers, in the Faubourg Saint-Antoine. On 21st November the two pioneers took off in earnest from the Parc de la Muette. Parisians of both sexes went down on their knees so that those behind them would not miss this historic sight. These 'Montgolfières', as they were called, were always filled with hot air.

423

427

425

426

Charles believed in hydrogen gas, and vouched for a new balloon (424). He made an ascent on 1st December from the garden of the Tuileries, amid the indescribable enthusiasm of 400,000 people crowding out the entire district, and landed near the forest of l'Isle Adam. On 19th September 1784 the Robert brothers again made an ascent from the Tuileries (425). Everything went balloon-mad: hats, dresses (426), menus, prints, shoes, snuff-boxes, clocks, caricatures. 139

In those days no gentleman was without his 'folly'. The word is not derived, as might well be imagined, from the gaudy extravagance of these pleasure houses: it comes from 'feuilles' (leaves), since it was above all a place where there were trees and thickets, like the Folie-Boutin and the Folie-Méricourt. In 1784 the gouty Beaujon (428), court banker, built the Folie-Beaujon at Roule, which was to charm Balzac and the Baroness de Rothschild, and in 1778 Philippe of Orléans, Duke of Chartres, ordered the organiser of his entertainments, the actor Carmontelle, to lay out a park in the English style of four hundred and seventy acres in the plain of Monceau. The 'Folie de Chartres' (430) had everything: an obelisk, a pyramid, a pagoda, a ruined temple, a Gothic dungeon, a Swiss farm, a Dutch wind-mill, a river, islands, a waterfall, a blue or yellow garden, and sea fights. The present Parc Monceau has lost nearly all these oddities and, alas, more than half its greenery.

429

'Follies' are another of the arts of Paris.

430

431

On 22nd October 1781 a dauphin was born, but there were such terrible memories of the catastrophe of 1770 in the Place Louis XV that the firework display at the Hôtel de Ville on 21st January 1782 (431) seemed rather wretched to those who watched. Very much more successful was the Palais Royal (433). In 1763 the building was given its present façade. In 1782 a new theatre (today the Théâtre Français) was begun. On three sides Philippe of Orléans had apartment houses built, their ground floors, which consisted of shops, opening out on to a garden through an arcade. In the wooden galleries enclosing the entrance court, curios and knick-knacks were sold and there were new attractions of all sorts, cafés and restaurants, which were all very successful. These galleries were much frequented by Parisian ladies who had the reputation of being fairly approachable.

The new reign started well. In 1778 Franklin, the American Ambassador, persuaded Louis XVI to recognise the United States, and the corporations of Paris all subscribed to build a vessel which would help to defend the new American liberties. The 'Parisian graces' were to be seen as far as the woods of Vincennes (432), where, in spring from 1781 to 1785, the first great races for which the King gave prizes took place.

LES GRACES PARISIENNES AU BOIS DE VINCENNE

432

433

141

It was decided to move the millions of bones in Paris, and the enormous underground quarries of the Faubourg Saint-Jacques took in an immense, macabre collection from the cemeteries and charnel-houses of the churches. Under the Second Empire the photographer Nadar was to take the first reporter's photograph in artificial light in these 'Catacombs' (435).

Louis XVI wanted to modernise Paris. By an edict of 1786 the houses on four bridges were destroyed, and the shops and dwellings on the Pont-au-Change, the Ponts Saint-Michel and Marie, and the Pont Notre-Dame (434) all vanished at the same time. The charnel-house of the Innocents, which for forty generations had swallowed up most of the Paris dead and was in danger of infecting the neighbouring district of the Halles, was closed as well.

435

434

436

Paris's water supply set another grave problem. The city's wells and fountains were inadequate, as were the water casks on the banks of the Seine that were filled by a machine which raised the water through long pipes (436). Eventually, on 8th August 1781, a steam pump began raising the river water up to the hill of Chaillot (437), whence it was redistributed to subscribers.

43

As Paris grew, its fiscal services, which were enforced from movable offices, became increasingly inefficient, so the Farmers-General, or revenue officers, had what amounted to a fiscal rampart built in 1785 (439). Ledoux, the architect, built posts and offices that were called 'barriers'.

The customs men's searches and inspections (438) exasperated the people, and there was widespread grumbling about the way the city was encircled.

Paris was long to remember these barriers or toll-gates, and they became part of the language of the city, in for example 'the barrier of Le Trône', or expressions like 'barrier keeper' or 'barrier prowler'. The barrier of Passy (440), one of the most beautiful because it was on the road to Versailles, has disappeared; but the pillars of the barrier of Le Trône (441) and the barrier of La Villette (442) still exist today; while these two great arcaded buildings at the barrier of Enfer (Place Denfert-Rochereau), once one of the busiest (442b), still testify to the heavy traffic there.

440

441

442 b

442

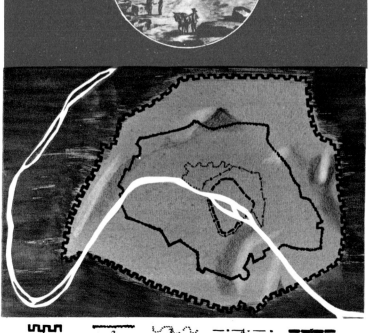

440 b

1. Thiers' fortifications of 1840

2. Wall of the Farmers General (1785)

3. Louis XIII's wall

4. Charles V's wall

5. Philip Augustus' wall

439

438

The craze for balloons did little to keep people's minds off the excitements of everyday life. The royal finances now seemed in desperate straits. One finance minister followed another: Calonne in 1786, Brienne in 1787, Necker (a Swiss), in 1788. When he suggested summoning the States General, representing the three classes of the nation, Necker achieved unprecedented popularity in Paris. The poor had suffered a great deal in the summer of 1788, and the winter, during which the temperature had fallen to well below freezing point, was terrible. A tense atmosphere accompanied the elections to the States General. On 28th April 1789 there was a sudden riot, with bloodshed, in the Faubourg Saint-Antoine. People were saying that the manufacturer Réveillon wanted to lower wages.

His workshops (443) were looted, wrecked and completely burnt out. The troops opened fire, causing 130 dead and 350 injured.

443

At the Palais-Royal, a young and unknown lawyer, Camille Desmoulins, declared that Necker's dismissal meant 'the Saint-Bartholomew of patriots'. He was cheered, and the busts of Necker and the Duc d'Orléans, taken from Curtius's waxworks museum, were cheered triumphantly in the streets. Insults were hurled at the Prince de Lambesc at the head of his cavalry, and he charged the crowd on the swing bridge of the Tuileries (445). The same evening, he withdrew to Saint-Cloud and Versailles. In Paris, panic and excitement ran high.

At the States General which met at Versailles, the Third Estate, which alone was as numerous as the nobility and the clergy, succeeded in being able to vote as individuals, an enormous success that frightened those nearest the King. On 12th July the population heard, with great indignation, that Necker had been dismissed. The Swiss and German regiments camping on the Champ de Mars were urged by the crowd (444) not to interfere in the battle that clearly threatened.

445

Twelve or fifteen men took over the toll-gate of the Gobelins, and Paris's fiscal wall was attacked on all sides. The barrier of La Conférence was burnt (446). Enormous excitement reigned on the night of the 12th. Robbers, never effectively suppressed in Paris, found a good opportunity for stealing; the tocsin sounded; priests headed patrols; and each electoral district organised itself into militia and elected leaders.

446

The whole of Paris was united against the court: high financiers who were friends of Necker, starving wage-earners, ambitious intellectuals, soldiers without a future, and the Duc d'Orléans, who was playing his own game.

448

Young people, later to spread the revolutionary spirit throughout Europe, flocked into the capital from the provinces (448). Everything was in the melting pot. This Parisian (449), who despises the costumes and manners of a society he believes abolished for good, thinks he has rid himself of them completely simply by wearing tricolour socks and tricolour cockades and knocking the heads off a few works of art in some nobleman's house. He cannot realise that many other heads – perhaps his own among them – will fall like theirs.

449

From a thousand follies the supreme form of Reason is born: its name is Revolution.

447

On 13th July, several hundred electors from the sixty districts formed a permanent committee at the Hôtel de Ville with the former town council and decided to organise a militia or National Guard. La Fayette, its chief, combined in his cockade the King's colour – white – with the blue and red of Paris. The National Guard needed arms. Someone suggested that they could be found in the old Bastille of Charles V, now a prison, and a fairly comfortable one, for offenders against the law amongst the nobility. Some French guards took the initiative and went there. Two rubbish carts and the stables were burnt and in the confusion and the smoke there was firing (447). The Governor, at the head of 114 Swiss guards and pensioners, surrendered. The riot caused 98 deaths.

Without bread, Paris grows its grim harvest of pikes.

The Assembly, which had feared being thrown into the Bastille, was the first to praise what had happened, and a delegation headed by La Fayette went to the Hôtel de Ville to compliment the electoral committee. Bailly, an astronomer, was proclaimed mayor; and as the Bastille, now open to everybody, had suddenly become a temptation to looters, it was decided to demolish it.

451

With its cornflowers of steel and its poppies of blood, it is the harvest of a long-felt fury.

On the morning of the 14th the rioters seized 28,000 rifles and 24 cannon from the Hôtel des Invalides (450). Thousands of soldiers on the Champ de Mars did nothing, and in the evening, with the Bastille taken, savagery reigned. In spite of assurances, the Governor was killed and his head stuck on a pike. The last of the merchants' provosts of Paris, Flesselle, was accused of playing a double game and murdered without trial on the steps of the Hôtel de Ville (451); his bleeding head was stuck on to the end of a pike too.

453

452

A megalomaniac contractor, Palloy, set 800 workmen (452) on to it and turned public work into a powerful piece of propaganda: he sold souvenirs, keys (453) that had been recovered, bullets and locks. From the stones of the demolished building, he had 88 models of the Bastille made and sent one to each department in France. Other stones were used to finish the Pont de la Concorde, so that the people of Paris could stamp on the remnants of despotism. On the following 14th July lanterns were put in the trees with notices saying 'Dancing' (454), and everyone celebrated for three whole days.

454

At dawn on the 6th the rioters invaded the royal apartments. The King gave way and with his family took the road to Paris. All round them the women waved poplar branches (457), and the men brandished the severed heads of the King's guards on the ends of pikes. At nine in the evening the King arrived at the Tuileries (458). Would this bring the Parisians more bread? In any case the monarchy and the assembly which followed it were the city's prisoners.

Paris still wanted blood. On the 23rd Foulon, the 74-year old Controller-General of France, was hideously executed, hung without trial from a lantern in the Place de Grève; afterwards his head was carted about the streets (456), its mouth full of hay because he had threatened to make Parisians eat it.

Revolutions repeat themselves. Montmartre, July 1789; Montmartre, April 1871; 82 years separated two identical scenes. The cannon of Paris were mounted on the hill (455 & 689). Since the 15th a rumour had been going about that the Court intended to make a platform on Montmartre to replace the Bastille, and from there would fire on Paris. In less than an hour, soldiers, middle-class citizens, workmen, women and children were climbing the hill, pushing cannon and carrying cannon-balls. Montmartre was held solidly. On the 16th the King recalled Necker. On the 17th he came to Paris. There was general excitement, even weeping, and Bailly said: 'The people have conquered their King.' Jefferson, the

456

His son-in-Law, Berthier de Sauvigny, Intendant of Paris, who was held responsible for the shortage of food, was murdered too. He was struck down with swords and his corpse set upon by the crowd.

458

457

new American Ambassador, was amazed. On the night of 4th August the nobility gave up its privileges. But the counter-revolutionaries took no more notice of this liberal gesture than the revolutionaries. Without having to cater for luxurious living, Paris was unemployed, and from the beginning of the autumn Parisians were short of bread. On the 1st October housewives queueing up vainly at bakers' shops heard indignantly that a great counter-revolutionary banquet was being organised at Versailles by the King's guard. On the 5th the most fanatical among them, 7 to 8,000 in number, started out for Versailles at six o'clock in the morning. It was a strange procession, noisy, uncouth and drunk with fatigue.

459

The cannon of a Summer storm

There was a pause in the Revolution. Parisians thought it had triumphed and peace had returned. The Assembly sat in the riding school of the Tuileries. Parties were formed, as well as popular societies or clubs whose importance was to increase.

Discussion was lively but not bitter. The traditional planting of the May tree (459), now called the Tree of Liberty, united everybody in a peaceful gesture.

Do not smile at this scene: for three or four years, Paris was often to lack bread, but it was to live, and presently to die, for slogans, symbols and emblems.

Jeunes gens courants pour le prix de la course à pied aux diverses fêtes que l'on donnait au Champ de Mars .... C'étoit vraiment un coup d'œil unique que plus de Soixante jeunes gens tous vêtus de mêmes et partant au même signal parcourir une longue Carriere, sans presque toucher la terre.

460

To replace the sacred person of the King, now becoming progressively less and less respected, and the Church's liturgy, for the present abolished, people developed an enthusiasm for youth and games – here we see a race (460) – and for Agriculture, Virtue, and Liberty. The pikes, the lictors' bundle of rods, the cockade, the red Phrygian bonnet which the Romans had given their freed slaves, became an everyday and necessary part of the Parisian scene. The name of a small unknown fortress in Piedmont, Carmagnola, was turned into a rallying cry, and became at once a civic uniform and a song.

thunder their salute to the tree of Liberty.

On 14th July 1790, for the Feast of the Federation, the Champ de Mars was turned into an immense amphitheatre. A procession of 18,000 delegates from the provinces crossed the Seine on a specially built bridge (461) (today the Pont d'Iéna). Talleyrand, the Bishop of Autun, said the Mass. La Fayette, the President of the Assembly, and the King took the oath to the Constitution, the Queen showed the Dauphin to the crowd, and enthusiasm was at its height. On the 6th December 1790, the Assembly wisely saved the country's artistic treasures from the vandalism that threatened to destroy them by creating a Monuments Commission. Depots were hastily organised to keep together the works of art that the revolution was beginning to scatter. In November 1794, the French Museum was opened at the Louvre with 537 paintings and 124 bronzes, before which everyone could place his easel as he liked (462). In 1795 the convent of the Petits-Augustins (today the Ecole des Beaux-Arts) became the Museum of French Monuments, thanks to the energetic architect Lenoir.

463

464

465

Mirabeau (464) died prematurely in April 1791. He had dominated the Assembly and Paris solely by his talent as a speaker. He was in the pay of the court, but no one knew it, and he was given a spectacular funeral. Manon Phlipon (465), the daughter of a craftsman in a Parisian jeweller's, married a scholar, Monsieur Roland, and came to settle in Paris in 1791. Her husband was soon to become Minister of the Interior. Madame Roland, soul of the Girondin party, supported the Revolution and was to be one of its victims.

But the tree of Liberty must still strike

What is all this excitement at Saint-Sulpice (463)? The curé is refusing to support the clergy's Civil Constitution. The Assembly had nationalised ecclesiastical property without provoking much opposition. But it was different when, in July 1790, it voted a new organisation of the Church in France.

Many Parisians stayed indoors except when they had burned down some of the toll offices. On 1st May 1791 the Assembly finally decided to suppress them. At the barrier of the Champs-Elysées (today the Place de l'Etoile) a strange procession pushed its way forward (466). Sheep, cattle and horses, carts of fodder or vegetables, baskets of eggs, all passed freely through. The heavy drinker no longer had to go out to the suburbs to drink untaxed wine: but he had to hurry to lay in stocks, for this new liberty disappeared even faster than the others, and the tolls of Paris still had 150 years of life before them.

466

BARRIERE DES CHAMPS ELISÉES

Premier May donné à la Ville de Paris par L'assemblé Nationale qui suprime tous les Droits d'entrées aux Barrieres

On the night of the 20th June 1791, the Royal Family, with the help of Fersen, a Swedish count who was greatly attached to the Queen, fled eastwards to join Bouillé's loyal troops. In a slow, heavy and far too noticeable coach they lumbered 125 miles. At Varennes the town council stopped the fugitives, and on 25th June they returned, accompanied by a Parisian crowd which was menacingly silent in its disapproval (467).

467

its roots deep within rebel soil.

468

Bailly (468), the Mayor of Paris, was a scientist who was ill-prepared for what was to happen. On 17th July 40,000 Parisians went to the Champ de Mars to demand that the King should be tried, and Bailly had this illegal meeting dispersed with the sword and rifle fire. For this he was never forgiven.

La Fayette (469), with all the prestige of the American War of Independence behind him, chief of the National Guard and undisputed master of Paris, often waited on events instead of directing them. His task was certainly very difficult. He was soon to go into exile, but was to return again.

469

On the 12th July 1791 Voltaire's body was taken to the Panthéon (470). Behind an army of citizens, clubs, toughs from the Halles, and Bastille victors or their widows; behind a model of the citadel, a bust of Rousseau, schoolchildren in classical costume, women dressed as the Muses, a gold coffin containing the great writer's works, and his statue carried by men in long Roman tunics; behind actors in costume, men of letters, magistrates, town councillors, deputies, ministers, ambassadors, and musicians with antique instruments, rolled the triumphal chariot with its wheels of bronze, bearing a coffin of oriental granite. Twelve white horses drew it through scented smoke. An entire cortège surrounded the great man's effigy, laid out and dressed in purple.

470

But Louis XVI refused to create in Paris an army of 20,000 provincial troops. On 20th June the Girondins fomented a riot, and, faced with the rioters (471), the King put on the red bonnet and drank the people's health (472). The northern frontiers were threatened. On 11th July the Assembly declared France in danger. Parisians joined the army; thousands of provincial troops reached Paris (those from Marseilles singing the 'Marseillaise'). On the 28th the Prussian General, Brunswick, threatened to destroy the capital if the King was touched. The King's double game was clear, and this threat infuriated the people. On the night of 9th August, the old electoral sections formed a revolutionary Commune at the Hôtel de Ville. The Tuileries were attacked (473), the Swiss guards massacred.

472

473

On 25th September 1791 the Constituent Assembly broke up, after the King, to the Parisians' joy, had accepted the Constitution. In the Legislative Assembly a group of young deputies, most of them from Bordeaux and called 'Girondins', formed the Left Wing. When they became ministers, they declared war on Austria on 20th April 1792, a decision pregnant with consequences.

152

Man of the hour was the Parisians' favourite orator, Danton (474). A bull had ruined his face when he was a child, so he was anything but handsome. He was crude, amorous, and fond of money – did it come from the King or from England? – and a man who always had his own way. As a Minister, there was little he could do. The revolutionary Commune became a force dominated by Hébert, Tallien, and Robespierre.

474

475

Defences collapsed. Verdun capitulated on 2nd September. Danton asked for a 'national upheaval' to defeat the invader. A horde of cut-throats (150 probably, not more) interpreted that in their own way. For two days and two nights, from the 2nd to the 4th, they plunged the prisons in blood.

476

The Carmelite church was the scene of a massacre. Three prelates and 115 priests were murdered (475). Drunk with blood, the 'Septembrists' attacked the women of the Salpêtrière and the children of Bicêtre (476). There were 1176 murders.

The Assembly justified the massacres after they had taken place. Fabre d'Eglantine, the gentle, corruptible author of the song 'Il pleut bergère', used them as an example to the provinces. The most savage of them all was Marat. When he emerged from the cellar (477) where he had long been hiding, he demanded 'plenty of executions'.

This is the sinister machine (478) that was to accompany the march of the Revolution. On the 21st August 1792 it beheaded the first political prisoner. How many last words,

477

478

LA VERITABLE GUILLOTINE ORDINAERE.
HA LE BON SOUTIEN POUR LA LIBERTÉ !

true or invented, it would soon inspire! Manon Roland: 'Oh liberty, what crimes are committed in thy name!' Edgeworth, Louis XVI's chaplain: 'Son of Saint Louis, arise to Heaven.' A soldier to Bailly: ' You're trembling.' Answer: 'It's the cold, my friend.' Madame Du Barry: 'One minute more, monsieur executioner!' Danton: 'Show my head to the people, it's worth it.' Malesherbes: 'If there was only some reason for all this!'

479   480

481

482   483

In August 1792 the great royal statues were hurled off their pedestals: Louis XIV on horseback (479) in the Place Vendôme, Henri IV on the Pont-Neuf, Louis XIV on foot in the Place des Victoires (480) were removed and sent to the foundry. Napoleon was to replace the latter with a colossal statue by Desaix (481), whose martial nudity (here veiled) was in 1822 replaced by an equestrian statue of Louis XIV.

The invasion was stopped at Valmy in September, and a new Assembly, the Convention, met. The Girondin group – Brissot and Roland, now hostile to Paris: 'This town nourished on blood and lies'– opposed the 'Mountain' composed of Danton, Robespierre, Marat, and the Duc d'Orléans, who had taken the name of Philippe-Egalité. On 13th August, on orders from the Commune, the Royal Family was transferred to the enormous tower (482) of the old Temple, where they followed a strict and gloomy routine; see the guard here pulling out his watch (483) to show that the meal is over.

Blood and wine are the same colour,

The King's fate divided the Convention. The Girondins hoped to spare him, the 'Mountain' to get rid of him. On 11th December the King appeared before the Convention set up as a court. On the 17th January the death-sentence was passed by a majority of five. There was no reprieve; the Duc d'Orléans, Philippe-Egalité, the King's cousin, had voted for his death. On 21st January 1793, in the Place de la Concorde at twenty-four minutes past ten, Louis XVI was guillotined close to the empty pedestal of the statue of Louis XV (484).

486

485

1793 was a terrible year. On 2nd
April, when the defeat and treason of
General Dumouriez was announced,
a Committee of Public Safety was
formed. On 2nd June the Convention
was suddenly invaded by armed
men. Under this threat, and swayed
by Marat, the deputies voted for the
arrest of twenty-nine Girondin deputies suspected of wanting to raise
the provinces against Paris. A macabre but very revealing event took
place at Saint-Denis, renamed Fran-
ciade (485), when on 12th October
the Convention exhumed, not without great difficulty, the royal remains (486). The architect Lenoir
had great trouble in saving a few of
the art treasures which had accumulated since the time of Dagobert.

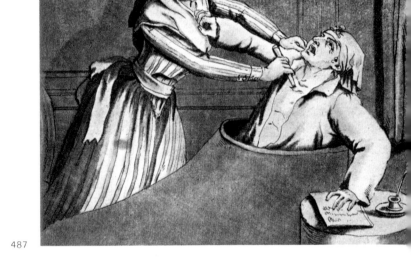

487

but now blood is more intoxicating than any wine.

488

The 'Mountain' controlled the political organisations, but it was the
extremists, led by Hébert, who ruled
the mob, and the mob laid down the
law. On 5th September the Convention was invaded and forced to put
'terror on the agenda'. House-to-
house visits and searches flung
thousands into prison. On 1st January 1794 there were 4,800 imprisoned in Paris, and in the months to
follow, 7,800. Charlotte Corday, a
girl of twenty-five and a passionate
admirer of the Girondins, arrived
from Caen on 13th July 1793 to see
Marat, with the excuse of telling him
about counter-revolutionary activities in Normandy. She murdered
him without witnesses in his boot-
shaped bath (487), and was executed
four days later wearing the red shirt
of the parricide.
The Revolutionary Tribunal condemned the Queen, Marie-Antoinette, to death. On 16th October
the sinister cart took her from the
Conciergerie to the guillotine.
30,000 soldiers kept order (488).

Until November 1793, the rites of the Catholic Church were celebrated without alteration, and, except in the case of obstinate priests who were forced to hide, without hindrance. But the Commune of Paris succeeded in making Archbishop Gobel give up his see. The churches of Paris were turned into temples of Morality, of Concord, of Commerce, of Hymen. The interior and exterior of Notre-Dame were damaged by rioters, and on 10th November the extremists Chaumette and Hébert organised a feast of the Goddess of Reason, whose part was taken by a dancer from the Opéra (489). The Committee of Public Safety,

struggling against starvation, disapproved of the spectacle, which risked arousing new antagonism. With Danton's help, Robespierre sent Hébert and his friends, oddly allied to the shadiest financiers of Paris, to the guillotine on 24th March 1794. Ten days later he sent Danton and Camille Desmoulins as well. On 8th June he entrusted the painter David with the organisation, on the Champ de Mars, of a great celebration to glorify the Supreme Being (491). Robespierre marched alone at the head of his colleagues, crowned with plumes that floated in the wind and looking like the pontiff of the new order.

Paris is a giantess glutted with carnage.

With the help of military experts like Carnot, generals under thirty years of age once more halted the invasion. An astonishing invention linked Paris with the towns at the front. On 15th and 30th August 1793 a machine with moving arms (490), invented by Claude Chappe, transmitted its first despatches by eye: the taking of two strongholds, Le Quesnoy and Condé. In fine weather it took three minutes to link up with Calais in 33 relays, and two minutes to link up with Lille. Saint-Pierre-de-Montmartre, the Château of Ménilmontant and the towers of Saint-Sulpice were the first to transmit telegraphic messages.

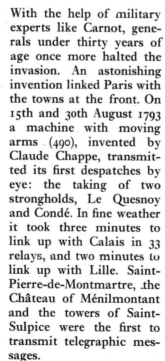

490

491

492

The law of the 21 Prairial (10th June 1794) suppressing all examination and defence in trials opened the Reign of Terror. In the Place du Trône (de la Nation), 1,378 heads fell in six weeks and Robespierre, to rally a majority in the Assembly, attacked the Committee of Public Safety.

On 9 Thermidor (27th July), in a heatwave, Tallien, dagger in hand, supported by Barras and Fouché, led a grandiloquent assault from the rostrum of the Convention against what he called 'the new Cromwell'. Robespierre and Saint-Just were arrested.

Two hours later, at seven in the evening, Robespierre and his friends, freed by Fleuriot, Mayor of Paris, were safe in the Hôtel de Ville. Had Paris really beaten the Assembly again? Hanriot, though, who with his National Guard was the real master of the streets, was dead drunk.

493

Dead drunk with death, she stumbles and falls at the foot of the scaffold.

494

Towards midnight a great storm scattered Parisians. Backed by the Convention and leading several detachments of troops, Barras soon managed to enter the Hôtel de Ville (492). Robespierre (493) had a broken jawbone (was it attempted suicide or a shot from a guard?), his friend Le Bas killed himself, and his other supporters were arrested. On the morning of 28th July the guillotine was moved to the Place de la Révolution (de la Concorde). Robespierre and all his supporters, like so many others, were beheaded (494 & 495).

495

496

Paris is transformed. After the brutal game of death

Stunned by the Parisians' delirious cheers of joy, the conquerors of 9 Thermidor realised that they had ended the Terror and opened a new age. All that had been lost in horror and bloodshed had now to be restored. Madame Tallien, called Our Lady of Thermidor because she had done all she could to soften the rigours of Robespierre's régime and hasten his fall, led the rejoicings. In 640 dance halls the waltz, which had arrived from Germany, was the rage in 1797. The gay world flocked into the Grands Boulevards and in front of the Pavilion of Hanover (496). What a story that place could tell! Since it was built in 1707, every reign and every régime had left its mark on it. The children of Madame de Montespan and Louis XIV had been the first to live there; and the Duc d'Antin built his famous causeway for it. Later the Maréchal Duc de Richelieu built this charming corner drawing-room with the fruits of his looting in Hanover; it had a view across the country as far as the windmills on the hill of Montmartre.

497

This pavilion with its shrubberies was now open to the public, and had become the main meeting-place of the young and wealthy; on 14th July 1798, Madame Tallien and Joséphine Bonaparte, a young general's wife, presided over the celebrations. There were gaming tables; and Velloni sold his delicious ice-creams. This romantic place ended sadly. The Pavilion of Hanover was bought in 1810 by a big firm of goldsmiths and in 1930 was removed to the end of the Parc de Sceaux to make room for the Berlitz Palace, which is only a palace in name.

499

It was Madame Tallien who did most to promote the success of the Parisian fashions of 1798–1800 as the 'Merveilleuse' (497), who wore all sorts of tunics – as Ceres, Galathea, or Omphale – all of them very transparent, and enormous hats. Her escort, the 'Incroyable' (498), had to appear ragged and uncouth. The Parisian working girl (499), who came to market in her simple morning dress, was luckily unaffected by these extravagances.

comes the waltz; after tragedy, the ballet.

498

500

501

The general public then lost interest in politics and applauded the satires that poked fun at those in power. At Nicolet's the actor Corse became a star as Madame Angot, a fishwife of the Halles, who became Queen of Paris (501). The Directors, who were now the first citizens of Paris and of France, lived in the palace of the Luxembourg (502) as the King had previously lived at Versailles.

Among them Barras was most in the public eye and was constantly being importuned for favours; but they had to struggle on two fronts, against the Jacobins led by Babœuf, and against the royalists led by Pichegru. On the night of 4th September 1797, Augereau brought 12,000 men into Paris, and arrested two Directors and all the deputies suspected of opposition.

Paris, goal of the ambitious. They stream up from the provinces

Paris might dance, but hunger and riot were still abroad. Twice, in April and May 1795, the people rose and surged into the Convention. On 5th October the royalists had the right bank in a state of excitement. The young General Bonaparte attacked the rebels and fired at them with cannon on the steps of the Church of Saint-Roch (500). Three weeks later the Convention dissolved, to be succeeded by five directors and a Legislative Council.

160

502

503

The expedition led victoriously into Egypt in May 1798 by the twenty-nine year old Bonaparte diverted public interest in Paris from political set-backs at home. Rameses conquered Paris. Prince Eugène de Beauharnais covered an old hôtel in the Rue de Lille with decorations in the Egyptian style, which have remained splendidly untouched (503). In the Rue de Sèvres, a fountain (504) was decorated with the statue of an Egyptian peasant. A whole new district, with streets bearing Egyptian names, arose round the Place du Caire. Sphinxes, lotuses, and hieroglyphics decorated one of the houses in this exotic area.

as if she were the one prize worth winning.

504

The Directory was powerless and completely lacked support. On 18 Brumaire of the year VIII (9th November 1799), Bonaparte, who was back from Egypt, managed with the help of his troops to get rid of the Legislative Council and took over supreme power. He became First Consul, and, in 1802, Consul for life. Every door was now open to him, including money (the Bank of France was created in 1800), and even the sciences. The Institute, which was founded in 1795, was delighted to welcome this new ruler of the day who, before his success in war and politics, had been an excellent mathematician: here he is seen in the Salle des Cariatides at the Louvre (505).

505

VUE DE L'EXPLOSION DE LA MACHINE INFERNALE, RUE S¹ NICAISE, A PARIS.

506

The first thing needed was to restore Paris to civil, social, and religious peace. Bonaparte re-opened the synagogue, and a great ceremony of atonement took place at Notre-Dame (508). The cathedral had been scheduled for demolition; on 9 Thermidor it had been saved, but it was used as a storehouse for wine. In 1802 it was restored to its religious purpose.

507

But opposition from the Royalists was not over. On 24th December 1800 there was a terrible explosion between the Louvre and the Tuileries (506). The First Consul was unhurt, but 8 people were killed and 28 wounded. Fouché, who had been an extremist in the Convention, was promoted Minister of Police and seized the opportunity to get rid of the Jacobin and monarchist opposition at the same time. In 1804, Cadoudal, a royalist conspirator, was guillotined, and the Duc d'Enghien shot—'Worse than a crime, a blunder', as Talleyrand said.

Conquerors have always known that only one thing brings lasting glory: the adornment of Paris.

The revolutionary period, though it had seen a great many industries started in Paris, had left no monuments apart from the Place de la Concorde (1790), and had done nothing to beautify the city. Bonaparte wanted to make Paris not only 'the most beautiful city there is, and the most beautiful there ever was, but also the most beautiful there ever could be.' Two architects, Percier and Fontaine (507), submitted to him a new town-planning scheme, but much of it remained on paper.

508

The Consul completed the Cour Carrée of the Louvre, which had remained unfinished since Louis XIV's day (509 & 901). The museum of the Louvre soon contained a magnificent collection, thanks to the numerous works of art brought from Italy, such as the Marriage of Cana, the Discobolus, the Apollo Belvedere, the Dying Gladiator and the Venus of the Capitol; but the horses of Saint Mark, removed from Venice, were to take the road back to Italy.

512

509

The Rue de Rivoli was driven along the northern side of the Louvre (511). The demolition of the Grand Châtelet left the entrance to the Pont - au - Change free; a square with a monumental fountain called the Palm Fountain was built there (512). There were many new bridges: the Pont des Arts in 1803, de la Cité in 1804, d'Austerlitz in 1806, and d'Iéna in 1813 – in all fourteen bridges at the heart of Paris in just over a mile. But the Abbey of Sainte-Geneviève, the tower of the Temple, the Abbey of Saint-Victor and the Convent of the Rue Saint-Jacques were all demolished.

511

The Emperor clasps bracelets of bridges round the arms of the Seine.

Usefulness overrode art and grandeur. Frochot, Prefect of the Seine from 1800 to 1812, completely re-organised the municipal services, and improved the sewers, the drains, the water supply, and the victualling of the city. The houses were numbered and a new cemetery, the Père-Lachaise, was begun on the slopes of Belleville. Before the barrier of La Villette a great basin was hollowed out (510), which became the junction between the Ourcq, the Marne, and the Seine, through the Saint-Martin and Saint-Denis canals. Bonaparte also demolished the old buildings and roads separating the Louvre from the Tuileries. In 1808 he built, on the esplanade of the Carrousel, a triumphal arch to commemorate Austerlitz.

510

514

Many provincial towns were linked with Paris only two or three times a week. The diligence, though very much better than the old coaches, was still only a lumbering heavy vehicle that did not do more than

515

four miles an hour on paved roads. It took another forty years for daily runs to be established from Paris to Rouen in ten hours. And the centre of the city was no better provided for. In 1640 a business man had started hiring out cabs at the Hôtel

The name of Paris makes Europe tremble.

516

Saint-Fiacre (515), but since then the number of public vehicles had hardly increased.

Besides, who wanted to go abroad? Paris was bursting with theatres, balls, and restaurants. Fighting might take place at Iéna or at Wagram, but at Frascati's, the Neapolitan ice-cream man's at the corner of the boulevard and the Rue de Richelieu, there was always entertainment to be found. People chatted as they drank refreshments or played furiously at roulette or at craps; in a third hall, there was room for 2,000 dancers (516).

Since the Middle Ages nothing had replaced the public baths. People had baths at home; but the Seine was always available. What a fine grenadier this swimmer would make (513)! War, for the time being, was not too demanding. In 1806, the year of Iéna, only 14,300 Parisians served with the colours, though the capital numbered 547,000. The Parisian of the First Empire might like sport but he cared little for travelling. He could see Europe in Napoleon's army, but as a civilian he travelled very little. A few dozen travellers and two or three carriages filled the yard of the national stage-coach office (514).

513

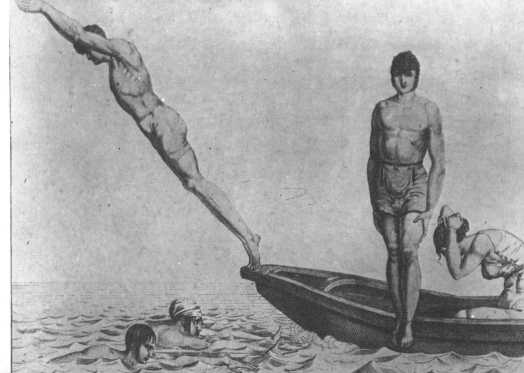

519

In a famous picture, the painter David immortalised the moment at which Napoleon crowned Josephine (517). Here is the Emperor in his great cloak of purple velvet that partly hides a long white satin robe in the antique style embroidered with gold. Marshals Murat, Sérurier, and Moncey are in attendance (518). Josephine, in her dress of silver brocade, kneels at his feet. David put Madame Mère, Napoleon's mother (who was in fact not present at the ceremony), in the place of honour. 'That's right, David, you've made me a French knight,' Napoleon was to say. In the Place de la Concorde, where four ballrooms had been built, people danced as long as they had breath

For Paris the names of Europe are as familiar as those of her own suburbs.

518

517

But the greatest entertainment of all was given by Bonaparte when he decided to have himself anointed Emperor under the name of Napoleon I. On the cold morning of 2nd December 1804, when France had been at war with England for more than fifteen months, the great occasion was announced by cannon and bells. A procession of 8,000 riders accompanied their Imperial Majesties from the Tuileries to Notre-Dame. Pope Pius VII, brought willy-nilly from Rome, enthroned the Emperor.

520

Far from Paris Napoleon's glory marched on, and the capital raised a monument to him made of the bronze of two hundred and fifty cannon taken from the Russians and the Austrians. Round a stone centre, a column a hundred and forty three feet high arose (521), in imitation of Trajan's column in Rome. In spite of the Emperor's wishes, a statue of himself as Caesar was placed on the top. The sixty bas-reliefs encircling the column glorify the soldiers of Austerlitz and give 'a historic record of the campaign of 1805', a record made by forty artists and weighing nearly 250 tons.

But there was a heavy price to pay for all this glory. The Emperor's 17 levies sent 1,660,000 men into the army, and Paris had had its fair share of casualties. Parisians did not always care for the brawls of the Hussars or riflemen who behaved like conquerors in the streets; yet there were Parisians, particularly those of the faubourgs, living comfortably under police protection, who never ceased to show boundless devotion to the Emperor.

Very much later, and under another political régime, the people of Paris were to make the Hôtel des Invalides (522) a temple to the glory of Napoleon. The Emperor was right when he said: 'The dying soldier has never cursed me (523); no man was ever more loyally served by his troops. As the last drop of blood leaves their veins they cry, "Long Live the Emperor!"'

Paris of the Grande Armée.

Capital of conquests and trophies.

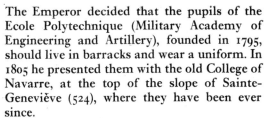

524

The Emperor decided that the pupils of the Ecole Polytechnique (Military Academy of Engineering and Artillery), founded in 1795, should live in barracks and wear a uniform. In 1805 he presented them with the old College of Navarre, at the top of the slope of Sainte-Geneviève (524), where they have been ever since.

As he suspected their political views, Monge said to him: 'Your Majesty should remember how hard we worked to make republicans out of them; and then, quite suddenly, there's an Emperor!'

Since 14th May 1802 the Cross of the Legion of Honour (525) has been awarded without distinction of rank or position to the best soldiers and the most deserving civilians. Many of the Empire's 48,000 crosses, of which 1,200 were given to civilians, were distributed by the Emperor in Paris at spectacular ceremonies. The first and the most formal of these took place on 14th July 1804, during a mass at the Invalides.

525

Victorious Paris. Her Caesar has overrun the world.

526

In order to complete the Rue Royale attractively, the Madeleine, the first stone of which was laid in 1764, did not face east as churches traditionally do. Under the new régime anything could have been housed there. In fact, it became the temple of the Grande Armée (526), and was to be as beautiful as Notre-Dame or Saint Peter's at Rome. Vigneau won the job out of a hundred and fifty competitors, and built a Greek temple in which the Emperor lost interest. After almost becoming the home of the Legislative Council, and later Paris's first railway station, the Madeleine was consecrated in 1842.

527

528

Every window between the Porte Maillot and the Place de la Concorde had been hired out to people who wanted to see the procession pass. Provincials and foreigners flocked into the capital. The Champs-Elysées, the new district of the Emperor, was at last accepted, and the aristocratic houses of the Faubourg Saint-Germain no longer sneered, since the head of the House of Hapsburg had set an example of friendship with the Emperor.

After his return from Austerlitz, in 1806, Napoleon had decided to build a colossal triumphal arch at the Neuilly toll-gate (today the Place de l'Etoile). In 1810, it had progressed no further than the foundations. But a full-scale replica of the arch, made of painted paper on a wooden framework (528), was built for the Emperor's entry into the city, celebrated with a great firework display in the streets of Paris, which were all decorated and lit up. All that year Paris danced. The Emperor and the Council grudged nothing for its entertainment. All the building in progress kept everyone busy.

The war in Spain was going badly, but on 20th March 1811 a hundred guns announced the birth of the King of Rome, the Imperial heir. Here we see him in his nurse's arms (529). The Municipal Council had a cradle, designed by Prud'hon, made for him in silver gilt, and today it forms part of the Imperial treasure of Vienna.

And Paris has become one long road leading up to the Arc de Triomphe.

When Napoleon's marriage to Josephine was annulled because she gave him no heir, he accepted Metternich's proposal that he should marry an Austrian princess, Marie-Louise, daughter of the Emperor Francis II and niece of Marie-Antoinette. The Imperial couple (he was forty and she eighteen) made their solemn entry on 2nd April 1810 (527). Napoleon was ceremoniously offered the keys of the city.

529

530

In the Salon of 1810, when the French Empire was at its height, the most successful picture was David's 'The Distribution of the Eagles' (530), from which he had just painted out the figure of Josephine. It depicts the great ceremony that took place on 5th December 1804 on the Champ de Mars, after Napoleon was anointed Emperor. In the presence of all the notabilities of the régime, civilian or military, he presented their colours to the colonels of his regiments and to the presidents of the electoral colleges.

The popular prints were no less enthusiastic than officially subsidised painting. Jean-Charles Pellerin at Epinal, and many others, made colour prints (531) that were sold by hawkers in the streets of Paris, and were to sell even faster after the downfall of their idol. Here we see Napoleon crossing the bridge at Arcole, the campaign in Egypt, Austerlitz, the Napoleonic code, his respect for the enemy's wounded, and his last farewells to his country; nothing is missing, and in effusions of this kind the people of Paris were applauding their own power and splendour.

169

Evil days were on Paris, though, and the first defeats. In spite of economic stagnation, the city provided Napoleon's army with the young recruits named after Marie-Louise, who, in the fierce battles of the first months of 1814, were to paralyse the invader. But from February onwards the remnants of the decimated regiments and their wounded filed through the streets of the capital (532). On 24th March the coalition armies (170,000 Austrians, Russians and Prussians) began the march on Paris, and on the 29th encircled it from Vincennes to Saint-Denis.

A Council of Regency decided that Marie-Louise and her son should leave. Baggage, private papers, personal treasure amounting to 18 million francs, and the Crown diamonds, all took the road to Blois, without ostentation.

A harsh awakening in the cold dawn.

The bugles no longer sound the charge.

The drums are muffled.

There had been no preparations to protect the city. 25,000 men defended it, though, on the morning of 30th March. Among peasants and refugees from the suburbs, General Moncey scored a success at the toll-gate of Clichy (533) that became legendary. With the Poles of the Vistula legions, he earned the respect of the Russians, commanded by an emigrant Frenchman. His headquarters were the well-known tavern called 'Père Lathuile' (today the Place Clichy). At the Trône toll-gate, students of the Polytechnique fired the cannon. On the night of the 30th, Marmont signed the capitulation, but Daumesnil, 'General Wooden Leg', dug himself in at the fortress of Vincennes. 'I'll yield my position when you give back my leg,' he told the representatives of the enemy. It took the Emperor's abdication to make him surrender.

On 31st March 1814, the soldiers of three nations entered the great avenues of Paris in ceremonial dress (534); the Tsar Alexander rode beside the King of Prussia and the Austrian Prince Schwarzenberg. Most of the Russian officers (educated by French tutors, whose language they spoke extremely well), admired Paris enormously. Parisians liked them too, especially the aristocracy, who saw in them the return of the monarchy. Along the faubourgs, 'among the ordinary people, there was an unspoken feeling of passive but gloomy consternation.' But in more fashionable districts, everyone celebrated whole-heartedly. In the Champs-Elysées, the beautiful Comtesse E. de Périgord, later the Duchesse de Duino, mounted behind a Cossack to get a better view of the parade.

Napoleon, abandoned by his marshals, abdicated at Fontainebleau on 11th April. On 4th May Louis XVIII entered Paris in an open carriage drawn by eight white horses. After the Te Deum at Notre-Dame, Henri IV's statue, hastily put up in plaster on the Pont Neuf, was solemnly saluted by choirs, a concert, and the release of a balloon decorated with white flags, the colours of the old monarchy (535).

537

The occupation went well. Chabrol, Napoleon's prefect since 1812, remained in office. The English (536) were not averse to the charms of the French capital.

In a few weeks slides on sledges called 'Russian Mountains' were having a lively success. Louis XVIII himself went to visit them in the park of the Folie-Beaujon where

they were erected (537). Doctors recommended them as healthy, and they continued to be found in parks until they were forbidden because of accidents on them.

Inconstant glory! The city hopes in vain. Glory has deserted it.

The occupation troops soon met the cocoa-sellers (538). A harmless infusion of liquorice in the cocoa hurt no one, and more than a century later, this great round leather barrel was still to be seen everywhere in the streets.

David now devoted himself to painting Leonidas and Thermopylæ, and the Rue Napoléon became the Rue de la Paix; but the Emperor was still everywhere. The reformed Paris National Guard hastened to adopt the Imperial uniforms (539) which had become legendary.

Napoleon was on the island of Elba, but Paris was filled with demobilised soldiers to whom peace had brought idleness and poverty. This Hussar (540), recognisable from the knot of hair which he wears defiantly, has to be content with hot sausages for a meal.

541

The Champs-Elysées and the Bois de Boulogne were a vast encampment, which the curious visited as if it were a theatre. Here we see a child making friends with a Cossack (541). 'It's so like a party that it's a pity it's a conquest,' said Madame de Coigny. The officers of the occupation had eyes for nothing but the galleries of the Palais-Royal. There at No. 113, the greatest gaming house in Paris, Blücher lost a fortune of 1,500,000 gold francs in a single evening. The occupation troops seemed to be leaving behind more than the French were paying them. At the exit, in the gallery, there were temptations of another kind. (542).

Paris accepts with a shrug. If she cannot live well, she must at least live.

543

A treaty was signed on 30th May 1814, and the coalition armies left the capital. But in March 1815 Napoleon suddenly crossed the distance separating Elba from Paris (543). On the 20th he slept at the Tuileries, hastily abandoned by Louis XVIII.

But during the Hundred Days that were to prove so tragic for the Empire Napoleon had to fight far from Paris. On 6th July the coalition troops made a victorious entry again; on the 8th the King returned. The Emperor's arrival had been wildly cheered, Louis XVIII's no less so; and Wellington, the victor of Waterloo, was cheered just as loudly. Could it be the same Parisians cheering each time?

General Labédoyère, aged 29, and Marshal Ney were executed for having gone over to Napoleon. Paris paid ten million francs in reparations, and the second phase of the occupation was less agreeable than the first. At the end of November 1818, a new Treaty of Paris was signed. The coalition armies withdrew (544). Though no one was sorry to see the last of the Prussians (they had wanted to blow up the Pont d'Iéna), the Russians were rather regretted.

544

Bon voyage, M. M. les Prussiens, n'y revenez plus au même prix.

545

Here a young Russian in civilian clothes and a beautiful Parisian girl are saying a touching goodbye (545).

Now that the epic is over, Paris consoles herself with games, plays, parties and politics.

546

Free once more, Paris learned to live again. At the Comédie-Française, Mademoiselle Mars (546) carried on the tradition of the great Parisian actresses who shone in society, as well as across the footlights. She had begun very successfully under the Revolution, and her fame continued until 1841. For those who preferred romantic music, there was comic opera, which since 1781 had been put on at the theatre of the Italian singers and actors. Boieldieu had great success there in 1825 with 'La Dame Blanche'. This theatre (547) gave its name to the Boulevard des Italiens that ran alongside it, but, so as to be distinguished from the little halls that abounded there, it whimsically turned its back on the street.

547

Another novelty, this time political, was the constitutional charter granted by the King in 1814 and renewed in 1815, which provided for two Houses, of which only the Chamber of Deputies was elected – by the richest. Its sessions were held in the Palais Bourbon, let to it by the Prince de Condé (549). Splendid oratorical battles took place there between the extreme royalists and the liberals.

Honi soit qui mal y pense: from the Palais Bourbon it is only a step to the glittering carnival, where the masks are even more numerous and the battles fiercer. Punch, Pierrot and Harlequin led a rout whose success grew yearly greater (550).

COURSE DES VÉLOCIPÈDES DANS LE JARDIN DU LUXEMBOURG.

548

Those who loved novelty probably preferred the curious races in the gardens of the Luxembourg and the Tivoli. As early as 1790 eccentrics had been seen at the Palais-Royal or the Pavilion of Hanover astride a two-wheeled stick. But in 1818 a German baron, Drais de Sauerbron, showed Parisians that the articulation of the front wheel gave the machine free movement. The draisienne or velocipede, which was still pushed forward by the feet, delighted the adventurous (548). Another thirty years were still needed to improve it.

549

Paris is still a child easily amused with a rattle.

550

Look at this handbill (551) of the spring of 1816. Mademoiselle Elisa Garnerin was jumping by parachute on to the Champ de Mars. What a family! Jacques Garnerin made his first parachute jump in 1797. His wife jumped too, from nearly 3,000 feet; then their adopted daughter, and their niece Elisa.

On 17th June 1816 there was great rejoicing: the Duc de Berry, second son of the Comte d'Artois, brother of the King, married the kind and lively Marie-Caroline de Bourbon, the seventeen-year-old daughter of the King of Naples. The Duke, though not very serious-minded, was deeply in love with his wife, and the young couple's unaffectedness delighted everyone. But misfortune came soon: on 13th February 1820, during the carnival, the Duke and Duchess left the Opéra at about eleven. At the theatre door a man leaped out and stabbed the Duke violently in the chest (552); he died at dawn. The murderer, one Louvel, had acted only through 'hatred of the Bourbons'. But seven months later, on 29th September 1820, the Duchess gave birth to the Duc de Bordeaux (the future Comte de Chambord). He was baptised with water from the Jordan, brought from Palestine by Chateaubriand.

552

What does she most enjoy?
Like a great baby,
she watches the passing show,
her nose
pressed to the window pane.

Lamartine and Hugo, like the advertisements for lotions and liqueurs (553), sang the praises of the Bourbon heir. It was a touching spectacle when he reviewed the troops at Bagatelle (554).

554

PETIT LAIT DU DUC DE BORDEAUX.

553

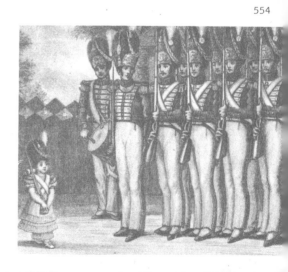

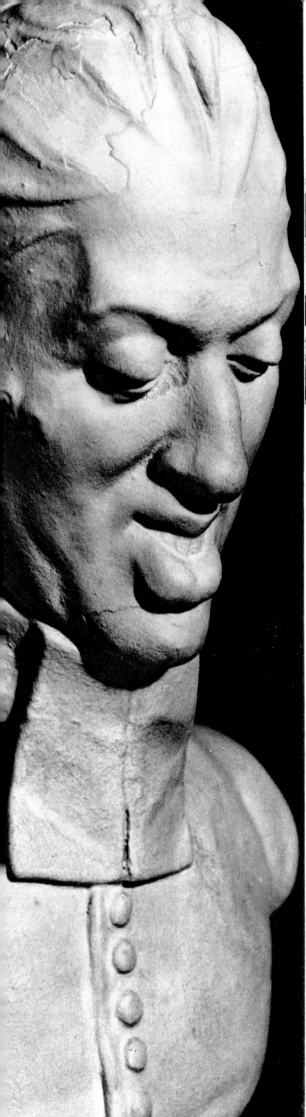

The caricaturist Dantan made a rather unflattering bust of Charles X (555), who entered the capital on 27th September 1824. Yet compared with the enormous, gouty Louis XVIII, the new King seemed delightful. But for how long? People adored novelty. A gasometer sprang up in the district of Poissonnière, and the painter Daguerre attracted crowds with his pivoted diorama. Romanticism soared.

556

Among all the discoveries of the time, that of the human body was progressing fastest. The King admired the first successful operation for cataract (556), performed by Dupuytren, chief surgeon to the Hôtel-Dieu. Other great doctors were Laënnec and Orfila.

Everyone found politics exciting too. The funeral of one of the leaders of the liberal opposition, General Foy (557), was an excuse for a striking demonstration, in which 50,000 Parisians took part on 30th November 1825, in the rain.

557

Paris buys her toys in the bazaar of the Present.

561

of taking India from the British, had wanted to put up as a fountain in the Place de la Bastille. Since 1810 a plaster model had stood on the banks of the Saint-Martin canal. A shed had been built round it and thousands of curious people visited it (561); it was not demolished until 1839. In 'Les Misérables' Hugo made it Gavroche's home.

558

In 1827 Cuvier, Geoffroy Saint-Hilaire and the whole Museum of Natural History were in a ferment. Mohamed Ali, Viceroy of Egypt, had offered Charles X a giraffe (558), and nothing like it had been seen in Paris before. It arrived on 30th June at the Jardin des Plantes, and the curious flocked to see it (559). In the theatre, in songs, in caricatures, even in hair styles, everything was 'à la girafe'. In spite of political unrest the government contributed to public entertainment by increasing the number of public holidays and authorising the travelling shows from the faubourgs. At the Champs-Elysées and the Trône toll-gate, crowds jostled to see greasy poles, tight-rope walkers, one-man bands, booths and shops going full blast. On the feast of Saint Louis, a national holiday, everyone who could fight for it had his share of sausage, bread and wine (560).

She knows there is always a circus in the street.
All she has to do is open her eyes –
and the procession marches past.

560

562

Built between 1822 and 1828, the galleries and covered passages of Colbert, Vivienne (564), Choiseul and Vero-Dodat were a great success. One of the new fashionable attractions was the iron Pont des Arts, which had a toll of one sou and a blind musician (565). The theatres in the Boulevard du Temple attracted crowds – especially the Funambules, which had been open since 1816, and where Debureau soon became famous as Pierrot; the Ambigu and Franconi's Olympic circus were also popular. Bobêche and Galimafré, two noisy and vulgar clowns, had been successful since 1814 and are seen here doing a turn on the balcony (566).

563

The columns of the Madeleine, at the corner of the boulevard, had been given some rather ugly straw hats (562), and the work got no further. The King, though, was providing very obvious protection for the Catholic Church. To the ambitious, success often came through the Church, and liberal and middle-class opposition, which had found nothing to oppose on a political level, undertook a campaign against clericalism. Following a rowdy parade on 29th April 1827, the National Guard was dismissed. But in 1828 Villèle, the minister, handed over to Martignac, who was more liberal. Béranger, an irreligious Bonapartist who had written songs against the régime, was condemned to nine months imprisonment; and his popularity grew.

564

Steam-boats started to furrow the Seine. The population of Paris reached 785,000; but there was no change in the roads. 17,000 vehicles and 340,000 horses used them every day. Though pavements were increasing, they were still muddy, and the water carriers still dragged their casks about and filled them at the few inefficient pipes (563).

565

566

The Restoration government, though not very liberal, opened up an era of freedom, at least of speech. Politics and literature were discussed in the aristocratic salons of the Faubourg Saint-Germain and in the rival district of the Chaussée d'Antin. Here is a woman who enlivened Parisian life, and who was famous without notoriety: the charming Madame de Récamier (567).

567

569

In her salon and library at the Abbaye au Bois in the Rue de Sèvres, Madame de Récamier devotedly followed the career of her 'great man', Chateaubriand (568), who had quickly become famous with a 'little American tale', 'Atala', and with 'René'; his 'Genius of Christianity' delighted even the irreligious in Paris. But Alphonse de Lamartine overshadowed him as he aged, and became the leader of the new romantics; while a newcomer, Prosper Mérimée, who soon became one of the personalities of Paris, made Spain the fashion.

The other Paris, adult Paris,

In 1829 Balzac decided to conquer the salons and the newspapers of Paris with a novel about Brittany, 'Les Chouans'. He soon became a notable figure whose famous cane with its gold knob set with turquoises (569), and whose coffee pot, debts and luxurious living were to become as famous as his works. Nobody painted provincial life as well as he did, and he was also quite unrivalled as a painter of the Paris of his day, for he kept his naïve faith in the city's supremacy. 'Every man of talent, every artist, every man worthy of the name, every cock with brilliant plumage, spreads his wings and flies to Paris,' he said. But Stendhal wrote: 'Everyone with any energy in Paris arrives there from the provinces at seventeen.' These two sayings, far from being contradictory, complement each other excellently.

568

570

goes to the theatre of Ideas.

Dona Sol (570) died on the stage and shouts filled the theatre. Nerval, Théophile Gautier, intellectuals and art students attacked the 'academic and classical'. Victor Hugo's new play 'Hernani' was famous even before the evening of 25th February 1830. Its author had deserted the royalist party for the liberal opposition, and in 1827 his preface to 'Cromwell' had begun the fight against official literature. In the preface to 'Hernani' Hugo wrote: 'Romanticism is nothing but liberalism in literature. And literary liberalism will be no less popular than political liberalism'.

LE PEUPLE RESTAURATEUR.

571

Paris knows what words can do –
and how they can turn into deeds once they are
in the streets.

It was a short step from fighting in the Comédie - Française to fighting
in the streets. On 28th July 1830 the paving-stones flew at the Porte
Saint-Denis (571). Barrels and carts were piled up at all the exits to
the city and the finest trees were chopped down to impede the movement of horses and artillery. What had happened to bring this about?
In August 1829 Charles X had dismissed the Martignac ministry,
which had liberal tendencies, and replaced it with one led by Polignac,
who favoured a monarchical interpretation of the constitutional charter but failed to get a majority in the Chamber of Deputies in March
1830. The Chamber was dissolved, but the opposition came out of the
elections strengthened. On 25th July Charles X made a real coup d'état.
He signed four orders, suppressing the freedom of the press, dissolving
the Chamber again, modifying the electoral law, and putting off new
elections. When they heard this, shopkeepers and manufacturers
decided to shut their shops and factories on the 27th. Marmont, who
was accused of betraying Napoleon in 1814 and offering the capitulation of Paris, commanded the garrison, which was thought to have
94,000 men.

Carte du jour.

572

573

In the afternoon of 27th July 1830, a few barricades arose and the guard-room at the Stock Exchange was set on fire. The troops killed several rioters, but in the evening were sent back to barracks. The disturbance seemed to have died down. All the same, in the Rue Saint-Honoré, a woman of thirty-five was killed by a bullet in the forehead. A butcher's boy carried the corpse into the Place des Victoires (573), harangued the crowd, and called for vengeance. The same thing was to happen one evening in 1848 (607).

574

575

On the 28th rioting broke out in the working-class districts, and traders quickly shut their shops (574). Barricades were raised with cries of: 'Down with the Bourbons! Long live the Republic! Long live the Emperor!' The Arsenal, the powder depot at the Salpêtrière, fell into the insurgents' hands. The Opposition deputies still hesitated to do anything illegal. At three o'clock Casimir Périer, Laffitte the banker, Mauguin, and Generals Gérard and Mouton went to demand the ministers' resignation and the withdrawal of the ordinances (575). Marmont dismissed them and flung four columns of troops against the rebel districts. They moved slowly ahead through rising excitement, and easily dismantled the barricades. But in the narrow streets the troops were powerless: people threw their furniture on their heads.

A thousand arms are raised in a single movement.

576

In the morning the Hôtel de Ville had been occupied by royalist troops. Entrenched on the opposite bank of the Seine, the insurgents fired on them all day. Here a young Parisian plants a red, white and blue flag, the revolutionary colours, in the middle of the bridge (576). Without cartridges the royalists had to retreat. Several detachments joined the insurgents. Marmont decided to place his troops round the Louvre and the Tuileries and to wait there for reinforcements.

182

577

Six thousand barricades transformed the districts of the centre and the east into an entrenched camp. After their triumph on the morning of 29th July at the Hôtel de Ville, the insurgents, led by a student of the Polytechnique, attacked the Tuileries and the Louvre. They pillaged the Museum of Artillery and, according to Louis Blanc, 'among them gleamed the helmet of Godefroy de Bouillon, Charles IX's flintlock, François I's lance'... side by side with top hats and caps (577).

The revolutionary flag of Paris is unfurled,

579

578

Children joined in the firing (578). The Louvre and the Tuileries were quickly taken. Marmont withdrew to the top of the Champs-Elysées. The King, who till then had not moved from Saint-Cloud, agreed to revoke his ordinances. But it was too late. On the 30th, Laffitte, Thiers and La Fayette, who by then was 74 and had again become commander of the National Guard after more than 35 years in retirement, hastened to hand over power to the Duc d'Orléans, Louis-Philippe. La Fayette appeared with him on the balcony of the Hôtel de Ville, and embraced him in the folds of a tricolour flag (579). This time there was to be no Republic.

the old flag whose silk is always new.

580

The 'Three Glorious Days' of July 1830 had cost the Royalist troops about 200 dead and 800 wounded, and the insurgents 1,800 dead and 4,500 wounded. To these defenders of freedom, the new government erected a commemorative column in the Place de la Bastille, instead of the elephant Napoleon had dreamt of (561). On 29th April 1840, with a broken chain in one hand, a torch in the other, and a star on his forehead, the spirit of liberty was hauled to the top (580). On the following 29th July a funerary temple was built before the entrance to the caves hollowed out under the column (581). The tenth anniversary of the July Revolution, the inauguration of the column, and the removal of the bodies of the victims of the 'Three Glorious Days' all took place at once.

581

582

James de Rothschild (582) had come to Paris in 1810 and, thanks to his international operations, became the capital's most important financier. Since 1811 he had been Austrian Consul-General, but was soon to be naturalised. He was financial adviser to Charles X, who failed to take his advice; he then put his bank at the disposal of Louis-Philippe and became his political collaborator, a hidden Minister of Finance.

584

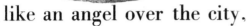

like an angel over the city,

583

After moving from place to place, the Bourse, or Stock Exchange, had a house of its own built between 1808 and 1826 to the plans of Brongniart (583). 'Get rich,' said Guizot. Sugar refineries, thread factories, and Mr MacAdam's bitumen all attracted capital.

Louis-Philippe, King of the French (584), was called the Grocer King and the Bricklayer King as well. He had eight children, carried an umbrella, and carved at table himself. Yet never had a king seen Paris more roused, more excited, more in a state of flux.

but in the wake of Revolution comes the tradesman…

The National Guard, before 1830 the instrument of opposition, now became the régime's best tool. Every citizen between the ages of twenty and sixty who was a tax-payer or a tax-payer's son was compulsorily enrolled. People mocked at it, caricatured it (585), but were proud of its fur busby and white trousers.

The real king of the day was the grocer (585b). He stood for the average Parisian who read Voltaire and Rousseau, admired the Legion of Honour, wept at melodrama, had fired in 1830, applauded the success of Béranger, elected opposition deputies, and blamed those who disturbed the peace.

585b

585

Paris has a new game: the railway, with its little trains

What was transport like in 1835? The mail-coach, carrying only four travellers, was expensive but fast and reached Bordeaux in 45 hours, Brest in 62, Lyons in 47, Toulouse in 72. The diligence, which was less expensive, took two days to Lille, three to Lyons, Rennes or Nantes, five to Bordeaux and eight to Toulouse. It took from sixteen to twenty passengers and on the way offered all the agreeable or annoying adventures you could possibly imagine. Following its success in the provinces, the railway from Paris to Saint-Germain was opened, but only got half way. On 26th August 1837 Queen Amélie, and the Dukes of

Aumale and Montpensier, took the first train in Paris. The ministers had warned the King not to undertake anything so absurd. How narrow the platform was in the Rue de Londres where the engine drove in (586) under the Place de l'Europe! But working girls could go and dance in the forest of Loges, which Diane de Poitiers had loved, for only 75 centimes. Rothschild backed this enterprise, so his rival Fould, who was piqued, built a line from Paris to Versailles along the left bank. And if you were to believe the great politicians of the day, Thiers and Arago, that was just about as far as railways would ever get.

dotting the surrounding countryside.

Quelques types des Spéculateurs des Chemins de fer.

(DESSINÉS D'APRÈS NATURE A LA BOURSE DE PARIS, PAR M. EUSTACHE LORSAY.)

587

In 1837, the government decided to link Paris by rail with all the frontiers so that it would thus become the centre of a great spider's web. This plan, unique of its kind in Europe, was to contribute enormously to the growth of the population of the city (786,000 inhabitants in 1831, 1,053,000 in 1851), and to the growth of the Parisian working class (587). The Stock Exchange was enthusiastic about this new means of transport, but a terrible accident seemed to confirm the forebodings of its critics. On 8th May 1842 the fifteen carriages of the fast train to Paris crashed, with 768 Parisians who had been to see the fountains at Versailles aboard. Running down from Bellevue, the axle of one of the two engines broke, and the next one, with four coaches, went right over it (588). Burning coals were flung about, the doors were locked, and the coaches blazed; there were 48 dead and 110 injured. The great explorer Dumont d'Urville, who had commanded two dangerous expeditions round the world and had faced the storms of the Antarctic, was among the victims. But this could not stop the advance of the railways. On 2nd and 3rd May 1843 the lines from Paris to Orléans (589) and from Paris to Rouen were opened. In 1846 the line from Paris to Creil was made practicable by the construction of a platform in the north of the city. Soon it was to take only nine hours to reach Calais. In 1849 Paris to Tonnerre was opened, a small beginning to the Paris-Nice line. In 1850 the Strasbourg platform was opened (Gare de l'Est), and in 1852 the Gare de Lyon (rebuilt in 1900).

588

589

'AUGURATION DU CHEMIN DE FER DE PARIS A ORLEAN

s exacts sur tout ce qui s'est passé sur la route et à l'arrivée du Convoi à Orléans, composé de 1500 personnes. — Brillante réception faite à S. A. R. le duc de Nemours ainsi qu'à monse
uc de Montpensier. — Rapidité avec laquelle le parcours de 30 lieues a été fait. — Discours du Maire d'Orléans. — Revue passée par le Prince. — Banquet offert à LL. AA. RR., où pl
ts furent portés à la gloire de la France. — Discours du duc de Nemours, et toast à la prospérité du chemin d'Orléans, à l'avenir des Chemins de Fer en France. — Retour du Convoi à Pa
o m. du soir, étant éclairé par les flambeaux des cantonniers. — Les Heures de Départs. - Les Prix des Places, et les Destinations. — Autres Détails sur le Chemin de Fer de Paris à Rouen

On 14th February 1831 the mob invaded the church of Saint-Germain-l'Auxerrois where a funeral service was being held in memory of the Duc de Berry. The crowd sacked the church and dressed up in the priests' vestments (590). Casimir Périer, an energetic left-wing banker, replaced the feeble Laffitte.

Liberty still has its champions, one being Daumier, who haunts its back streets.

What gloomy scene is this, stinking of camphor and chloride (591)? A terrible epidemic of cholera, that took people back to the Middle Ages, had begun in the delta of the Ganges in 1817 and now devastated Paris. The first victim succumbed on 19th February 1832. On 5th April there were 503 cases; on the 8th 707; on the 12th 1,020. Everyone went in fear of his life; social life was disrupted; the Opéra-Comique was turned into a hospital. Casimir Périer visited the cholera patients at the Hôtel-Dieu and died of it. Lamarque, the Deputy-General, died too.

591

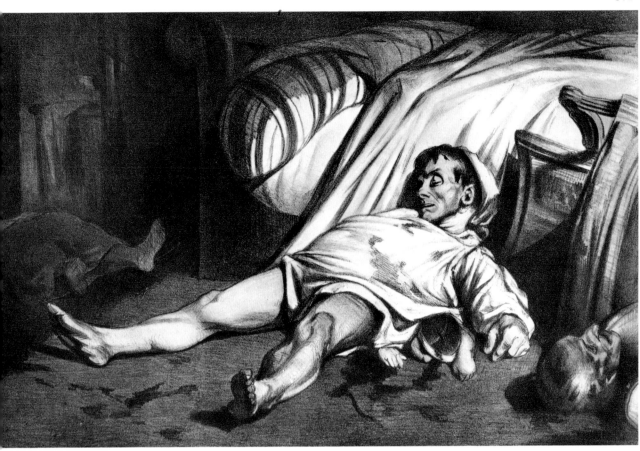

So much bitterness, so many newspaper campaigns against the king, had their effect. There were seven attempts at violence in 1834 and 1835. On 28th July, when the King was watching a parade to commemorate the Three Glorious Days from a window in the Boulevard du Temple, a device composed of several gun barrels loaded with grapeshot exploded (593). Mortier, who had previously blown up the Kremlin, fell down dead, and thirteen others were killed in the crowd and in the royal circle. The man responsible, an Italian called Fieschi, was arrested with two of his accomplices, members of the Society of the Rights of Man, who had acted without orders from the Republican Party. They were executed. Every press attack on the King was in future punished. Censorship of caricatures and plays was re-established.

On 5th June 1831 the funeral of General Lamarque, who was considered both a liberal and a Bonapartist, provoked more revolutionary scenes. 2–3,000 insurgents, many of them young people, took over half Paris. Cannon were turned on them. Some 200–300 were killed: no one will ever know exactly how many.

On 13th and 14th April 1834 there were further riots, more serious this time, because they were planned and co-ordinated with Lyons by the Republican societies that were beginning to spring up. The ringleaders were quickly arrested. Only the centre of Paris resisted, and in a house in the Rue Transnonain, the troops mercilessly butchered innocent people. Altogether there were 25 victims, which was far fewer than in 1831. The Republican party was flung into confusion, but a drawing of Daumier's immortalised the massacre of the Rue Transnonain (592).

Is it caricature? No, said Baudelaire.

'It is history, the trivial and terrible reality.'

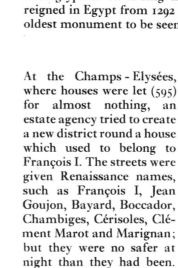

Since 1795 people had worked out, on paper, various ways of replacing the statues of Louis XV and of Liberty in the great Place de la Concorde. At first, in 1800, a national column was envisaged; then, according to the régime of the day, statues of Charlemagne, of Louis XV and of Louis XVI. Louis-Philippe decided to make this monument entirely non-political, and Hittorf, the architect, redesigned it, with an obelisk brought from Egypt at the centre between two great fountains, and statues representing the main towns of France on the eight small pavilions at the corners. At the instigation of the Egyptologist Champollion, Louis XVIII had already agreed on the transfer of the obelisk to Paris. Like Cleopatra's Needle in London, it was a gift from the Viceroy of Egypt, Mohamed Ali.

On 25th October 1836 the royal family and more than 200,000 spectators attended the erection of the colossal needle (594). Apollinaire Lebas, a marine engineer, directed operations. It took three hours to raise the enormous mass, which weighed 230 tons and was over 75 feet high. Hieroglyphics on it sing the glory of Rameses II, who reigned in Egypt from 1292 to 1225 B.C. Clearly this is the oldest monument to be seen in Paris.

595

At the Champs-Elysées, where houses were let (595) for almost nothing, an estate agency tried to create a new district round a house which used to belong to François I. The streets were given Renaissance names, such as François I, Jean Goujon, Bayard, Boccador, Chambiges, Cérisoles, Clément Marot and Marignan; but they were no safer at night than they had been.

Do not be taken in by the easy-

596

The year of 1836 was certainly eventful. On 9th January Lacenaire, a cynical murderer whose exploits had for a long time been discussed in the Parisian newspapers, was executed. The Arc de Triomphe de l'Etoile (596), unfinished for twenty years, was finally opened. It was a memorial to the wars of the Revolution and above all to those of the Empire. The great frieze round it showed a procession of conquerors over six feet high bringing home the spoils of the conquered nations.

The whole of the Grande Armée, dressed in their glorious old uniforms, came out in the cold on 5th December 1840 to accompany the mortal remains of the Emperor, which had come from Saint Helena on the frigate Belle-Poule, escorted by 500 sailors. Victor Hugo wrote: 'From a distance, through the mist and the sunshine, against the grey and russet background of the trees in the Champs-Elysées, among the great white ghost-like statues, a kind of golden mountain was moving slowly (597) . . . wrapped, as it were, in sound; a coffin that brought with it the acclamations of the city, as a torch brings with it its smoke.' Sixteen horses drew the enormous chariot to the Invalides, where under six successive coffins Napoleon would later rest in the crypt specially arranged in 1861. The Prince de Joinville thought that the authorities had not done enough for the occasion. 'Everything the public did was splendid; everything the government did was wretched.'

What is a sleigh doing in the Place de la Concorde and in the Champs-Elysées (598)? The winter after the abortive Polish rising against the Russians in 1831 was very severe and Poland was the fashion. Many Poles, including Chopin, had taken refuge in Paris.

The oldest parts of Paris began to be demolished, and the Rue Rambuteau was driven through them. In 1841 Thiers decided to build a new ring of defences about 25 miles long, divided into 94 bastions with 16 forts (the scene was set for the siege of 1870). The government tried to exploit its Algerian successes; the capture of the retinue of Abdel Kader in 1843 by the Duc d'Aumale was followed, in 1844, by victory over the Moroccan army. At the Tuileries the Emperor of Morocco's tent, captured at Isly, was the object of lively curiosity (599).

going ways of Paris. She can always

find stones and gold for her

victories and

trophies.

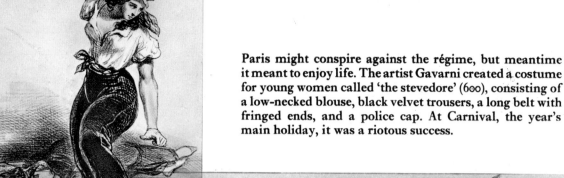

Paris might conspire against the régime, but meantime it meant to enjoy life. The artist Gavarni created a costume for young women called 'the stevedore' (600), consisting of a low-necked blouse, black velvet trousers, a long belt with fringed ends, and a police cap. At Carnival, the year's main holiday, it was a riotous success.

Mon adoré, dis-moi ton petit nom.

At dawn on Ash Wednesday, after enjoying themselves at the inns in Belleville, thousands of masked figures, pelting one another with sweets and plaster eggs, went down without stopping till they reached the toll-gate of La Courtille. A new slope, down to the Boulevard du Temple, opened out before the crowd, and there they waited for the Parisian bacchanalia (600b).

The 'grisette', the working girl who earned thirty sous a day, made up the gentle, modest charm of romantic Paris; while the 'lorette', who lived on for posterity through Gavarni (601), was rather less respectable. Alexandre Dumas tells us that during the two months of Carnival she danced at least 611 hours out of 1,440. She had even a district dedicated to her – a middle-class district, since Monsieur Thiers lived there – where the church of Notre-Dame-de-Lorette was built in 1836.

602

And the Paris of pleasure never dies either. It can lose its head over a grisette.

Smart Parisians celebrated Carnival too. Here is a dandy crossing the Place de la Concorde in his elegant open carriage (602). The most eccentric dandy of them all was a certain La Battut, son of a London chemist and a French émigrée. Popular opinion confused him with another well known figure in Paris, Lord Seymour, and applauded all his absurdities with shouts of 'Hurrah for Milord Blackguard!' But he was soon to be ruined. The printer Rouchon covered the walls of Paris with elegant posters that, among other novelties, showed that one could get from Paris to Meaux (about 32 miles by road) by the post-boat in five and a half hours (603).

BATEAUX~POSTE
POUR MEAUX,
par le Canal de l'Ourcq, 4 lieues à l'heure.

GRANDE BAISSE DE PRIX.
1.er SALON, 1.f 25. – 2.me SALON, 1.f
DÉPARTS:
De la Villette, à 8 h. 1|2 du matin. De Meaux, à 8 h. du matin.
2 h. du soir. » 2 h. du soir.

BUREAUX: A PARIS.
FAUB.rg S.t DENIS, 12. ET BOUL.rd S.t DENIS. 22
à MEAUX, sur le PORT.
Les Salons sont chauffés en Hiver.

603

Demandez la séance de la cour des pairs!

People were tense again. The corn harvest was bad, and Europe was in the grip of an economic crisis. Things were worse in high places. On 26th June 1847 the newsboy (604) found it easy to sell his papers, as they told how the former Minister of Public Works, Teste, president of the Court of Appeal, and General Cubières had obtained a concession in a rocksalt mine for a bribe of 94,000 francs. Excitement was still high when, in August, a terrible crime shook Paris: in the Faubourg Saint-Honoré, the Duc de Praslin, a peer of France, murdered his wife and committed suicide.

Behind the songs of Paris is always the muted anthem of revolution, practised in secret,

Republican intellectuals increased in number, but Guizot, the Prime Minister, refused all reforms, parliamentary or electoral. During the summers of 1847 and 1848, the Opposition launched a great propaganda campaign by means of banquets given in Paris and all over France.

On 9th July 1847, at the restaurant of Château-Rouge, the first reformist banquet took place, attended by 1,200 people, among them 86 deputies. But would the majority of revolutionary-minded people put up with gastronomical stunts for long (605)? On 19th January 1848 a reformist banquet in the 12th arrondissement was forbidden.

605

then suddenly ringing out like a war song.

The organisers of the forbidden banquet warned the National Guard and the people that on Tuesday 22nd February they would stage a demonstration. The excitement was so great that Guizot resigned. On the 23rd a cheerful crowd thronged the centre of Paris. Here, where the boulevard crossed the Rue des Capucines (606), a procession of demonstrators marched past the Ministry of Foreign Affairs. The 14th regiment of the line, thinking their chief was threatened, fired, and twenty fell dead in the street.

Heaped up on tumbrils or stage-coaches, the corpses ended up in the Place des Victoires where, as in 1830 (573), the rioters called the people to arms and to vengeance (607). During the night, the King formed a ministry which included moderate opposition members, like Thiers and Odilon Barrot, but to balance these concessions he gave the unpopular Bugeaud the command of the armed forces of Paris.

608

During the night of 23rd February 1848 barricades went up everywhere. The cry was no longer 'Long live reform', but 'Down with the King'. Bugeaud threw four columns of 27,000 men against the rioters, but the King hesitated, and gave orders to cease fire. The National Guard, with the students of the Polytechnique in front, went over to the insurgents. A violent skirmish with the loyalist municipal guard took place at the post-house of the Château d'Eau, in the Place du Palais-Royal, and this enabled the King to escape. He abdicated in favour of the Comte de Paris. At one o'clock, Louis-Philippe and Queen Amélie hurried out of a side door in the terrace of the Tuileries which gave on to the Place de la Concorde, then being held by General Bedeau (608). A carriage drove them pathetically away to Saint-Cloud.

A city of extremes. Pleasure one day,

death in the streets the next.

609

196

The rioters broke through the railings of the Tuileries, where there was a large body of troops (609). A lieutenant advanced as spokesman to the Duc de Nemours' staff. 'Monsieur', he told the Prince, 'six legions of the National Guard are surrounding the Tuileries, with the citizens in arms behind them. Bloodshed, terrible bloodshed, is imminent, and it will all be upon your head, for brothers will be butchering brothers.' The Prince withdrew his troops.

The mob invaded the Tuileries and hurled itself on the trappings of royalty. Sofas and armchairs were flung through the windows, the portraits of the King, of Soult, and of Bugeaud were ripped to pieces, and busts, even Voltaire's among them, were defaced with rifle fire and thrown down into the courtyard.

610

612

LE GAMIN DE PARIS AUX TUILERIES.
Cristi!..... comme on s'enfonce là dedans.

611

The revolutionaries of 1830 had fought against the church as well as the régime. But in 1848, many marched under the banner of Christ. When the crowd invaded the chapel of the Tuileries a student from the Polytechnique cried: 'Have some respect for Christ and for religion!' and a well-behaved procession took the great crucifix to the nearest church, Saint-Roch (615).

A city which takes sides, with barricades

Women and children dressed up in the valuable tapestries (610). Looters were however executed on the spot; and a workman in rags kept quantities of jewels in a bathtub covered with a sheet.

On the throne an infantry officer wrote: 'The people of Paris to the whole of Europe: liberty, equality, fraternity.' Jokes and horse-play (611 & 612) went on for a while, then the royal throne was borne in triumph along the boulevards (613). At each barricade the crowd stopped and the throne was put down to serve as a stand for some extempore orator. Finally, at the foot of the July Column in the Place de la Bastille, it was set on fire (614), and the great crowd danced round it.

613

as one of its products.

614

RÉPUBLIQUE FRANÇAISE. 1848.
TRAIT TOUCHANT
DU POUVOIR DE LA RELIGIO

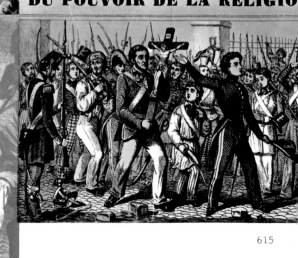

615

616

At eleven o'clock in the morning a group of workers and students from the Polytechnique had forced Rambuteau, the prefect, to flee from the Hôtel de Ville, and had hoisted the tricolour flag (617). But excitement grew in the squares and lobbies. The new ministers laboriously completed the provisional government, including in it two socialists put up by the crowd. The distribution of portfolios caused violent quarrels, and the students with drawn swords had to protect the debate. Here are the ministers from top left to bottom right: Dupont de l'Eure, Lamartine, Arago, Ledru-Rollin, Garnier-Pagès, Crémieux, Armand Marrast, Louis Blanc, Marie, Albert, and Flocon (618).

Riot, a force long dimmed, lights up at last,

In the afternoon of 24th February 1848 the Duchesse d'Orléans went with her two sons, the Comte de Paris and the Duc de Chartres, to the Chamber of Deputies for the regency to be proclaimed. There was a noisy session, with the legitimist Right in league with the republican Left. Workers and students shouted from the galleries. Lamartine mounted the rostrum and bowed to the touching sight of the princess and her children, but recognised the rights of the rioters and proposed the constitution of a provisional government. Armed insurgents poured into the chamber (616), and there was general confusion. The names of the new ministers, selected that morning in the editorial offices of the two republican newspapers, were hastily thrown to the crowd, and everyone went to the Hôtel de Ville, the temple of revolutions in Paris.

617

618

and in its glow can be seen the man who has never shared in the city's pleasures: the workman of Paris.

619

On the morning of 24th February 1848, when the Republic was established, the workers flocked to the Hôtel de Ville. They made the government guarantee everyone a living by promising work. In the afternoon they came back with the red flag, previously the flag of martial law, as an emblem of their rights. Lamartine stood on a chair and persuaded the crowd to keep the tricolour flag, 'which has sent the name, the glory, and the freedom of our country round the world'. On the 26th the government created national workshops to provide work for the unemployed (619). Did the moderate minister, Marie, who was responsible for them, sabotage the experiment so that the Socialists could be blamed for this failure? The numbers in the workshops kept growing (by 15th June there were 118,000), but they had a daily salary of two francs for unproductive work, and this could only lead to disorder.

620

On 10th March, however, a tree of liberty (621) was planted joyously in the Place de l'Hôtel de Ville symbolising the dawn of universal brotherhood and social peace. The workers had accepted 'three months of poverty in the service of the Republic'; the clergy supported the new régime and blessed the tree; the Bonapartists, who had turned up again, were not complaining; and the middle classes felt reassured and joined in the general enthusiasm. Yet this revolution, much more than that of 1789, had been a rising of the slums and the workmen's districts, and of a doctrinaire minority. Paris and the big towns had no idea what the provinces and the countryside thought. On 2nd May the result of the first general elections in France came through. In Paris Lamartine got most votes, 259,800, and nine other departments elected him as well; Proudhon, Barbès, all the workers' candidates were beaten. Louis-Napoleon Bonaparte, the Emperor's nephew, was elected five times in the provinces. Moderate republicans and monarchists had united to achieve a great majority.

621

The Assembly met on 4th May 1848 and replaced the provisional government with an executive commission without the Socialist Republicans, who rushed into the Chamber and unleashed the greatest uproar in French parliamentary history. But Blanqui, Raspail, and Barbès were arrested, and the extremist clubs were closed. On 21st June the Assembly gave the workers in the national workshops the choice between joining the army, having their pay stopped, or going to the country. On the 23rd barricades rose again in the east of the city and around the Panthéon, and held the army in check.

On the 24th General Cavaignac was invested with almost dictatorial powers. Sixty-five barricades barred the Faubourg Saint-Antoine, and with some difficulty the troops moved up the Rue de Charenton (622). Five generals were killed; and it took three days, 30,000 troops and 16,000 guards to restore order.

Paris, city of factories, workshops and warehouses,

facing the ugly mouth of the cannon with nothing.

On 25th June the Archbishop of Paris, Monsignor Affre, was authorised by General Cavaignac to go to the Place de la Bastille with two priests and a worker carrying a palm branch, in order to try to end the fighting (623). There he was fatally wounded, and died two days later. The official figures, which underestimated the facts, said there were 914 killed among the government troops, and 1,435 among the insurgents. Throughout the Saint-Marcel and Mouffetard quarters Sister Rosalie was famous for her untiring goodness, which had already been shown in the revolution of 1830 and during the cholera epidemic. On 24th June an officer of the mounted police who was the sole survivor of an attack on one of the barricades took refuge in the courtyard of the convent and was saved by Sister Rosalie's popularity (624). Once the rebellion was over she sheltered innumerable outlaws and orphans, and an avenue in Paris perpetuated her memory.

623

624

DÉVOUEMENT de la MAGNANIME SŒUR ROSALIE

The Republicans were persecuted, and the régime was everywhere discredited. By universal suffrage, three-quarters of the voters elected Louis-Napoleon Bonaparte as President, and on 20th December 1848 he took the oath to the Republic (625). In the new Assembly of May 1849, the Republican party was much smaller than it had been and on 13th June rashly tried to seize power, failed, and brought on itself a new wave of repression. Louis-Napoleon formed a ministry composed entirely of loyal friends, and on 2nd December 1851, under the pretext of monarchist threats, he dissolved the National Assembly and had the military and civil leaders of the Opposition arrested. Several Republicans tried to raise the people in the eastern districts of Paris and Baudin, a deputy, was killed while putting up a barricade (626) in the Rue Saint-Antoine.

625

A German artist painted this gloomy picture of the evening of 2nd December, when the Prince-President rode down a narrow street full of the wounded and the dying (627). Resistance had been short-lived. The people of Paris, who were at least as Bonapartist as they were Republican, retained painful memories of June 1848, when the troops in the street had quite pointlessly opened fire on an unarmed crowd and caused a hundred deaths.

627

but its soiled hands.

Out of this unequal struggle,

Paris now knows this other Paris,

knows what it is, that it exists,

and that it will continue to exist.

626

The Second Empire was to foster many brilliant and imaginative talents. In the first rank among them was Félix Tournachon, called Nadar (629), playwright, man of letters, caricaturist, painter, and above all great balloonist and photographer. Jules Verne based the character of Ardan, the extravagant hero of 'A Voyage to the Moon', on him.

628

630

On 29th January 1853 the Emperor, who was 45, married Eugénie de Montijo (630), a beautiful Spaniard of 28. In spite of the political difficulties of the régime the Empress was very popular among the people of Paris. Joseph Prud'homme, a character created by Henri Monnier, reigned supreme in the theatre (631), in novels and in caricatures. He was the incarnation of the average Parisian who argued about the government, loved order, comfort, progress, serious conversation, the theatre, the newspapers, and new household inventions like gas-cooking and sewing machines.

On 20th December 1851 a plebiscite gave Louis-Napoleon a large majority (628). 15,000 of his opponents were interned or deported overseas. After a grand tour of the provinces, where he declared 'The Empire means peace', the President was welcomed into Paris on 16th November 1852 with cries of 'Long live the Emperor'. A plebiscite approved the re-establishment of the Empire, and on 2nd December Louis-Napoleon was solemnly installed in the Tuileries under the name of Napoleon III.

632

633

631

Daumier drew a portrait of 'the muse of the Brasserie' (632). Cafés had become the leaven of the new Parisian life, and literature, painting, tourists, and family outings all fell under their influence.

The Duc de Morny (638), second in the hierarchy of the régime and ambassador extraordinary to Moscow for the coronation of the Tsar Alexander II, there married, at 45, the lovely 18-year-old Sophia Trubetskaya (639). He was a man of parts who promoted sugar-beet and railways, launched Deauville, 'the beach of Paris', encouraged literature and the arts, wrote vaudeville sketches with Alphonse Daudet and Ludovic Halévy, founded the Paris Grand Prix, and supported the right to strike. But he loved gambling, luxury, risky speculation, and shady business deals, and was politically quite unprincipled.

638

639

634

640

No one could paint Paris's high society better than Constantin Guys; the best and the worst were to be found in those whose great carriages rolled down the Champs-Elysées or along the Avenue du Bois (634). In 1855 a Parisian called Michaux invented the bicycle with pedals (635), which provided people with a new, and above all healthy, enjoyment. The Exhibition of 1867 was to make these bicycles known to sportsmen all over the world.

In 1855 Alexandre Dumas fils launched the word demimonde, which the Parisian vocabulary had previously lacked. Many of the heroines of this demi-monde (636 & 637), such as Païva, who was Polish, or the English girl, Cora Pearl, were born far from Paris; and few made respectable marriages.

635

Offenbach (640), a German from Cologne, soon became a naturalised Frenchman and Parisian, and as a composer of comic operas was the capital's best entertainer. His 'Belle Hélène', 'Vie Parisienne' and 'Grand Duchess of Gérolstein' gave Paris its reputation as a town of pleasure, where everyone lived the gay life.

636

641

637

The Imperial Court often went to Saint-Cloud, Fontainebleau, Compiègne, and even to Biarritz, its summer resort, but the Tuileries remained its favourite residence, both for work and as the scene of its frequent receptions. At the Empress's 'little Mondays' she received up to 600 people, and four times a year there were large receptions for 3–4,000 guests. The municipal council of Paris also organised great balls at the Hôtel de Ville (642), where the green, blue, purple and gold-frogged uniforms of soldiers and diplomats jostled the rare civilians, who wore embroidered Court dress and carried swords. The ladies had very low neck-lines and wore double skirts until 1856 when a frame appeared made of ten steel rings, called a crinoline, which held skirts out to an exaggerated width. 'It was a curious mixture of dynastic luxury, Cæsarian ostentation, and the jumped-up middle-classes,' quite without elegance, natural or acquired; but foreigners loved it. In 1847 a man called Bullier, tired of working as a lamplighter at the 'Grande Chaumière', a dance-hall in Montparnasse, bought an open-air dance-hall nearby, where he planted a thousand lilac trees (643). Thanks to their delightful scent, the 'Closerie des Lilas' attracted all the students, who danced the cancan, the polka and the mazurka there. It became known as the 'Bal Bullier' and was one of the institutions of Paris, lasting up to 1914. Those who were too old to dance enjoyed the café concerts. The success of the Alcazar, the Eldorado and the Bataclan was to outlive the Second Empire. There the comic singer Thérésa acquired a great reputation with songs that had bewildering titles: 'It tickles my nose', 'The

642

Dancing by gaslight

balloons, bubbles

The kings and queen

The moths of an evenin

644

bearded lady', 'But he oughtn't to have gone there', 'Nothing is sacred to a sapper'. It was the people of Paris who created the reputation of the innumerable eccentrics in the streets: Hercule Damourette, nicknamed Iron Jaw; Tripoli Son of Glory, pedlar of scouring powder: Baptiste the clown, nicknamed Little Chicken; Liard, rag-picking philosopher; Mangin, the pencil seller; and Jacob, a zouave healer.

Nothing was stranger and more frenzied than the Mabille dance-hall (644). Right in the heart of the Champs-Elysées, or, more exactly, in the Allée des Veuves (today, 51 Avenue Montaigne), it had long been a country inn; then in 1844 a dancing master's son called Mabille modernised it and launched it with a great many advertisements and articles in the press. It was 'lit like a government reception'. Olivier Métra and his orchestra of fifty played in a Chinese pavilion surrounded by fake palm trees with globes of gas hanging among the leaves. Several young polka dancers made their name, and even their nickname, there: Rosita Sergent, nicknamed Queen Pomaré, an enormous girl with jet-black hair; Céleste Veinard, nicknamed Mogador; Rigolette; and especially Marguerite the Huguenot, nicknamed Rigolboche. Several male polka dancers were no less famous: Lévêque, nicknamed Chicard and made famous by Gavarni and Nadaud; Brididi; and Pritchard. The dances so happily started under the July monarchy went on at Mabille's under the Second Empire. 'The young will dream of it, foreigners will bring their wives there, historians will mention it,' Taine predicted, and he was right.

trailing crinolines,

popular refrains.

of the fleeting moment

dancing the polka.

In 1852 Napoleon III put a vigorous administrator of Alsatian origin, Haussmann, in charge of the Prefecture of the Seine. The capital needed everything: indoor markets, churches, public buildings, cemeteries, fountains. Soon public works were starting up all over Paris. Masons from Limousin, Auvergne or Savoy were quickly snapped up (645). There was everywhere a fury of expropriation, demolishing and building, and unskilled labourers became big contractors by dint of sheer hard work.

645

Haussman got the Emperor to approve a decree (646) by which on 1st January 1860 Paris annexed the eleven communes inside the surrounding fortifications (647 & 900). 500 miles of new water-mains were built, 260 miles of new sewers, and 32,000 gas lamps replaced 15,000 lanterns. A new underground city was created and came to life (648).

648

It was a time for change. The city was breaking out everywhere. Under Louis-Philippe, Eugène Sue had acquired an enormous reputation with his description of the 'Mysteries of Paris' and its underworld. The suburbs had developed haphazardly, and the suburban population had risen from 13,000 in 1806 to 351,000 in 1856.

647

_ Dire que nous v'là parisiens !....

650

On the right bank, a great new square was planned and in it, in 1861, the foundation stone of a new opera house was laid. In 1863 it was proposed to link it to the Seine, but there were such densely built districts in between that the avenue was not finished until 1877.

Most of the toll-gates of the Farmers General were demolished (650) under Haussmann's plan, which envisaged lines of concentric boulevards, roads fanning out from the centre to the suburbs, and great crossroads with side streets linking up the various districts. On the left bank the Boulevard Saint-Germain and the Rue de Rennes were built by destroying many old houses in this aristocratic faubourg (902).

Out of her old material, Paris cuts new clothes to fit her.

The Vaudeville theatre, in the Place de la Bourse (649), where 'The Lady with the Camellias' and 'The Romance of a Poor Young Man' were performed, gave way to the Rue Réaumur (today the Rue du 4 - Septembre), which joined the Opéra to the Bourse. The theatres whose melodramas had given the Boulevard du Temple its nickname of the 'boulevard of crime' disappeared as well to provide a link between the Place du Trône (de la Nation), the Gare du Nord and the Halles, and to make way for the Place du Château d'Eau (today the Place de la République). But the new buildings put up there were unattractive. The church of the Trinité was in a pseudo-Renaissance style, the church of Saint-Augustin in pseudo-Romano-Byzantine on a metal framework, and the church of Sainte-Clotilde, in pseudo-English Gothic.

649

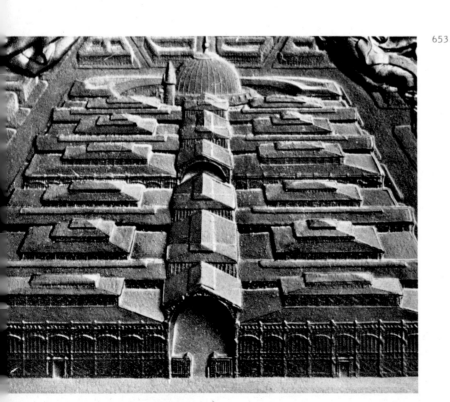

Haussmann enlarged and lengthened the great Gallo-Roman crossroads. From the Gare de l'Est to the Enfer toll-gate (Place Denfert-Rochereau), he cut wide boulevards from north to south (Sébastopol, Saint-Michel). From east to west he lengthened the Rue de Rivoli as far as the Rue Saint-Antoine. These pictures show the difference between the view from the top of the Arc de Triomphe today (651), and the view in 1848 (652). The decree of 1863 envisaging a circus with twelve roads reaching out from it like the spokes of a wheel, and uniform houses designed by Hittorf, transformed three whole districts. At the Roule toll-gate (652 above), the Place des Ternes was created, the plain of Monceau was divided up, and the Boulevard Haussmann joined the Opéra to the Etoile by the Avenue de Friedland. Abandoning the blocks of flats to the middle-classes on the first floor, and the artisans and working-girls on the fifth and sixth floors, the rich built small private houses in the new districts on the west of the city that did not begin to disappear until after 1945.

651

On the blackboard of their city, Parisians again learn to draw the figures

653

654

The crucial problem of victualling Paris had not been given serious consideration since the time of Philip Augustus. Between the Halle aux Blés, dating from Louis XV's time, and the Marché des Innocents, dating from Louis XVI, other buildings had been put up haphazardly. 'I just want huge umbrellas, nothing more,' the Emperor told Haussmann. In 1854 Baltard built ten, of cast iron and glass, with deep cellars which were so satisfactory that they were copied in the provinces and abroad (653). At night the 'stomach of Paris' presented a scene so completely new and fascinating that Zola made a novel out of it.

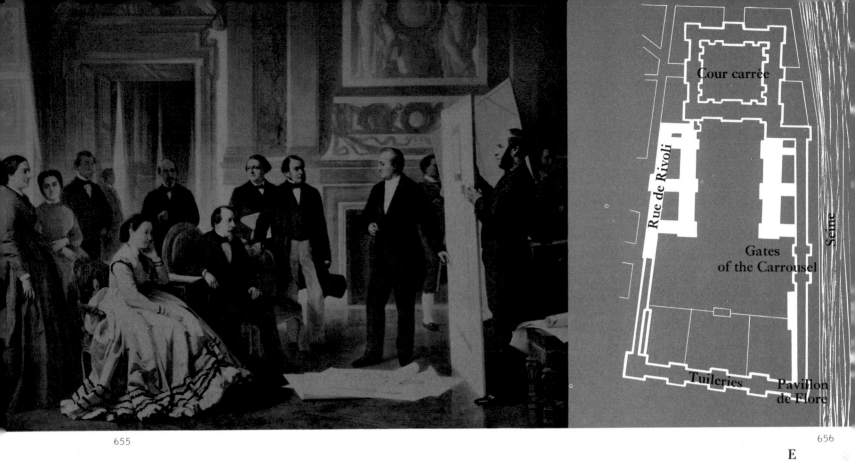

E
N + S
W

of elementary geometry: the circle, the square, the rectangle.

Following Visconti's plans (655 & 656) carried out by Lefuel, Napoleon III ordered the Tuileries and the Cour Carrée to be joined by a north gallery along the Rue de Rivoli. He also rebuilt the west part of the riverside gallery, dating from Henri IV's day, and the Pavillon de Flore beside it, replacing the narrow gates of the Pont du Carrousel with great arches (657). The north link was opened in 1863; it had been awaited two centuries (901) and was to last eight years, until the Tuileries were burnt down by the Communards in 1871.

N
W + E
S

Between 1858 and 1868 the Ile de la Cité was a great mound of rubble. Most of its residents left, and it was broken up, pulverised and flattened. Anything not destroyed was restored, or rather transformed. These pictures show the difference between Turgot's plan (658), made under Louis XV, and a present-day aerial view (658b). Some of the changes, of course, were made before the Second Empire. Napoleon III did not remove the houses from the bridges or the big buildings from the quayside roads. The view of the Sainte-Chapelle was unattractively altered after the burning of the Palais in 1776; but, apart from these, no stone was left unturned by Haussmann's pickaxes. Even the Pont au Change and the Pont Saint-Michel were moved so that they would face each other exactly.

A straight line is the shortest distance between two points;

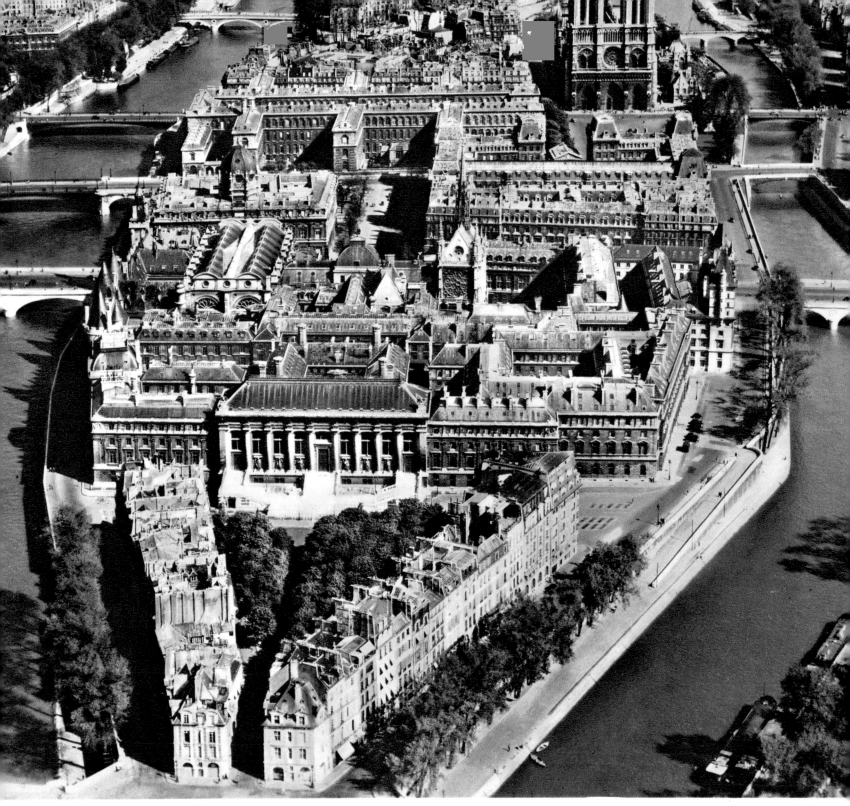

658b

Three large roads now crossed the island, along the lines of the three bridges (658b). The old Cité had been like a ship on which everyone – simple folk, canons, magistrates – embarked; and, one must admit, some frightful slums went with them. Haussmann made it a sort of captain's bridge in which he concentrated all the accumulated administrative powers of Paris: the Prefecture of the Seine, the Chamber of Commerce, a barracks (today the Prefecture of Police), side by side with such ancient institutions as the judiciary power of the Palais and the religious power of Notre-Dame. He destroyed the base of the beautiful triangular 17th century Place Dauphine, and replaced it with a gloomy pillared façade and a useless monumental staircase. Only a few private houses remain on the island.

but the poet wonders if it encourages meditation.

Haussmann's thorough reconstruction of the capital deserves criticism, though. The Halles, which were outside Paris when Philip Augustus opened them, today swallow up the whole of the centre of the city. The railway stations have become obstacles that break into the avenues. Haussmann had the excuse that he could not foresee the continuous increase in car and train transport, and the scale of the victualling of the city. His new Paris was built as the social and administrative centre of 1,825,000 Parisians.

Out of all the angels and saints surrounding the base of the spire of Notre-Dame (660), one only, instead of looking at Paris, looks upwards (661). It is the architect Viollet-le-Duc in person. He had no qualms about setting himself up at the highest point in Paris, and it is to him that we owe this new spire and the complete – rather too complete – restoration of the cathedral that took place between 1841 and 1864. But he was not responsible for the disproportionate increase in the open space in front of the cathedral (662), two hundred and twenty yards long and a hundred and sixty-five yards wide, which was to serve as a parade-ground for the neighbouring barracks (today the Prefecture of Police).

660

659

Well may you wonder, poet. The city of your dreams is being ill-used.

Here is the Ile de la Cité during its reconstruction (659). On the north bank the walls of the new Hôtel-Dieu were beginning to rise. The doctors wanted to remove it from the Cité – but the Emperor and public opinion brought pressure to bear to keep it there. Haussmann was content to follow a scheme of 1838 which moved it from the 661 right of Notre-Dame (91) to the left (662), and one cannot criticise him for this, because today doctors are anxious to keep a great hospital in the heart of Paris for urgent cases and for purposes of study.

212

662

In future Paris must do the impossible:

remain beautiful in spite of all the mistakes that have been made.

'Paris changes, but nothing in my melancholy has changed.' A true Parisian wrote this – Baudelaire (663), who, until his death in 1867, often wandered in spirit 'from the cold quays of the Seine to the burning banks of the Ganges'. An important section of his 'Fleurs du Mal' was entitled 'Parisian Pictures', and there he evoked the 'teeming city, city full of dreams', and the 'pipes and belfries, these masts of the city'. City: the word becomes a leit-motiv. Baudelaire knew the world of the slums, the hovels, the hospitals, the world of poverty, filled with hungry, downcast creatures wasted by suffering and vice; but he knew Haussmann's Paris as well: 'The shivering dawn in its dress of pink and green Moved slowly over the deserted Seine; In the dark Paris rubbed its eyes And picked up its tools, an old working man.' But the town was perhaps already too large and too crowded (664). In his 'Spleen of Paris', Baudelaire expresses the vague disquiet of the individual in the enormous capital who seems to have no contact with others of his kind.

663

664

213

Windsor Castle was shown in one of the most beautiful of the firework displays, and forty years after Waterloo the Queen of England bowed over Napoleon's tomb while the organ of the Invalides played 'God save the Queen'. Five million visitors admired, as she did, the products of 9,500 French and 10,500 foreign exhibitors, and a great show of the work of Ingres and Delacroix.

On 29th December 1855 the Imperial Guard and the troops of the line back from the Crimea marched down the Grands Boulevards (667). Once again the balconies of the Pavilion of Hanover were crowded with Parisians cheering the end of a hard war. Paris gained several famous names from it: the Boulevard de Sébastopol, the Avenue de Malakoff. When he gave the Black Sea regiments their colours, on 2nd April 1856, the Emperor opened the Pont de l'Alma, so-called in memory of the little river Alma, the crossing of which had opened up the road to Sébastopol. Four statues of soldiers stand on it: a zouave, the most famous because it marks the rising of the water when the river floods, a grenadier, an infantryman and an artilleryman.

666

Paris is constantly being cured by its vitality.

The first Paris Exhibition, the idea of F. de Neufchateau, took place in the Champ de Mars in 1798. Since then there had been ten others up to 1849. In 1851 London opened the first universal exhibition at the Crystal Palace, and France was represented there, taking second place. At the first universal French exhibition, opened in Paris in 1855, England took second place. The two nations were very friendly. In August Queen Victoria and Prince Albert crossed the Channel. Paris had not received an English sovereign since the distant and troubled days of Henry VI. The young queen aroused great enthusiasm by going about in an open carriage (665, 666).

It is a city
that never stops,
that always attracts
the curiosity
of the world.

On 14th January 1858 an Italian outlaw, Orsini, who thought the Emperor had not done enough to free Italy from the Austrian yoke, threw two bombs at the Imperial carriage (668) in front of the Opéra, from the Rue Le Pelletier. He was executed. The Emperor reserved quite a different fate for the lovely Comtesse de Castiglione, whom Cavour had entrusted with a special mission. French troops at last intervened, and their ceremonial entry on 15th August 1859 aroused delirious enthusiasm. On the banks of the Seine, a new universal exhibition in 1867 created a magical world. There were crowned heads in plenty: the Tsar Alexander II, William I, King of Prussia, escorted by the gigantic Bismarck and the dry Moltke, the great Sultan of Turkey, Abdul Aziz, the Mikado's brother, the royal couples of Belgium and Spain, and Francis Joseph, Emperor of Austria. The Bal Mabille never

stopped, and at the Variétés the 'Grand Duchess of Gérolstein' was played to packed houses. People were dancing everywhere... on a volcano if you were to believe the pessimists, Rochefort the main one, who growled: 'Paris has been called France's head, but is now nothing but its legs.' An attractive innovation was when the whole of the Champ de Mars was transformed into an enormous park, with woods, waterfalls, aquariums and buildings where every country offered the most exotic entertainments and drinks. Frédéric Le Play, metallurgist and sociologist, and Michel Chevalier, economist, organised the serious side of the entertainment. Between the Pont d'Iéna and the Ecole Militaire, they built an enormous Coliseum (669) of iron and glass. For the first time a group of exhibition stands was devoted to working-class houses and social work. Thirty million visitors looked at 52,000 exhibitors.

669

LE RÈGNE DE LA CRINOLINE.

On the sites of Paris, whorls of multicoloured flowers: crinolines.

673

674

In 1852 a clever man with a beard like Jupiter called Normand Boucicaut (673) started a shop on the left bank in which he sold 'novelties', that is, everything to do with clothes, fashion accessories, and furniture. His prices were not varied according to the appearance of his customers, and he went in for small profits and clearly-marked price-tags. He established specialised branches which were free to buy and sell as they chose, and the trade of his shop, which was called the 'Maison du Bon Marché', grew cease-lessly. This first of the big stores soon occupied an entire building (674) and had numerous enterprising imitators.

Department stores,

where the traditions of a thousand little

shops are found under one roof.

In 1855, Chauchard, a lowly employee of a shop called 'Au Pauvre Diable', opened the 'Louvre' in the new district of the Rue de Rivoli. By the end of the century he was one of the business tycoons of Paris. 1855 also saw the launching of the 'Bazar de l'Hôtel de Ville', where Ruel, who came from Lyons, specialised in household goods. Jaluzot, who was from Nice and had been employed by Boucicaut, in 1865 started a new shop, the 'Printemps', on the Boulevard Haussmann. In 1869 a pedlar from the Pont-Neuf called Cognac founded the 'Samaritaine'.

The progress of the railways and of transatlantic shipping urged industry on to unprecedented efforts, but steam was still the only form of energy. Far from the sources of iron and coal, Paris was badly placed in the race. A humble coppersmith, Cail, founded a great mechanical engineering works at Grenelle (675), and in the northern suburbs the chemical industries which had grown out of bleaching works and tanneries abounded.

But Paris in the Second Empire, Paris without petrol or electricity, drew its power not from its industrial capacity but from its brilliant social life, its political, financial, and literary prestige, and its modernity. Haussmann realised this quite clearly. The boulevards lost their countri-fied, artistic, bohemian air and became the centre of important financial houses, luxurious shops, newspapers, and elegant cafés – the Café Anglais, the Café de Paris, the Maison d'Or, the Café Riche, the Café Cardinal (676). Their golden age was beginning, and it was to be a long one.

675

676

679

677

The remains of the great Gallo-Roman forest of Rouvray and later a royal hunting forest, the Bois de Boulogne, had suffered in the Revolution of 1789 when the abbey of Longchamp and the Château of Madrid were destroyed, and many of the trees were chopped down during the occupation of 1815. Napoleon III decided to make it the biggest public park in Paris, in the English style on the model of Hyde Park, which he greatly admired, and ordered Alphand, the engineer, Davioud, the architect, and Barillet-Deschamps, a horticulturalist, to make it so. They formed two lakes (680), planted 400,000 trees or bushes, made winding roads, bridle paths and walks for pedestrians, and scattered it with pavilions and chalets.

The Avenue de l'Impératrice (today the Avenue Foch), that links the Champs-Elysées to all these marvels, is 150 yards wide, with a road, paths, trees and grass. All the smart 'carriage-folk' in Paris have lived there. And for the eastern districts of Paris the Emperor laid out, not without difficulty, the woods at Vincennes.

Haussmann was backed by an important group of engineers and intellectuals, disciples of Saint-Simonism, which sought to improve the human condition with technical developments. Among them the Pereire brothers, Emile (677) and Isaac (678), themselves financed a good deal of the modernisation and construction of the new Paris.
The hotels of Paris developed (679). The Pereire brothers built a vast hotel, the Louvre, in the Place du Palais-Royal for the exhibition of 1855. On the Boulevard des Capucines the Grand Hotel arose in 1867, and with its 750 rooms it was for a long time the largest in Europe.

Luxurious carriages in the beautiful new avenues of the Bois...

678

680

681

After all this enjoyment, all this active prosperity, the picture changes: Paris suddenly appears to withdraw, surrounded by fortresses and enclosed by the bastions that Thiers had built (681). On 19th July 1870 Napoleon III declared war on Prussia, and in six weeks he had lost it. Defeated at Sedan, he was taken prisoner by the Prussians. On Sunday 4th September the crowd broke into a meeting of the Legislative Council. The thirty-two year old Gambetta, Jules Favre, and several republican deputies formed a government of National Defence under the presidency of General Trochu, and proclaimed the Republic in the Hôtel de Ville. The Empress fled. But the war was not yet over: Jules Favre and Bismarck met in vain near Meaux.

. . . then suddenly a new kind of traffic: cannon under the walls.

682

A cold āwakening to a morning of siege.

684

'Paris's courage, devotion to duty, unselfishness and

patriotism have all been highly praised.

In a word – Paris does without butter!' (Théophile Gautier, 1870–1871).

RÉPUBLIQUE FRANÇAISE

LIBERTÉ — ÉGALITÉ — FRATERNITÉ

MAIRIE DU 18ᵐᵉ ARRONDISSEMENT

La Municipalité du 18ᵐᵉ Arrondissement proteste avec indignation
contre un armistice que le Gouvernement ne saurait accepter sans
trahison.

Paris, le 31 Octobre 1870.

LES ADJOINTS,   LE MAIRE DU 18ᵐᵉ ARRONDISSEMENT,
J.-A. LAFONT.   G. CLÉMENCEAU.
A. SIMONEAU.

Paris. — Imp. PRISSETTE, passage Kumaer, 17. Maison passage du Caire, 17.

The Government of National Defence decided not to leave Paris, but
sent a delegation to Tours. On 15th September the Germans were in
sight. On the 19th they surrounded the capital completely. On the
morning of 7th October, Gambetta flew off in the balloon 'Armand
Barbès' from the Place Saint-Pierre in Montmartre to organise
resistance in Tours (683 & 684). The besiegers tried to blockade Paris
completely. Along a continuous front of about 52 miles, with 150,000
men and 700 guns (685), they cut off all contact between the town and
the outside world. Paris became a fortified camp. On 27th October the
army of Metz capitulated without fighting, and thus freed the best
part of the German army. After Thiers had visited the capitals of
Europe, there seemed to be some possibility of an armistice (686).
An attempt to break out at Le Bourget failed lamentably; and a
similar heroic attempt by the Parisian garrison at Champigny on
2nd December was no more successful.

220

685

Paris's two million inhabitants, without food or fuel, suffered severely. The horses were slaughtered, and even the Rothschilds went on foot. Domestic pets and the animals in the zoo were eaten. Queues formed before Félix Potin's grocery in the Boulevard de Strasbourg (687) and waited from eight o'clock in the evening to three o'clock the following afternoon. Butchers sold dog, rat, mule, bear, camel, cat, and tiger meat. The rich suffered less than the workers, the lower middle-classes, the employees, and the craftsmen of the suburbs.

The Prussian batteries opened fire against the forts in the south on 5th January 1871, and for the first time shells fell on Paris. The cemetery of Montparnasse (688), the left bank, and the Latin Quarter were hit. The garrison failed in its effort to break out at Buzenval.

On 23rd January Jules Favre obtained a general armistice. The conditions seemed reasonable. After four months and ten days, resistance in Paris ceased at midnight on the 26th. As for the provinces, the government behaved as if all was lost because Paris had capitulated. Gambetta resigned from his post as Minister of the Interior. On 8th February the whole of France voted. Paris elected Victor Hugo, Gambetta, Garibaldi, Littré, Ledru-Rollin, Louis Blanc, etc., but the candidates who stood for peace carried the day. At its first meeting at Bordeaux the Assembly decided to move to Versailles. On the 18th in the Gallery of Mirrors at Versailles the King of Prussia was proclaimed German Emperor. On 1st March he reviewed his troops along the racecourse at Longchamp. Then the Prussians marched down the Champs-Elysées (689), although they occupied only the outskirts of the city. On 3rd March they evacuated Paris. It was a short occupation, but was to be followed by tragedy.

688

689

Paris was no longer hungry, as food was being supplied from London, but the National Guard, which had kept its equipment, had illegally formed a Federation under the direction of a Central Committee. On 1st May 1871, as in July 1789 (690 & 455), the Federal troops took their cannon up to the hill of Montmartre. The rumour, which was untrue, had gone about that they were to be handed over to the Prussians. At dawn on 18th March 1871 Thiers, named chief of the executive power of the Republic, ordered General Lecomte to retake these batteries. The operation failed. At six p.m. in the Rue des Rosiers the rioters shot old

691

Clément Thomas who, in June 1848, had commanded the National Guard against the insurgents; they also shot General Lecomte. The Central Committee repudiated these murders, but everywhere the barricades went up. Thiers, who had only a small number of troops at his disposal, retired to Versailles with the authorities.

Victor Hugo, who had been elected deputy for Paris, had joined the Assembly at Bordeaux. There his son Charles died of apoplexy. He went back to Paris on that tragic 18th March. It is a long road from the Gare d'Orléans to the Père Lachaise cemetery, and as the funeral procession passed, led by the poet, the barricades opened up and the Federal troops saluted it (691). 'The people in arms are sad, and their great battalions make a hedge of silence,' Hugo wrote later.

Elections were held on the 26th. 229,000 electors out of 485,000 on the voting lists elected the 90 members of the General Council of the Commune; but the moderates refused to sit. Blanqui's small group and about thirty revolutionaries governed Paris, although they were a minority. On the 27th the Commune of Paris was proclaimed (692 & 693) at the Hôtel de Ville, which was decked with red flags. It meant war between Paris and Versailles (694). Old historic bitternesses revived. The Commune government respected the coffers of the Bank of France and borrowed money from Rothschild. There were 80,000 active troops and 115,000 militia, but only about 20,000 of them had any idea of military discipline.

692

Liberty – the only bread Paris cannot do without.

693

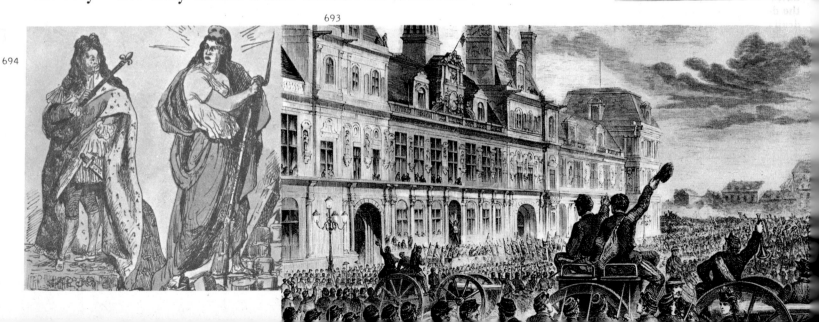

695

696

Without civil or military leaders, the Commune of Paris, strung between the Central Committee and those elected at the Hôtel de Ville, took no proper measures. When the Versailles troops were already at Neuilly, it knocked down the Vendôme Column (695). Painter Courbet was accused of this act of vandalism.

The people shout for the 'Commune', an old word that since the Middle Ages has meant Liberty.

The troops from Versailles (696) occupied Paris from Neuilly to Saint-Cloud. On the afternoon of Sunday 21st May 70,000 men entered through the unguarded Porte du Point du Jour, and a week of carnage began. Most of the Commune's troops scattered, but a small number fought on until the end. On 24th May the slaughter began in the Place du Carrousel (697). Flames rose from buildings where cases of powder and demi-johns of oil had been placed.

697

698 On 24th May 1871 the men from Versailles took the left bank. Everyone who belonged to or was suspected of belonging to the Federalists was summarily shot. Both parties were seized with a murderous frenzy. This strange picture (698), taken from a series called 'Crimes of the Commune' which was brought out to justify the repression, is a composite photograph which attempts to reconstruct the atrocities of the Rue Haxo. On 24th May the Communards had shot the Archbishop of Paris. On the 26th several dozen hostages, priests and laymen of all kinds, were shot in the courtyard of the Rue Haxo by a frenzied crowd, in which the women were the wildest.

Liberty, yielding to force, is deprived of every weapon but despair and madness.

Street battles raged everywhere, with swords, rifles, revolvers and cannon. A handful of desperate men decided to set fire to the public buildings. The staff of the Louvre saved the collections in the Museum, but the magnificent old Hôtel de Ville was burnt down on 24th May (699). 'It was a splendid ruin,' wrote E. de Goncourt, 'a ruin of sapphire, ruby, emerald, blindingly bright because of the chemical action of the stones roasted in the petrol.' Several streets were severely damaged, especially the Rue du Bac, Rue de Lille, Rue de Rivoli, and the Quai de la Rapée. Including only the buildings either partially or completely burnt, the damage amounted to 114 million gold francs. The Tuileries, the Palais-Royal, the Louvre, the Ministry of Finance, the Palais de Justice, the Préfecture de Police, the Conciergerie, the Hôtel de Salm, the Gobelins, the Arsenal and Thiers' house were the main buildings to be burned down.

699

700

Slowly the Federal troops were pushed further and further into the eastern districts of Paris. At the end of this terrible week, Sunday 28th May, they were huddled together in the Père Lachaise cemetery with several pieces of artillery (700). The smoke from the fires rose over the city in a dark fog. Soon they were fighting with swords among the tombs, and in the apocalyptic twilight the living battled desperately among the dead.

Pushed back against the wall of the cemetery that was thus to achieve a horrible fame, the last defenders of the Commune were pitilessly shot down (701). The death of 480 people had been answered by that of 18,000 Parisians, men and women, guilty or innocent, Federal sympathisers or reputed to be so, on the vaguest possible counts. The total losses in this one week in Paris were greater than those of the Revolution of 1789 during 6 years and throughout the whole of France.

And from now on Paris has its wailing wall,

like Jerusalem of old, for those who died for Liberty.

701

702

703

The Tuileries, whose main structure was still intact (202), was demolished and sold by auction. But Napoleon I took his place again on top of the Vendôme column (702). The Hôtel de Ville was entirely rebuilt. A statue of Joan of Arc was put up in the Place des Pyramides. Sir Richard Wallace, a great friend of Paris, presented the city with eighty public fountains.

Everything returns to normal: the rich man is rich,

the poor man is poor,

705

And so life began again. Parisians hastened to lend their money to free their country of the Prussians. The Third Republic felt its way carefully.

704

privilege is upheld. Meanwhile, the city gathers its strength.

The liveliness of the boulevards (704) and of the racecourse at Longchamp (705) showed that social life had returned to its former gaiety, but on pay day in the evenings the poor flocked to the pawn shops to retrieve their mattresses (706). Once more they had suffered harshly and they were not interested in politics while politics ignored them. In 1872 there were 550,000 workmen out of a total of 1,794,000 Parisians. Masons and carpenters were the best paid among them, because Paris was proud of its rich and varied buildings (707 & 708).

706

C'est une grande et puissante dame que **Sa Majesté la Ville de Paris**. Ainsi qu'on va le voir, c'est une véritable souveraine que bien des rois couronnés doivent envier tous les jours.

Elle possède en premier lieu son palais, l'Hôtel-de-Ville : incendié pendant les heures sombres de notre deuil national, il vient de renaître de ses cendres : sa valeur est de 35 millions.

Elle possède 20 mairies blanches et coquettes, une par arrondissement. Ce sont de véritables monuments qui représentent plus de 27 millions, un joli denier n'est-ce pas.

Elle possède 64 églises catholiques, 9 temples protestants et 2 synagogues israélites, représentant 191 millions. Si on ne prie pas le bon Dieu à Paris, franchement, c'est qu'on y met de la mauvaise volonté.

Trois grands établissements d'instruction supérieure, et six établissements d'instruction secondaire, valant 40 millions, sont ouverts tous les jours aux savants et aux écoliers.

Ses écoles primaires au nombre de 143, et valant 65 millions, reçoivent une armée de 50,000 enfants de toutes nationalités, puisqu'on y compte plus de 4,000 petits Allemands, hélas!

Ses fameuses halles valent 20 millions. C'est là que s'entassent chaque matin les denrées venues des quatre coins de la France et que Paris dévore en 24 heures.

La Ville de Paris possède 3 théâtres municipaux valant 12 millions. Elle en possèdera bientôt un quatrième où elle invitera son peuple d'artistes à entendre l'opéra populaire.

Pour veiller à sa sécurité, elle possède 20 casernes dont la valeur est de 28 millions, et où elle peut loger plus de 100,000 soldats.

Elle possède 183 postes d'octroi et magasins destinés à l'assistance publique, valant 188 millions de francs. C'est là que tout ce qui entre dans Paris paie un droit d'entrée proportionnel.

Paris possède 19 cimetières qui ont une valeur de 33 millions, et ils sont presque tous pleins. Il meurt près de 50,000 Parisiens par an, de quoi peupler une grande ville.

Paris possède 44 parcs merveilleux, squares, pépinières, serres, etc, valant plus de 272 millions. C'est la parure et le charme de la grande cité.

La Ville est ornée de 96 statues, bassins, fontaines monumentales, représentant 5 millions. C'est le luxe des souverains : Paris n'est-il pas un véritable roi?

Plus de 120 millions ont été consacrés aux canaux et aux divers établissements hydrauliques qui alimentent d'eau la grande cité. On doit y consacrer encore pareille somme, car l'hygiène publique le demande.

Parlerons-nous des terrains à bâtir et des maisons isolées que la ville possède un peu partout, pour plus de 60 millions ?

En dehors de toutes ces propriétés qui représentent près de 1100 millions, la ville de Paris possède un revenu annuel de près de 300 millions, c'est-à-dire plus que les royaumes de Portugal, de Grèce, de Danemark, de Bavière, de Wurtemberg, de Hollande, de Suède et

Typ.-Lith. de Ch. PELLERIN à Épinal.

The astonishing range of the human voice can almost bring down the chandelier.

228

On 5th February 1875 Marshal MacMahon, President of the Republic, officially opened the Opéra (709). Thus the dream of the architect, Charles Garnier, was realised after fourteen years of work. It was Napoleon III who had decided to give to Paris a thirteenth and definitely Parisian theatre. When Garnier had presented his plan to him, the Empress cried, 'And what is this style? It isn't Greek, it isn't Louis XIV, it isn't Louis XV.' 'It's Napoleon III, your Majesty. Are you complaining of that?'

709

Escaliers de service.   Foyer de la danse.   Couloirs et loges Administration.   Cour et Porte
      Salle du corps de ballet.   d'artistes.   sur leboulevard
      Salle d'étude des choristes.   Haussmann.

713

The ballet dancers see themselves in

the monocles of their admirers.

Thirteen painters, seventy - three sculptors and fourteen decorators took part under Garnier's direction in the adornment of the Opéra, for which variously-coloured marbles had been brought from all the quarries of France. The façade was ornamented with statues which Garnier commissioned from his friend J. B. Carpeaux, a charming group of dancers round an inspiring genius (710) symbolising the Dance. The foyer of the Opéra was long to be a kind of annexe to the Jockey Club (711).

711

The Opéra, whose foundations caused a great deal of trouble because the prehistoric bed of a northern tributary of the Seine was found there, is about 184 feet high, about 565 feet long and about 330 feet wide, and covers 3 acres of ground. Its stage (712) is 50 feet wide and 105 feet deep; it has nearly 12 miles of passages; and its electrical equipment contains 13,000 bulbs allowing for 5,000 combinations of lighting. There are only 2,156 seats because of the numerous staircases and exits (713). The chandelier weighs over 6 tons. The hangings at the back of the stage, which were meant to show enormous landscapes, have been replaced by a panorama in sheet-metal weighing nearly 22 tons.

712

710

Seven years after the Commune, the Universal Exhibition of 1878 celebrated France's revival. Extraordinary things, so new that they seemed almost to anticipate the future, were to be found there: electric light, which also lit the Avenue de l'Opéra; the telephone; the gramophone. On the slopes of Chaillot, which since the Restoration had borne the name of Trocadéro, Davioud built a palace that was at the same time a water-tower, a large theatre and concert hall, and a green hill. Its composite style was rather disappointing: Hispano-Moorish, with touches of Italy, Marseilles and the Auvergne about it (714). Another marvel was the Palace of Industry on the Champ de Mars which was a milestone in the history of metal construction and a triumph of ceramics.

714

717

In the Place du Château d'Eau, which had become famous 50 years earlier thanks to Daguerre's diorama and to the laboratory where he and Niepce invented photography, the basins of the great fountains were replaced by a statue of the Republic, unveiled on 14th July 1883 (717). In 1884 the 150-feet-high statue of Liberty, which was presented to the port of New York, raised its gigantic torch high over the roofs near the Boulevard de Courcelles (718) before its departure for the United States. Bartholdi designed it, and it was made of 300 sheets of hammered copper nearly an inch thick and weighing about 80 tons. Its interior framework of iron weighed nearly 120 tons and was constructed by Gustave Eiffel.

718

719

720

In his laboratory in the Rue d'Ulm on 6th July 1885, Pasteur and his assistants vaccinated a small Alsatian boy called Joseph Meister and cured him of rabies. People who had been bitten flocked in from everywhere: 19 men, cruelly mauled by a mad wolf, came from the depths of Russia (719). The vaccine was so successful that an international subscription was raised and made possible the foundation of the Pasteur Institute, opened in 1888.

Zola was forever painting the darkest sides of Parisian life. In 'Nana' he described the demi-monde; in 'L'Assommoir,' the slums; in 'Au Bonheur des Dames,' a big store; in 'Le Rêve,' the painter's life; in 'Le Ventre de Paris,' the Halles; in 'Paris', social life. In April 1889 he climbed up on the engine of the Paris-Mantes train at the Gare Saint-Lazare, in a frock coat (720); and then he wrote 'La Bête Humaine'.

Sarah Bernhardt (1844–1923) had become the golden voice of Paris. In 1875 she was elected a member of the Comédie-Française (721) and was immensely popular on both sides of the Atlantic in the 200 roles she played in her 61 active years.

The Breton Renan (722), a Parisian from the age of fifteen, quarrelled with the Imperial régime because his course at the Collège de France risked 'arousing regrettable disturbances'. He became the flag-bearer of liberalism and until his death in 1892 was extremely popular in Paris.

722

721

On Victor Hugo's 80th birthday, 26th February 1881, 600,000 Parisians marched down the Avenue d'Eylau before the poet's house (723). Between his grandchildren Georges and Jeanne, Hugo spent the whole day at the open window greeting the endless lines of wellwishers. There was a mountain of flowers on the pavement outside, and the street was renamed the Avenue Victor-Hugo. The author of the 'Legend of the Centuries' and of 'Hernani' died on 22nd May 1885. Before he was buried in the Panthéon, Hugo's body was exposed during the night of 31st May under the Arc de

723

Paris, the poet! The people know that a poet is as glorious as a conqueror.

Triomphe, and watched over by twelve young poets. Below are some of the comments on the occasion.

Barrès: 'From a very great distance people could see the enormous urn that reached as far as the arch, and stood on a double platform of purple velvet. Great waves of people, delirious at having created a god, beat against the frightened horses, all the way from the Place de la Concorde.'

Romain Rolland: 'Around the Arch at the Etoile, where the god slept like a conqueror, on the field of glory snatched from his great rival Napoleon, there were no tears, no grieving. It was a village fair by Jordaens' (724).

Before daybreak the humble hearse in which Hugo had wished to be buried appeared. Two million Frenchmen accompanied it along the Seine, and along the Boulevards Saint-Germain and Saint-Michel. 'Down at the end of the Rue Soufflot,' wrote Claretie, 'the Panthéon was draped in black, and its two giant tripods sent their green flames up into the wind .... The simple, striking, black hearse appeared in the wide road (725), and every head was uncovered. The noise went before and after him, enfolding him as he passed.'

724

725

726

Paris was now shaken by political excitements. In 1887 a young general, the 48-year-old Boulanger, Minister of War (726), became the idol of the anti-Republicans and of the Nationalists who wanted revenge on Germany. The Rouvier ministry got rid of him by sending him as commander of the 13th Army Corps to Clermont-Ferrand. The 'Boulangists', as they were called, overran the Gare de Lyon on 8th July and lay on the railway tracks. The general left Paris on an engine (727). Dismissed from the army in 1888, Boulanger, who wanted Parliament dissolved and the Constitution revised, led a fiery campaign in Paris that ended in his victory in the by-elections. On 27th January 1889 he could have been master of Paris and of France. But he hesitated; and the Republicans pulled themselves together. Boulanger was divided between love and politics, and he chose the first. He left France on 1st April 1889, and committed suicide on the tomb of his mistress at Brussels in 1891.

727

Paris, the conqueror! She raises the spires of her modern cathedrals.

728

729

As Boulangism expired, a new Universal Exhibition was held during the centenary of the Revolution, from 6th May to 6th December 1889, on the Champ de Mars. The Gallery of Machines, a metal building 147 feet high, was dwarfed by M. Eiffel's tower (728, 729, 730), which was 984 feet high (1,043 feet since it has been topped by a television mast). 2,500,000 rivets assembled its 15,000 pieces of iron, which weighed 7,000 tons, but its density per cubic inch is incredibly light.

730

731

733

732

The 'boulevard' remained the centre of Parisian life. Fashions came and went: after the Muscadins, the Incroyables and the Gandins – so called because the Boulevard des Italiens was at one time called the Boulevard de Gand – came the Raffinés, the Beaux, the Dandies, the Fashionables, and the Gommeux. And here with their monocles and their cigars are the Fops and the Snobs (732 & 733). The newspapers, as much as the theatres, were at the centre of this boulevard life, and Paris had 46 of them.

During the Second Empire painters had reconciled painting with Paris, which thus became, and was long to remain, the centre of the world of art. In the first rank among them, Manet painted Parisian subjects like 'Music at the Tuileries', 'Races at Longchamp', 'Fancy Dress Ball at the Opéra', or 'At the Café Concert'. 'The Bar at the Folies Bergère' (731) was painted two years before his death, when ataxy had already gained a cruel hold on him.

Paris, the palette.

734

735

736

As a protest against the great sprawling city, Impressionist painting, which would hardly have existed without the life of the cafés and the brasseries, took as its subject everything that provided an escape from the capital, such as the nearby suburbs, and the steamboats or rowing boats on the Seine. After the 'Regatta at Argenteuil', Monet painted and repainted the Gare Saint-Lazare in 1877 (736).

Students fought the police and, ironically enough, there was an affray (738) between the mob and the police in front of the Charité hospital. But this was just a skirmish compared with what the anarchist dynamiters were doing. Ravachol blew up a large private house and some blocks of flats; Vaillant threw a bomb into a full session of the Chamber. In 1894, 'the accursed year', bombs exploded everywhere. President Carnot was assassinated in Lyons. It was the anarchists' last fling, but something else was soon to set Parisians at loggerheads.

In December 1892 the law was kept busy. Charles de Lesseps and the administrators of the Panama Company went to prison. His 83-year-old father, Ferdinand de Lesseps, who had created the Suez Canal, wanted to cut through the isthmus of Panama and antagonised 40,000 creditors in doing so. Shady go-betweens had bribed a Minister and several deputies in order to get permission to float public loans, and the result was a resounding political and financial scandal.

No fraud or scandal can tarnish the unsullied glory of her painters.

739   740

Here is a charming family scene: 'They've sworn not to discuss the Dreyfus affair' (739); 'They've discussed it' (740). A few Parisians saw Dreyfus's sword broken and his military badges torn off on 5th January 1895, in the quadrangle of the Hôtel des Invalides (741). Had this artillery captain really sold Germany important documents connected with national defence? Or had he been framed, and would the army's honour be compromised if the truth were known? The business was passionately argued, and in 1898 Zola launched a powerful campaign against Dreyfus's enemies, thus gaining considerable popularity. Dreyfus was innocent: this was officially stated in June 1899. But who was guilty? It is something people still argue about . . .

741

742

Under the Second Empire an Englishman called Worth had 'invented' the 'haute couture' of Paris. But it was a firm founded in 1892 at 5 Rue de la Paix by the banker Isidore Paquin and his wife that employed most work-people. It was quite an event when its 2,700 employees, men and women, left at the end of the day (742); and painters, like the popular song writers, were not slow to make use of it.

Who will ever describe the toil of her sempstresses

or the researches of her inventors?

A canary sings in its cage, a cat watches under the fading light of a paraffin lamp, and the tired anæmic sempstress sleeps on her sewing machine, while day dawns over the Eiffel Tower and the Palais du Trocadéro (743). This is the courageous and exhausting Parisian life which Willette, who painted Pierrot, Mimi Pinson, and curvacious women too, could so well evoke. In 1900 Gustave Charpentier immortalised this small world of sempstresses and midinettes, girls struggling with the temptations and difficulties of Paris, in his musical play 'Louise'.

743

Paris celebrated Franco-Russian friendship. In October 1896 the pale, thin 28-year-old Tsar, Nicholas II, and the Tsarina were greeted very warmly by the people of Paris. Accompanied by the President, Félix Faure, the Tsar laid the first stone of the bridge opposite the Hôtel des Invalides, named after his father Alexander III (744).

On 28th December 1895 several idlers who had gathered in the basement of the Grand Café, in the Boulevard des Capucines, were delighted with the moving images projected on a screen by the Lumières, from Lyons. The cinema was born (745).

744

A whole people labours

to make the city famous.

746

It soon had its victims. On 4th May 1899, at a fashionable charity bazaar in the Rue Jean-Goujon, a projection lamp caught fire. In the conflagration which followed 140 people died (746).

745

CINÉMATOGRAPHE LUMIÉRE

Perhaps because it had not been encircled by the tax wall in 1785 and was a free commune from then until 1860, the top of the Butte Montmartre became the home of the eccentrics of Paris. Since Mercury, Saint Denis, and Ignatius Loyola, it had been an inspired place, but as well as that it had its windmills, with their pleasant millers and millers' wives, who on Saturday evenings or Sundays welcomed visitors to dance, drink and eat. In about 1900 there were still four windmills on the Butte (747). Today there are only two: the Blutefin and the Radet, which are known by the single name of the Moulin de la Galette (747). With the windmill at Longchamp and that in the cemetery at Montparnasse, these are the only survivors of that girdle of fluttering sails which, under Louis XIII, encircled Paris (234). A man called Debray, whose father, it was said, had been cut to pieces by the Cossacks in 1814 – and the pieces attached to the wings of the windmill – turned the Moulin de la Galette into a public dance hall. And this is what it has remained.

Montmartre-over-Paris.... From the top of the hill

At 4 Rue des Saules (748) an inn called the 'Lapin Agile' (Lively Rabbit) – after the sign of a rabbit jumping into a saucepan with a bottle in its hand, painted by André Gill – prospered, though not without disturbances. Other inns were set up at the foot of the Butte. Rodolphe Salis began the 'Chat Noir' where people sang topical songs, and at the 'Mirliton' Aristide Bruant (749), with his big hat and boots, evoked the frail pitiful creatures of the Parisian streets.

the city is a river whose sounds climb the slopes.

751

750

In the Place Clichy in 1889, in the rambling garden of M. Forest's summer residence, the twenty-five-year-old Comte de Toulouse-Lautrec is carefully painting (750) a woman with an umbrella. This unhappy and cynical aristocrat had been crippled since childhood – he had broken both thighs – and he immortalised a humanity still young but already worn by life, that flung itself frantically into artificial pleasures. Toulouse-Lautrec also painted the singers and dancers of the day: Yvette Guilbert (751) in a green dress and long black gloves, and Jane Avril, nicknamed

752

Mélinite (752). In 1890 Zidler reopened the Moulin Rouge (753), with his French Cancan and his 'naturalist quadrille', where dancers with extraordinary names frisked about: 'La Goulue' (The Glutton) (754 right), 'Grille d'Egout' (Drain Grating) (754 left), 'Valentin le Désossé' (Boneless Valentin).

753

754

'The larvae of vice and poverty', says one newspaper of Toulouse-Lautrec's figures. 'A lesson in moral surgery', says another.

The wheel is one of the symbols of Paris: cab wheels, bicycle wheels,

the wheels of the travelling fairs.

The 'horseless carriage' now began to rival the railways. Paris had long known it. In 1771 Cugnot, an engineer, had launched his steam truck in the court of the Arsenal, going at just over 2 miles an hour. In 1834 the German Dietz and his steam-tug went from Paris to Saint-Germain in 2 hours 28 minutes. The arrival in Paris of Amédée Bollée's 'Obéissante' from Le Mans was a sensation in 1875. Albert de Dion and a mechanic, Bouton, opened a small factory near the Porte Maillot in 1887. In the Rue Spontini in 1889 Léon Serpollet took the first driving test in a steam vehicle he had invented. In 1891 a petrol-driven car produced by Peugeot at Le Doubs followed the bicycle race from Paris to Brest and back. In 1894 the first car race from one town to another was run: Paris-Rouen, 77 miles (756).

But the motor-car had not yet become part of the Parisian scene. The Place Clichy shows this (757), since it was the crossroads for every sort of city transport, including the cab, the omnibus which since 1853 had been given a top deck, the elegant open carriage of the well-to-do, the sportsman's bicycle, and the rails of the horse trams.

On 22nd October 1895 an extraordinary accident took place at the Gare Montparnasse. The express from Granville did not stop (755), and the engine went through the wall and crashed down some 30 feet into the Place de Rennes.

758

759

Since doctors said that bicycling, like all forms of exercise taken in moderation, was good for women, anæmic young ladies had taken it up and the number of women cyclists in the Bois de Boulogne greatly increased (758).

Paris itself spins round like a lottery

wheel, awarding prizes at random.

760

On 1st April 1900 a Universal Exhibition opened the century. On the Esplanade des Invalides were the exhibitions of interior decoration, furniture, and the home (759); and on the other side of the Pont Alexandre III were the Grand Palais and the Petit Palais, halls of cast iron where the fine arts were shown. An imaginary city sprang up on the banks of the Seine where nations vied with one another over the richness of their exhibits. 50,859,955 visitors to the exhibition never tired of praising the immense bouquet of metal (760) that sparkled with electric lights near the Ecole Militaire. Another attraction was the Great Wheel (761).

761

As a result of the vow taken by French Catholics after the French defeat in 1870, the Archbishop of Paris decided to build a church consecrated to the Sacred Heart of Jesus on the top of the Butte Montmartre. On 23rd July 1873 the National Assembly declared, by 393 votes to 164, that the scheme was one of public utility, and conferred powers of compulsory purchase.

Abadie's design, chosen by competition, was inspired by the church of Saint-Front at Périgueux; but there was great difficulty with the foundations because of the innumerable plaster quarries there. Work began in 1876. The Savoyarde (762), one of the biggest bells in the world and weighing 19 tons, was pulled up to the church by 28 horses. It was cast at Annecy in 1895 and presented by the diocese of Savoie. But the Sacré-Cœur (763) was not consecrated until 1919. It is about 330 feet long and about 165 feet wide. The lantern of the dome (764) is 212 feet high, and the campanile 308 feet; from the gallery the view over Paris extends to over 30 miles. The merits of its Romano-Byzantine style are questionable, but at a distance its tall white form fits in perfectly with the horizon of the capital.

Perhaps under the influence of Loïe Fuller's dances, performed in floating veils, the 'flower-woman' was everywhere to be seen – in painting, in sculpture, in furniture, in advertisements (767), in the exterior decoration of blocks of flats. But the Parisian girl who remained untouched by fashion or the great world was still completely captivating (768).

767

In the seams of the métro
man begins to develop his underground thoroughfares.

In July 1900 the underground metropolitan railway took only 25 minutes instead of an hour and a half to go from Maillot to Vincennes. Fulgence Bienvenüe, a Breton trained at the Polytechnique, directed the work on the métro which for years was to tear up the pavements of Paris. The Seine was crossed eight times (three times by viaduct, five times by tunnel). At the

Place Saint-Michel a metal tunnel was built on the surface (765), then sunk about 75 feet under the ground. By 1930 the Paris métro system was complete.

In the approaches to the Place de l'Opéra (766) the traffic, in which motor cars were beginning to join the horse-drawn vehicles, was already congested.

768

765

No sooner had the fanfares of the exhibition of 1900 died down than Paris had new cause for excitement. In 1904 Emile Combes, President of the Council, suppressed the schools run by religious organisations. In 1906 Church and State were separated and the state administrators made an inventory of ecclesiastical possessions. There was much quarrelling over it, and a recent convert, François Coppée, poet of the people of Paris and of idylls in the public parks, ostentatiously took the part of the expropriated monks and nuns (771).

'You are weary of this old world at last', says the poet Apollinaire;

'Le Tout-Paris', which replaced the former royal or imperial courts, welcomed Sarah Bernhardt (769), who played Edmond Rostand's 'L'Aiglon' (769), and applauded the Isola brothers, who performed astonishing feats of calculation (770), Réjane, the clowns Footit and Chocolate, Polaire and Mistinguett.

A Brazilian, Alberto Santos - Dumont, the son of an engineer from the Ecole Centrale in Paris who had become a coffee king at Sao Paulo, used his fortune to promote aerial navigation. After various attempts, he lifted his canvas aeroplane about a yard off the ground on the lawn at Bagatelle at dawn on 13th September 1906, and covered a distance of over 20 feet; on 23rd October he rose 9 feet and flew for nearly 200 feet (772). The whole of Paris celebrated the first officially verified flight.

769

770

and Paris repeats his words

as it gazes up at the first aeroplanes,

14 bis

772

244

After the famous automobile race from Paris to Bordeaux in 1895, the elegant Comte de Dion (773), with a number of motorcar enthusiasts, founded the Automobile Club de France. In 1901 there was a race from Paris to Berlin, in 1902 another, starting at night, from Paris to Vienna. In the towns each competitor was preceded by a cyclist going at 8 miles an hour (774). Marcel Renault reached Austria as the winner, but was killed in 1903 in the race from Paris to Madrid.

773

774

The public had a great affection for the Paris trams, which since 1890 had used steam and then electricity instead of horses. Thanks to the petrol engine, the omnibus regained its popularity. The first regular line, from Montmartre to Saint-Germain-des-Prés (775), was opened in June 1906. But the tram did not completely disappear until 14th August 1938.

778

775

a Paris curious about the new century.

In 1902 two young scientists, Marie and Pierre Curie, succeeded in preparing a decigram of pure radium in a shed at the School of Physics in the Rue Lhomond. But Pierre Curie was run over by a horse-drawn van, and Madame Curie was appointed to her husband's chair. On 5th November 1908 a woman spoke in the Sorbonne for the first time (778).

779

776

There were dozens of famous Parisians. Here are some (779): from left to right, Robert de Montesquiou, a snob in the new fashion; the two famous artists Forain et Caran d'Ache; Polin, the military comedian; Boni de Castellane, the last of the dandies; Eve Lavallière, a delightful actress; and the poet Apollinaire.

'The Apache is the plague of Paris,' said the Petit Journal in 1907 (780). Here we see the elaborate precautions taken in 1912 to arrest Bonnot, the formidable chief of a gang of bank thieves at Choisy (781).

780

777 Since Marchand's mission had clashed with Kitchener in the heart of Africa, Paris had disliked the British. It had supported Kruger and the Boers. But Edward VII (776), who loved the pleasures of Paris, came to the throne in 1901, and on 1st May 1903 visited the city (777). People cold-shouldered him at first, but his good humour soon won their hearts. The 'Entente Cordiale' was born.

781

After the 'belle époque'

Paul Déroulède, cloaked and bearded for the fray (782), aroused the Parisians with his mighty voice. In February 1899, the year when the Dreyfus case was being reconsidered, the fiery president of the League of Patriots took advantage of President Félix Faure's funeral to try – not too seriously – to overthrow the régime. He was arrested. His friends, who had taken refuge at a printer's in the Rue Chabrol, resisted troops and police for forty days. Déroulède was exiled to Spain and was granted an amnesty in 1905.

disaster comes again. The river floods the streets. The enemy is at the gates.

783

784

785

786

In January 1910 Paris was flooded by torrential rains. Here in the Boulevard Haussmann a sailor sculls along towards the Gare Saint-Lazare (783), where the river has gone back to its old channel. The water reached the parapet of the Pont Sully (784) and the famous zouave's beard on the Pont de l'Alma. The Rue de Seine had never deserved its name so well (785). The lowest part of the 'Parisian basin' took on its prehistoric appearance. On 28th January not a single pavement was to be seen in the Cité, the gardens of the Champs-Elysées were a lake, and the Ile Saint-Louis was under water.

Raymond Poincaré, to whom Armand Fallières has just transferred his powers as President of the Republic, is seen here saluting the Parisians (786). He was elected on 17th January 1913, and was to have a dramatic seven years in office.

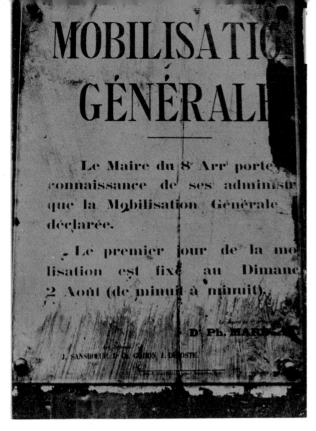

788

Raoul Villain, a fanatic with a morbid passion for Alsace-Lorraine, thought that Jaurès' opposition to three years' military service meant abandoning the annexed provinces, and he murdered the Socialist leader in the Café du Croissant (788). On 2nd August France was mobilised (789). On the following day Germany declared war on France. The Gare de l'Est became the most crowded place in Paris (790 & 790b). The Germans attacked on a front stretching from the Somme to the Vosges. On 2nd September von Kluck's army was 15 miles from Paris.

789

The war begins with the death of two great men:

Jaurès, who was murdered; and Péguy, who was killed in action.

790b

790

On 28th July 1914 Austro-Hungary declared war on Serbia. On 30th there was partial mobilisation in Russia, on the 31st general mobilisation in Germany.

791

Charles Péguy, a young poet from the Ecole Normale Supérieure, had started a review called Les Cahiers de la Quinzaine, which tried to reconcile tradition with Socialism (791). Among young intellectuals his influence grew. Called up on 4th August 1914, he wrote: 'A train heaped with flowers took me to Coulommiers on Tuesday. I was the only officer in charge of 3,000 Parisians.' With the Parisians and the soldiers called up from Seine-et-Marne he fell, on 5th September, some 25 miles from the threa-

tened capital. The German general staff, whose lines of communication with its forward troops soon became distended, made no effort to take Paris, as it had done in 1870, but decided to destroy the various armies. 850,000 French and British troops were battling with 750,000 Germans from Verdun to Meaux. It was the British, commanded by Sir John French, side by side with Maunoury's army corps, who protected Paris on the east from its assailants.

794

793

The defence of Paris, which had become an entrenched camp, was entrusted to General Galliéni, and the government retired to Bordeaux (792). The capital's only defence was the fortifications of Thiers, which had already been badly damaged in 1870, various walls made of paving stones hastily erected at the main gates (793), and the enthusiasm of the Parisians, who marched past the Gare de l'Est in patriotic processions (794).

With its rifles

garlanded

with flowers, Paris sets out for what it thinks will be the last and easiest of wars.

795

796

Von Kluck crossed the Marne and descended on the south-east of Paris to envelop the Fifth Army. This little girl played sadly in the Tuileries (795), while hordes of refugees from the north and east poured into Paris (796), which waited in anguish for the results of the gigantic struggle at its gates. Galliéni ordered Maunoury to attack von Kluck's right flank on the Ourcq. Joffre persuaded the British to do the same and put Franchet d'Esperey at the head of the Fifth Army. On 6th September he ordered a general counter-attack. Galliéni reinforced Maunoury with everything he could find: the Parisian taxis (797) took reinforcements right up to the front on the Ourcq and the Marne. In the south General Foch bore the whole German attack and made his famous remark: 'My right flank is smashed, my left flank is yielding, but everything's fine and I'm attacking.' Von Kluck's army was separated from von Bülow's, and on 13th September the whole front moved back. The battle of the Marne had saved Paris.

GOUVERNEMENT MILITAIRE DE PARIS

Armée de Paris, Habitants de Paris,

Les Membres du Gouvernement de la République ont quitté Paris pour donner une impulsion nouvelle à la défense nationale.

J'ai reçu le mandat de défendre Paris contre l'envahisseur.

Ce mandat, je le remplirai jusqu'au bout.

Paris, le 3 Septembre 1914

Le Gouverneur Militaire de Paris,
Commandant l'Armée de Paris,

GALLIÉNI

Paris - Imprimerie MARCEL PILARD, 140, rue du Faubourg-Saint-Martin (Tel. 132-34 et 432-75)

792

797

It will soon have to call on the strength it has long known : the strength of despair.

The cellars

in the city

are a continuation

of the trenches

at the Front.

From now until the end of 1916 the war was confined to the north and east of France, where it settled down into a battle of positions and trenches. The invasion of the northern departments forced Paris to open a great many munition factories and chemical works. The city's industrialisation dates from this period. In 1917 Poulbot designed this charming poster (798) for the benefit of the wounded, of whom there were large numbers. Things were going very badly: there was no Russian front left, the Italians were defeated, and in France both the Right and Left were ready for peace. In November the 76-year-old Clémenceau became President of the Council and Minister of War. He wanted 'to wage war, nothing but war'.

'The Zeppelins have passed over, and Paris smiles', (799) said the Petit Journal reassuringly in the spring of 1915. The aeroplanes, called 'taubes', had appeared on 30th August 1914, and had hardly

ceased their raids when the Zeppelins began to become a nuisance at night. On 31st January 1918 another kind of aeroplane, the Gotha, appeared. Defences were meagre, lights much too numerous; they dropped 91 bombs, causing 51 deaths and 204 injured. On 12th April the Rue de Rivoli was hit by an aerial torpedo weighing 700 lbs. Altogether, until 15th September 295 projectiles had been dropped on Paris, 325 on the inner and 43 on the outer suburbs. Life went on in the cellars (800). On 24th March 1918 at seven in the morning people were astonished to see large shells bursting. A gigantic cannon was firing from the region of Laon, 75 miles off. It was called 'Big Bertha', after Frau Krupp. Until 29th August it was to cause 256 deaths and 620 injured. On Good Friday, 29th March, it hit the nave of the church of Saint-Gervais during the evening service. A buttress was broken, the side walls collapsed, and 75 were killed and 90 injured (801).

A city of Victory, rapturous at having been spared.

During the spring of 1918 Ludendorff launched four successive attacks. The Germans reached the Marne again. On 18th July, while the Parisians were anxiously listening to the firing of the guns, Foch counter-attacked and forced the enemy to retreat. The arrival of fresh American reinforcements favoured a general offensive on 26th September. The front moved a little further from Paris each day. On 7th November the Germans asked for an armistice. On 11th November at eleven o'clock there was a general cease-fire.

At four o'clock, Clémenceau (802) stood on the rostrum at the Palais-Bourbon. He said, 'Let us pay homage to our great dead, who have given us this victory. Those still alive will march down our boulevards to the Arc de Triomphe when they return and we will cheer them. Thanks to them, France, which yesterday was the soldier of God and today is the soldier of Humanity, will always be the soldier of the Ideal.'

Also at four o'clock, the crowd gathered in the Place de l'Opéra

(803) and on the boulevards (804), making an enormous uproar. There were demonstrations in the Place de la Concorde before the statue of the town of Strasbourg (805); and celebrations went on for several days.

807

806

Paris, resting place of the Unknown Soldier, to whom she owed her victory.

808

810

811

812

On Sunday 13th July 1919 at the Hôtel de Ville, Poincaré distributed the colours of 22 regiments (806). On 14th July a gigantic review of troops was held in honour of the French soldier (807). Foch (808) and Joffre, with Generals Weygand and Belin, followed by the Allied General Staff (809), led the parade after passing under the Arc de Triomphe. First came the Allied armies in alphabetical order: the Americans with Pershing (810), the Belgians, the British with Haig, the French with Pétain (811), the Italians with Montuori; right on to the Siamese.

809

Paris is worth dying for, since it is so good to live there.

813

The war seemed never to have happened. Paris plunged greedily into the pleasures of yesterday. The winner of the Prix Goncourt of 1919 was Marcel Proust, the most Parisian of novelists (813), with his 'A l'ombre des jeunes filles en fleurs' ('Within a Budding Grove').

But everything had changed. To find the old Paris Utrillo had to climb up to Montmartre, and he kept on returning to the Rue Saint-Rustique as if the 'wines and liqueurs' and the dome of the basilica had cast a spell over him (814). He met again all those artists and writers who had from 1900 to 1914 brought new glory to the Butte: Juan Gris, Max Jacob, Modigliani, Mac Orlan, Vlaminck and Picasso, who took their talents and their hopes to the 'bateau-lavoir' (washing-boat), a warren of studios at the top of the steps leading to 13 Rue Ravignan.

Paris was now to make the fortune of those who had survived their previous poverty. Van Dongen, Dutch but very much the Parisian, painted elegant coupés, big limousines and thoroughbred riders, but did not forget to add the traditional figures in the Bois de Boulogne: the soldier and his girl, runners, nurses or mothers with their children, and rowing boats (815).

815

After the war Paris also recognised those who were in fact her most valuable assets. Before 1914 the philosopher Bergson had attracted large audiences to his courses at the Collège de France. Illness forced him into semi-retirement (816), but in 1928 the Nobel prize crowned his reputation both in Paris and abroad.

The music-hall stars were hardly less famous, it is true, but in 1925 Paris enjoyed itself. The 'Revue Nègre' at the Théâtre des Champs-Elysées started Josephine Baker on her career. The Moulin Rouge with Mistinguett rivalled the Casino de Paris with Maurice Chevalier. Everyone was astonished and delighted by the couturier Paul Poiret (817): but he was to die in poverty. After having had a great deal of fun, the Parisians begged Poincaré to save the franc in 1926. This stern expert brought Paris back to her pre-war prosperity – a mirage that until then had seemed impossibly remote.

816

817

818

At five minutes past ten on the night of 21st May 1927 a small aeroplane landed on the runway of the aerodrome of Le Bourget. Troops and police (818) had to snatch its pilot, Charles Lindbergh, from the exuberant crowd: he had just crossed the Atlantic alone in the 'Spirit of Saint Louis'. A flight lasting thirty-three hours with a single motor, two sleepless nights, and more than 3,500 miles without radio or parachute, made Lindbergh into a hero whom Marshal Foch (819) congratulated and whom the Parisians greeted with admiration and delight.

819

On 6th May 1931 the President of the Republic inaugurated a colonial exhibition open to all nations. In the woods at Vincennes, around the lake of Daumesnil, Marshal Lyautey created an exotic imaginary city dominated by a vast model of the temple of Angkor (821). Thirty-three million people visited it. Two of its attractions survived: the Zoological Gardens or Vincennes Zoo, and the Museum of France Overseas.

Paris celebrates everything simultaneously, and as well as having its Giraudoux, a writer notable for his intelligence, imagination, logic, and vivacity, it also had its Giraudoux of painting, Dufy, who took the panorama of Paris as the flowery theme of this delightful screen (822).

'In the twenty square miles I can see before me there has been more thinking, more discussion and more writing than anywhere else in the world', wrote Jean Giraudoux of the Eiffel Tower.

822

In 1897 Marcel Renault and his 20-year-old brother had installed a drill, a lathe and a forge in an old boathouse on the island of Seguin (823) at Boulogne, in the Billancourt district. In December 1899, helped by two locksmiths, they had built their first car. Thanks to them Boulogne, which in 1872 had only 17,343 inhabitants, in 1931 had 85,188, and in 1936, 97,379. The Renault works became the greatest enterprise in the Paris region (824).

André Citroën, another car manufacturer, has also done a lot to industrialise the south-west of Paris. In January 1915 he bought some market gardens in the Quai de Javel, not far from the Champ de Mars, and there started an ammunition factory. He began producing cars in 1918, and the boldness of his industrial enterprise and methods of publicity became the talk of Paris. It was he who thought of illuminating the famous buildings of Paris at night and of decorating the Eiffel Tower with his gigantic luminous signs (825). He brought to the banks of the Seine a working population as big as that of Soissons (826).

824

The craftsman's city is now surrounded by dreary suburbs bristling with factories.

825

826

Between ballots for a new Chamber of Deputies on 6th May 1932, Paul Doumer, the President of the Republic, opened the annual sale for ex-service writers. A madman of Russian origin, Gorgulof, fired on him several times with a revolver; he was taken to the Beaujon hospital (827), and died during the night.

A league of ex-servicemen, 'the Cross of Fire', led by Lt.-Col. de la Rocque (828), proposed to restore authority while repudiating the traditionalism of the old Right. Then in January 1934, a monumental swindle was discovered, the work of a stateless person called Stavisky, who had as accomplices various politicians, who were shielded all the way up to the circles immediately surrounding the President.

On 6th February thousands of ex-servicemen or militants of the extreme right set out in a protest march which degenerated into a sanguinary battle in the Place de la Concorde and on the boulevards (829).

828

829

The old struggle breaks out again between privileged and under-privileged Paris; the machines slow down and stop.

830

The trades unions and left-wing organisations carried out violent counter-demonstrations on 9th and 12th February. They soon joined forces under the name of the 'Popular Front', and triumphed in the elections of May 1936. Immediately afterwards, the workers of 1,286 firms in the Paris region went on strike and occupied their work places (830). At the Pont d'Austerlitz even the barges were at a standstill (831). It was a 'sit-down' strike.

831

The Palais du Trocadéro, built in 1878, was demolished in order to open up the steep perspective over the Champ de Mars. The Eiffel Tower reappeared. But on the site the workmen remained sitting or gave the closed-fist salute (833), in reply to the Fascist or Nazi salute. The opening was put off from 18th to 24th May, and even then it took place among the rubble; and when the exhibition closed, in November, the Mexican pavilion was still unfinished. All the same, it was a great success. The architects Carlu, Azéma, and Boileau planned the new palace as a monumental entrance to the exhibition. They were blamed for demolishing the old Trocadéro and for depriving the city of its one great hall (4,665 seats), but in answer to their critics they opened up and deepened the old quarry that had been used for building stone on this slope of the hill of Chaillot (834) at the beginning of the 18th century. And so, under a great central terrace, a theatre was built capable of holding from 1,500 to 3,000 spectators, and – in contrast to the old hall – with excellent acoustics. Pools and fountains linked the new Palais to the Seine and the Pont d'Iéna, on a line with the Eiffel Tower, the gardens of the Champ de Mars, and the Ecole Militaire. It is the most splendid view in Paris.

Paris invites the world to its festivities –

but there are rumbles of unrest in the background.

833

On 8th June 1936, owners' and workers' representatives signed agreements that satisfied the chief claims of the workers: this took place at the Hôtel Matignon, the residence of the President of the Council. The leaders of the Popular Front (832) – from left to right, Léon Blum, Maurice Thorez, Roger Salengro, Maurice Viollette, Pierre Cot – are here seen applauding their fighting men. But political tension was still high, and public feeling was inflamed by the civil war between Franco's troops and the Spanish Republicans. When Léon Blum's government took office, the currency was devalued, production was low, and there was unemployment. In these unfavourable circumstances preparations were made for the International Exhibition of 1937.

834

835

837

The Exhibition of 1937 took over and extended what had been done in 1878, and made the Palais de Chaillot (835) into a complete city of museums: the Naval Museum, the Museum of Man, the Museum of French Monuments. Modern art was generously treated, and its building, not far from the Exhibition, still exists (836). Beside the Trocadéro Auguste Perret built the Museum of Public Works. With the Cité Universitaire, dating from the same period, they constitute one of the rare groups of buildings that appeared between the two wars. The Exhibition celebrated the third centenary of Pascal's 'Discourse on Method', in which he affirmed that 'good sense is the most widely shared thing in the world.' But the pavilions of Stalin's U.S.S.R. (837), and of Nazi Germany (838) defied each other at the foot of the Palais.

Armed men are marching

rank after rank

through the streets of Europe.

838

836

What can the people of Paris do against those who have given up Liberty?

The position of Czechoslovakia, now gravely threatened, caused great anxiety. Hitler demanded that the Germans on the Czechoslovak frontier should be incorporated in the Reich. France and England had guaranteed this frontier but on 29th September, at Munich, Chamberlain and Daladier agreed that Czechoslovakia should be dismembered and deprived of its defences. An intensive press campaign transformed this retreat into a diplomatic

On 11th September 1937, a bomb blew up the building of the Federation of French Employers, and other terrorist acts followed. They were the work of a revolutionary secret society called 'La Cagoule', an anti-Communist movement that was preparing to go as far as a 'coup d'état'. On 12th March 1938 Hitler's annexation of Austria aroused great excitement. However, on 19th July Paris put out her flags to welcome King George VI and Queen Elizabeth, and a picturesque flotilla gaily accompanied the royal guests down the Seine as they went to sign the Golden Book in the Hôtel de Ville (839).

success. On his return, Daladier was the first to be surprised by the cheers that greeted him in the streets (840).

The French naïvely imagined that war was definitely averted. But in March 1939 the Nazis occupied the whole of Czechoslovakia. On 23rd August the German-Soviet pact freed Hitler from serious danger and he then demanded the incorporation of Danzig and the Polish Corridor into Germany. At dawn on 1st September his troops invaded Poland. At five o'clock in the afternoon, France entered the war against Germany. Paris covered its monuments with sandbags (841) and dug trenches in the parks as shelter from air raids.

What can a people which is not thinking of war do against those who are preparing for war?

Invaded simultaneously by Germany and Russia, Poland capitulated at the end of September 1939. The conflict then entered a phase of deceptive calm which was called the 'phoney war'. Defiant slogans appeared on the walls: 'We will conquer because we are the stronger' (842). Life was normal in Paris, and people no longer feared air raids.

In spite of Nazi propaganda, which tried to drive a wedge into Franco-British friendship, the British paraded in the Place de la République (843). On 21st March, Paul Reynaud replaced Daladier as President of the Council. He announced that mines had been placed in Norwegian territorial waters where German ships loaded with ore passed. 'The iron road is cut,' he said. But it was not to be cut for long.

In April, Hitler's troops quickly took over Norway and Denmark. On 10th May they flung themselves on Holland, Belgium and Luxembourg. Parachutists, tanks, and German aeroplanes put an end to all resistance. On 14th May the French front was broken at Sedan. The Dutch army and then the Belgian army capitulated. The Germans left Paris alone, and tried to encircle 235,000 British and 115,000 French troops in the region of Dunkirk, who, by abandoning an enormous amount of equipment, avoided capture and escaped by sea. But Paris was now insufficiently protected. On 3rd June it was bombed: 254 were killed and 652 wounded (844).

844

On 6th June the front of the Somme collapsed. Paris was no longer able to produce a Galliéni, or a Joffre, or the soldiers of the Marne. On the 9th to the 10th, the ministers moved out of Paris without warning, requisitioning an enormous number of the vehicles available. With the 'Mona Lisa', the 'Marriage at Cana', and tons of useless office files, they set off for the south. The government had been transferred to Tours, but by the 15th it had reached Bordeaux. In his message of the 10th to President Roosevelt, Paul Reynaud declared: 'We shall fight before Paris, we shall fight behind Paris.' Vain words! Hundreds of thousands of Parisians abandoned the capital by every possible means of transport, and thousands of fugitives camped in the stations. The sky clouded over: it was the thick smoke of the petrol stocks burning at Le Havre. Paris was out of bounds to the defeated soldiers, who tramped along the roads on foot.

845

General Dentz remained in Paris to keep order and maintain food supplies. When the Germans reached the north-east of the capital on the evening of 13th June, the people showed complete apathy. At 6.30 on the 14th, German troops began to cross Paris, and the swastika flag appeared on buildings and ministries.

The invasion went on methodically. On the 17th Marshal Pétain, who had replaced Paul Reynaud in the government, asked for the conditions of an armistice. Hostilities ceased on the 25th at 1.35 in the morning. These Parisians have loaded their grandmother into a perambulator and are coming home on foot (845).

To the sound of heavy boots tramping its streets,

846

847

849

Paris at first answers with silence.

On July 2nd Marshal Pétain's government was transferred to Vichy, which became the capital of the zone left free by the German army. Paris, which Hitler visited briefly (846) to see Napoleon's tomb, the Palais de Chaillot and the Opéra, was now only the centre of the German occupation in France: there were German signposts (847), German posters (848) and German parades (849).

848

The capital of France at war was London, where General de Gaulle tried to reorganise all who wanted to continue the struggle. Paris was full of soldiers and officers of the Third Reich (850), who were astonished to find an abundance of goods which their country had forgotten. Solidly held by the police and the German administration (851), Paris became the centre of the Wehrmacht in Western Europe. In fact, cut off from the southern zone, the northern zone and the eastern zone, it was a capital only of 'Gross Paris'.

850

854

Paris is silent so that it can hear the voice of honour.

851

The Germans requisitioned an increasingly large part of French production. Taxicabs disappeared and gave place to bicycle cabs (852), and queues lengthened in front of food shops (853). In 1941 the Germans even requisitioned the bronze statues: Rouget de l'Isle (854) went for scrap.

853

852

Paris of the Resistance. There is defiance in its elegance, in its smiles.

The struggle goes on in secret.

Hitler decided to make a spectacular gift to France – the remains of Napoleon's son l'Aiglon, which had remained in Austria. They reached Paris (855) on a freezing day in December 1940. The ingenuity with which Parisians of both sexes managed to dress (856) and eat produced results which looked wonderful, but took no one in. Hitler's attack on the U.S.S.R. on 22nd June 1941 made the atmosphere of Paris more tense and feeling against Nazism began to grow.

856

857

264

CE JUIF ET LA FRANCE

PROCHAINEMENT

858

August 1941 was a tragic month: there were the first incidents against the occupation troops, the first executions (860) and the first curfews. A Lt.-Commander of the Free French Forces, H. d'Estienne d'Orves, was executed. The terror began: those who resisted, or were suspected of doing so, were arrested in thousands. The persecution of the Jews increased, with exorbitant fines (December 1941), the compulsory wearing of the yellow star (May 1942) (857), confiscations, and mass deportations for systematic murder.

859 860

861

862

A Communist deputy of the region of Paris, Gabriel Péri, was executed in December 1941. On the 150th anniversary of Valmy, 20th September 1942, there were incidents against the occupiers which were answered with the execution of 116 hostages. In 1943 forced labour in Germany toughened opposition, but Paris reflected every shade of opinion: there were those who waited, to whom Anglo-American successes or German difficulties in the U.S.-S.R. gave food for thought; there were those who collaborated with the occupation by working in the political movements of Déat or of Doriot, in the press, on the radio or in any of the organisations set up by the Nazi régime; there were Black Market profiteers and 'zazous' who cared for nothing but their own comfort. Most people, though they wished for a speedy liberation, were fully taken up with the daily struggle for survival. A handful of secret agents and active members of the Resistance kept up a merciless struggle in the background. The Paris forts – Vincennes (861), Mont Valérien or Issy-les-Moulineaux (862) – were the scenes of ruthless reprisals. On 6th June 1944 the Allies disembarked on the beaches of Normandy. The battle seemed to drag on and on 120 miles from Paris, but the capital never lacked drama.

On 28th June Philippe Henriot, Vichy Minister of Information, was executed by the Resistance. Marcel Déat and Laval put in a gloomy appearance at his funeral at Notre-Dame (863). Only the old deputy mayor of Saint-Denis, Doriot, wearing his German uniform of the Legion of French Volunteers against Bolshevism (864), seemed optimistic.

But antagonsm to Hitler was widespread. In Paris the bombardment of the station of La Chapelle caused 641 deaths. Badly fed, their nerves on edge with waiting, at each air-raid warning Parisians took refuge in the métro (865). On 30th July they learned with relief that the German front in Normandy had been broken at Coutances.

863

864

865

866

The Swedish Consul-General, Mr Nordling, managed to obtain a truce from von Choltitz and from those who were holding out in the Prefecture of Police for the night of the 19th and for Sunday the 20th. An announcement was put up in shop windows (867). But the extremists of both camps were against a truce and it was broken on Monday. On the 22nd Colonel Rol ordered everyone to the barricades (868).

In horse-drawn carts, hastily camouflaged, the defeated German armies crossed the streets of Paris, going east (866). On 12th August, Pierre Laval brought Edouard Herriot, president of the Chamber of Deputies of the Third Republic, back to Paris and asked him to summon the National Assembly, to whom he wanted to transfer his powers before the arrival of the Allies: in vain. Those Frenchmen who had played an important part in the occupation took the road to Germany on 17th August, whether they wanted to or not.

868

Heroic attacks and guerilla operations against buildings that were still occupied, arms depots, isolated vehicles or German convoys went on ceaselessly (869). On Wednesday the 23rd von Choltitz received direct orders from Hitler to carry out 'on the territory under his command in Paris as extensive destructions as possible'. He disobeyed.

869

On 10th August the Paris railwaymen went on strike, followed on the 15th by the police and on the 18th by all the public services. On the 19th the National Council of the Resistance called on the people to rise, and the police who had struck occupied the Prefecture of Police, while the French Forces of the Interior (the F.F.I.) of the Paris region, commanded by Colonel Rol, occupied official buildings and the newspaper printing presses. What would be the the next move of the new German Governor of Paris, General von Choltitz, with his 12,000 men?

870

On the morning of Friday 25th August Leclerc's entire division entered through the Porte d'Orléans, the Porte de Gentilly, and the Porte de Saint-Cloud. The centres of German resistance, the Palais-Bourbon and the Opéra (871–873), yielded one by one. General von Choltitz refused an ultimatum from Colonel Billotte, but at three o'clock in the afternoon he was captured in the Hôtel Meurice and taken to General Leclerc in the Prefecture of Police.

871

General Eisenhower did not intend to attack Paris directly, but to encircle it. The military and political undesirability of war in the streets of the capital was explained to him. On the evening of 22nd August the order was given to the French Second Armoured Division camped in Argentan and under the command of General Leclerc (870) to move on Paris.

872

'Through the power of a word,
I start my life again.
I was born to know you,
and to name you, Liberty'.
The voice of the poet Paul Eluard
is the voice of Paris.

873

On Thursday the 24th at seven o'clock in the evening, while skirmishes continued in the streets, Colonel Billotte arrived within 7 miles of the capital. At 8.45 a few armoured cars which had found a way through were wildly cheered, and at 9.22 emerged into the Place de l'Hôtel de Ville, where they joined up with the National Council of the Resistance.

In spite of the general joy, the conquerors were not entirely in agreement. General von Choltitz had to surrender twice: to General Leclerc and to Colonel Rol. Full of enthusiasm at their liberation, the Parisians gave a frantic welcome to Leclerc's tanks and the French army (874). On 25th August at 5 p.m. General de Gaulle was received in triumph at the Hôtel de Ville. The next day he went on foot from the Arc de Triomphe to Notre-Dame to hear the Te Deum. The National Council of the Resistance and many of those who had played an important role in London, Algiers, and Paris, accompanied him all along this victory parade (875). From left to right, they are: Paul Bastid, Laniel, Admiral Thierry d'Argenlieu, General Koenig, G. Palewsky, General de Gaulle, General Leclerc, Georges Bidault, Alexandre Parodi (concealing General Juin), Georges Marrane, Jean Marin, etc.

Paris exultant. Her liberators have a right to her embraces.

The war receded, and France emerged from the abyss into which she had plunged. Paris breathed again. But peace on earth was still a fragile thing. In the autumn of 1948, the Trocadéro was chosen as the seat of the General Assembly of the United Nations. Its president, Mr Trygve Lie, was symbolically offered the key of this new UNO territory, the key that had once belonged to the old convent of Chaillot (876). But in spite of its size, it found it hard to open all the delegates' hearts to peace.

General de Gaulle only briefly advised the provisional government set up immediately after the Liberation. Frenchmen voted, and voted again: politically, things were in a state of flux. 1945 and 1946 saw two constituent assemblies and two referendums. Meanwhile dancing went on – down in the cellars of Saint-Germain-des-Prés, where existentialism held brief though hectic sway. The Fourth Republic was born officially at last in January 1947, when Vincent Auriol was elected President. When he ended his term of office in 1954 to make way for his successor, M. René Coty (877), the face of the world had changed.

And Paris herself, just after joyously celebrating her two thousandth birthday, now sprawls so far along the loops of the Seine (878) and has such an exuberant amount of energy, such an amazing number of activities, that to recount her present-day history would mean describing the life that goes on in all the cities and all the worlds that compose her: something attempted a hundred times, but never with complete success. So our tour of Paris is nearing its end.

One word more: the history of Paris and its inhabitants continues in the history of France and in the history of the world. All the beauty, all the grace and wit for centuries found along the banks of the Seine have not disappeared (879–884). And the more devouring modern life and its demands become, the harder Paris tries to find a more human proportion in the midst of them (885–893).

876

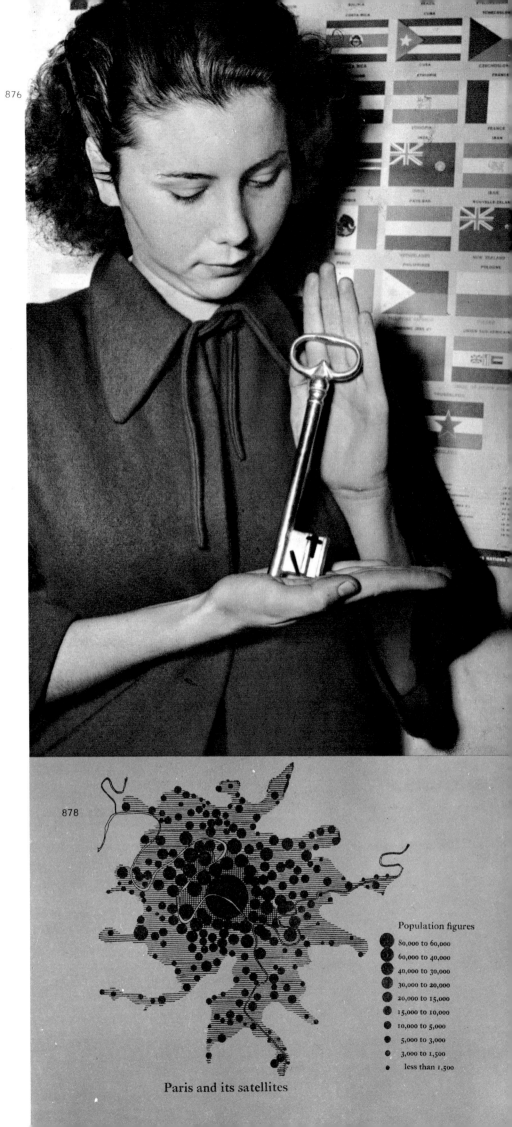

877

878

Paris and its satellites

Population figures

- 80,000 to 60,000
- 60,000 to 40,000
- 40,000 to 30,000
- 30,000 to 20,000
- 20,000 to 15,000
- 15,000 to 10,000
- 10,000 to 5,000
- 5,000 to 3,000
- 3,000 to 1,500
- less than 1,500

In art, in fashion, in literature, Paris is everywhere famous. The Paris theatre has often had periods of brilliance, but rarely has one man dominated it like Louis Jouvet, who, during a career too early ended in 1951, acted ten thousand times before the public. Jules Romain's 'Knock' and the works of Jean Giraudoux were his favourites. He brought Molière to new life in plays like 'L'Ecole des Femmes' and 'Don Juan' (879).

The 'haute couture' of Paris is in the tradition of two centuries of brilliant social life, and its models bring this supremely difficult art to the entire world. Models like those shown below (880), dressed by Dior, practise the curtseys they are to make to

Laboratory of ideas.

Some are expressed in movement,

880

Queen Elizabeth II. Ballet, which came from Italy as a court entertainment, is a living, lyrical art that has been decisively transformed in Paris. It was there that, in 1909, Diaghilev put on the Russian ballets that revolutionised choreography. And when they founded a new company, Roland Petit (a true Parisian, born in the district of Les Halles) and Zizi Jeanmaire (881) called it the 'Ballets de Paris'.

881

From the U.S.S.R. to Mexico, France's theatrical ambassador is the company of the Comédie-Française, which is Paris's first company too. From 1812 to 1946 it was administered under a statute signed by Napoleon in Moscow; from 1799 it has occupied the southwest wing of the Palais-Royal (Salle Richelieu), and from 1946 has also been at the Odéon (Salle Luxembourg), a building dating from 1782. The Comédie-Française has performed Molière's 'Tartuffe' more than 2,000 times and has put on more than 2,500 plays, including a number by contemporary playwrights like Paul Claudel, François Mauriac and Henri de Montherlant.

some in words; but all attack dullness,

all serve the two-edged word: 'Esprit',

which means grace,

both spontaneous and deliberate.

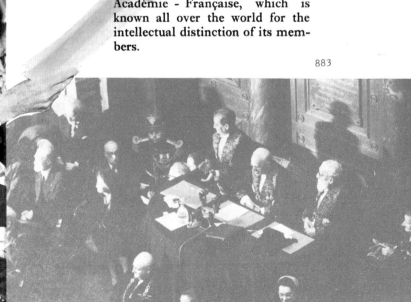

Georges Lecomte, André Maurois, and Marcel Pagnol (883) are here receiving a new Academician, Jean Cocteau (884), under the dome of the Institute (322). This 300-year-old ceremony assures the continuation of the oldest Parisian institution, the Académie - Française, which is known all over the world for the intellectual distinction of its members.

883

884

February 1954: the thermometer was well below freezing point. In a miserable encampment in one of the suburbs, a child froze to death. How many others might suffer this terrible fate? How many homeless thousands walked the streets of Paris, or huddled together in freezing hovels? A missionary, the Abbé Pierre (885), took the lead in an almost superhuman campaign for mutual help. 1,854 families with five children or more were living in a single room. For Paris and the Seine department this was a running sore: four square miles of huts, of which only about a quarter, divided into sixteen blocks, was scheduled for any real improvement.

Paris faces

the problems of today, especially that of housing the rich harvest of its people.

The only space that has been added to Paris since 1920 is Thiers' fortified zone, now demilitarised. The speculators have profited by wiping out the slums in this area and building places like Aubervilliers (886), the Porte de Châtillon and large blocks of flats. There is still a lot of argument about how the best use is to be made of it, as green spaces, schools, playgrounds and public parks had all been planned. What in fact is the use of building and rebuilding if the growth of the population never stops?

Paris itself has only 2,850,189 inhabitants, but the department of the Seine totals 5,154,834, or 14 per cent of the population of France and more than the 33 largest towns of France together. The outer suburbs, which extend to a radius of nearly 22 miles from Notre-Dame, have since 1920 been covered haphazardly by dwellings and industry. Most of these agglomerations are only dormitory towns, without any autonomous existence, whose inhabitants work far from their homes (887). Each morning the Gare Saint-Lazare pours 260,000 commuters into Paris, the Gare du Nord 110,000, and the Gare de l'Est 65,000. The fresh air of the suburbs, their quietness, so soothing to jangled nerves, and their low cost of living, are now nothing but pleasant memories.

Paris, the magnet, attracts the whole of France, as well as travellers from all over the world.

Paris, which is visited by more than 600,000 tourists every Summer and in three months has 500,000 air passengers in transit, has been able to find a piece of land of about 7 square miles in area at Orly in the south-eastern suburbs (891) on which to build an airport which will gradually be given all the most

889

modern equipment. With its other airport at Le Bourget for freight and mixed traffic and the helicopter terminal at Issy-les-Moulineaux for short journeys, Paris aims at becoming the hub of European air traffic. It has airport facilities to fit its size, but it has grown out of all proportion, and has become 'the most

891

beautiful example of human congestion' (Giraudoux). Its million cars have brought about parking and traffic problems almost impossible to solve.

The department of the Seine has 302,920 employers, 573,600 salaried employees, 1,021,740 wage-earners, among whom there are nearly 650,000 women. 29 per cent of all French civil servants, 23 per cent of all doctors and 39 per cent of all lawyers are to be found there. A third of the French metal industry,

though there is neither iron nor coal, is centred there; and also a third of the chemical industry, a third of the clothing industry and half the rubber industry. The Parisians' income, which is the highest in France, stands at an index figure of 162 compared with 126 in the north. Each Parisian is on an average three times as rich as a man in the provinces. But what of the problem of housing all the people who are attracted by this super-abundance of wealth and energy in such a small area?

890

892

Look at Paris from the air. If you fly over the Hôtel des Invalides, the Eiffel Tower and the Palais de Chaillot (892), you will see three centuries: 1710, 1889, 1937. To whom do we owe this great trinity of monuments? The circle is now complete. Right at the beginning of the story are the fairies who leaned over the cradle of the capital: the plancton of many thousands of years ago that made the stone used in building the Invalides; the Seine that left a great carpet of alluvial soil at Grenelle on which Louis XIV's choice fell; and the island, attached to solid ground early in its history, where Eiffel placed the pillars of his tower. All the rest was the work of the architects, engineers, masons, smiths, navvies and slaters of Paris.

Cross the Seine to the Place de la Concorde and the Champs-Elysées (893). Again you see three centuries; but this is no longer the Paris built with skill and hard work, but the Paris of pleasure and display, of military parades, motor-car sale-rooms, tasteful shop windows, and elegance. Yet the same fairies and the same Parisians have made this Paris as, yesterday, made Notre-Dame and the Pont-Neuf.

These are things which have been created in spite of the ruinous wars of Louis XIV, the illusions of the reign of Louis XV, the tumults of Boulangism, the crisis of 1930, the social struggles of 1936 and almost permanent difficulties over revenue.

All sorts of plans are already shaping the Paris of the future. There are big public works which will help to speed up the flow of traffic, such as underground roads, a circular motor route 26 miles long, wider thoroughfares, etc. And here are plans which are even more ambitious: a Palace of Industry at the Rond Point de la Défense with an exhibition hall over 400,000 sq. ft. in size; a new Faculty of Medicine at the Salpêtrière; a new Faculty of Science on the site of the Halle aux Vins; a stadium to hold 100,000; an international city of the arts with studio-flats; a Radio House. The Halles are to be reorganised or removed elsewhere, and markets are to be made at stations; the slaughter-houses of La Villette are to be rebuilt; the public services are to be re-grouped and the Ministry of Finance is no longer to be housed in the Louvre. And that is not all. The surrounding towns are to become autonomous social and economic units, and the stifling industrialisation of the department of the Seine is to be slowed down.

A city that defies death and chooses life.

'The glory of France, and one of the noblest and

chief ornaments of the world.'

All this, of course, will not happen tomorrow morning. But Paris was not made in a day. For instance, the Faculty of Medicine in the Rue des Saints-Pères took so long to build that when it was finished it was too small. It is no longer easy in Paris either to build or to destroy. Two thousand years of privileges, strange regulations, traditions that cannot be checked, rules that, although out of date, are still obeyed, and prejudices at once respectable and absurd – these do not allow much free expansion to building. Money is needed, too, and this is not a wealthy age. But perhaps funds are not needed as urgently as bold administrative and political solutions, together with the men who will apply them in the face of difficulties and opposition.

893

894

A new building arose near the Eiffel Tower, the Ecole Militaire and the Invalides: the Unesco Secretariat (894). The shape of a three-pointed star, with its windows overhanging the concrete shell of the conference rooms, it is the first important new building in Paris since 1945, a signpost of progressive architecture and a cross-roads of world intelligence. Seven centuries after the great cultural impetus which created the Sorbonne, Paris can still conjure up the same spirit. And if she can play hostess on great cultural occasions, she can arrange gayer festivities just as well. In April 1957, Queen Elizabeth II and the Duke of Edinburgh paid a visit to Paris (895). The Seine was aflame with rockets (896).

Where man lives in friendship

with streets and squares,

trees and statues,

895

hills and river banks, and with the sun which wears the colours of Liberty.

896   897

MAPS

List of
ILLUSTRATIONS

INDEX
of buildings
streets and people

PARIS: ORIGINS TO 17th CENTURY (898)

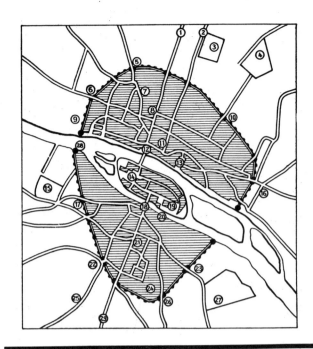

PARIS IN THE 17th AND 18th CENTURIES (899)

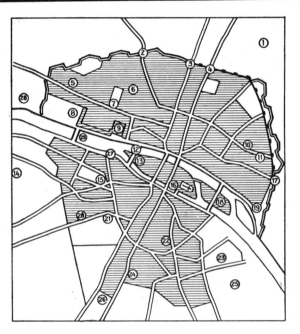

CONTEMPORARY PARIS (900)

Shaded area: boundary of Paris before the decree of 1860.
Nos. 1 to 17, communes absorbed into Paris after the decree of 1860.

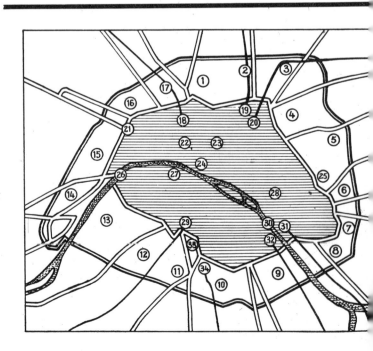

LOUVRE (901)

Fortified castle and donjon of Philip-Augustus (1200), courtyard modernised by Charles V. — 1

West and south wings (diagonally shaded) begun in 1527 under François I and completed under Henri III. — 2

From left to right: Petite Galerie, Galerie du Bord de l'Eau (riverside gallery) and the Tuileries, planned by Catherine de' Medici (1578) and completed under Henri IV. — 3

Galerie du Bord de l'Eau and Pavillon de Flore built under Henri IV (1595) and much restored (even reconstructed) under Napoleon III. — 4

Pavillon de l'Horloge and west wing of the Cour Carré built under Louis XIII (1624). — 5

On the right: Pavillon-Saint-Germain-l'Auxerrois, Perrault's colonnade, wings of the Cour Carré. On the left: Pavillon de Marsan; all built under Louis XIV. — 6

North gallery begun under Napoleon I and finished under Napoleon III and the Third Republic. — 7

Pavilions of Turgot, Richelieu and Colbert, built under Napoleon III (1852-1877). — 8

Arc de Triomphe du Carrousel. — 9

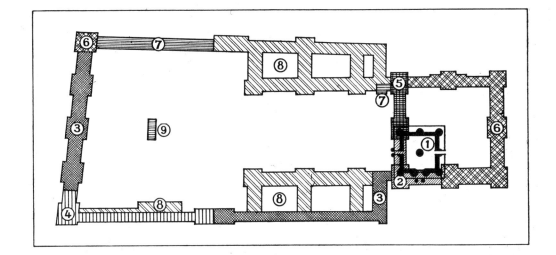

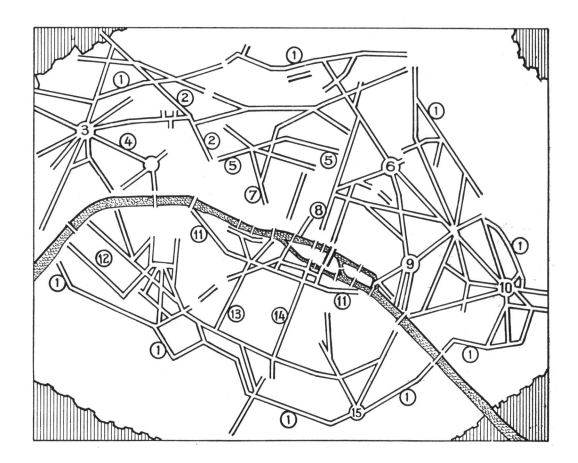

LIST
OF
ILLUSTRATIONS

The illustrations are numbered 1 to 902. Most of these numbers are given in the text so that the reader can at once place the picture in its historical and dramatic context. Others do not appear there because the illustrations they refer to are intended to supplement the narrative by acting as 'walkers-on', or as a backcloth to a period or an event. Precise details of these are given in the list that follows.

The illustrations have been chosen from every period and source. In this vast fresco a distinction must be made between evidence taken down on the spot by people who participated in or witnessed the events described (this was of course most frequently the case during the last sixty years, when photography was able to seize the passing moment) and that which has been imagined subsequently by painters, miniaturists and engravers—who were often great if unrecognised artists.

It should not be forgotten that realism in the miniature dates only from the 13th century, printing and the popular demand for the wood engraving only from the end of the 15th century—whereas Paris is more than 2,000 years old.

Abbreviations

SOURCES:

ARCH Archives de France (Paris).

CAR Musée Carnavelet (Paris).

CHA Chalcographie du Louvre.

CLU Musée de Cluny (Paris).

CP Private collection.

EST Cabinet des Estampes, Bibliothèque Nationale.

IMP Département des Imprimés, Bibliothèque Nationale.

LOU Musée du Louvre.

MAN Département des Manuscrits, Bibliothèque Nationale.

MED Cabinet des Médailles, Bibliothèque Nationale.

P.R. Library of Editions du Pont Royal.

VER Musée du Château de Versailles.

TITLES OF BOOKS:

G.C.F.V. *Grands chroniques de France;* by Vérard, 1493. Bibliothèque Nationale.

G. de GEN. *Histoire nationale de Paris et des Parisiens;* by Gourdon de Genouilhac (1884).

G.C.F. *Grandes Chroniques de France* (title of various works in the 15th century, illustrated by different hands).

PHOTOGRAPHS:

(BN) Photographic department of the Bibliothèque Nationale.

(APH) Photographic archives of historic monuments.

(MON) Monde et Caméra Agency.
   The many illustrations in black-and-white or in colour which bear no indication of their origin or of the photographer all belong to the Cabinet des Estampes of the Bibliothèque Nationale and were photographed by the photographic department of the Bibliothèque.

FRONT ENDPAPERS engraved by G. Poillot after a view by Mathieu Mérian (1631).

The buildings are: 10 Saint-Bernard; 11 Sainte-Geneviève; 12 Saint-Gervais; 13 the Temple; 14 Notre-Dame; 15 Hôtel-de-Ville; 16 Porte du Temple; 17 Saint-Séverin; 18 the Sainte-Chapelle; 19 Saint-Jacques-la-Boucherie; 20 Saints-Innocents; 21 Saint-Augustin; 22 Saint-Sulpice; 23 Saint-Magloire; 24 Saint-Nicolas; 25 Saint-Martin; 26 Porte de Nesle; 27 Saint-Germain-des-Prés; 28 Saint-Germain-l'Auxerrois; 29 Saint-Eustache; 30 Louvre; 31 Saint-Sauveur; 32 Saint-Honoré; 33 Galerie du Bord de l'Eau; 34 Porte Saint-Martin; 35 Porte Saint-Denis; 36 Porte Montmartre; 37 Porte Saint-Honoré; 38 Saint-Roch; 48 Faubourg Saint-Germain; 52 Pré-aux-Clercs. In the foreground, the Hôpital Saint-Louis.

Illustrations facing the half-title: the Pont Royal, Galerie du Bord de l'Eau, Quai des Théatins (Quai Voltaire). Turgot's plan. Detail. (1739).

Coloured endpapers: Paris from the air, view looking towards the Ile de la Cité (Ektachrome Henrard).

The photographs numbered as follows have been kindly lent to us by the photographic library of the 'Documentation Française': 45, 127, 128, 304, 411, 485, 490, 502, 637, 671, 672, 725, 740.

The photographs of the documents with the following numbers have been authorised by M. Destailleur-Chantereine, their owner, to whom we tender our thanks:
455, 467, 468, 484, 509, 526, 576, 577, 607, 614, 616, 618, 619, 620, 624, 625.

INDEX
of buildings
streets and people

As well as being a history of France and her people, this book is at the same time a comprehensive historical guide to Paris. The index gives the reader not only the numbers of the pages on which a particular building is described in the text but also the numbers of the illustrations in which it appears, showing what it was, what it has witnessed and what it is like now.

To make reference easier, these numbers have been printed in two different types: in ordinary type and without any other indication when they refer to a building or person mentioned *in the text*; in bold type and in brackets when they refer to *an illustration* in which the building or person appears, even if they are not mentioned in the text accompanying the illustration.

For example, Pont Neuf 11 (9) means that on page 11 there is a reference to the Pont Neuf, and that it appears in illustration No. 9. (392) means simply that illustration No. 392 shows the Pont Neuf as part of the background of some historical event.

288

d

e

f

g